MW01088172

Land of Our Lady Series

Prayer

LITANY. According to a pious tradition, Mary's house in Nazareth was transferred to Loreto, Italy. Here began a devotion called the Litany of Loreto or the Litany of the Blessed Virgin. The forty-nine invocations comprising this prayer are taken from the holy Bible and the Fathers of the Church. These beautiful invocations apply to everyone's lives as exemplified in the seven pictured among these pages.

THE NEUMANN PRESS

Mary's Influence on Life

MEANING. These words of the Bible can be applied to Mary: "He that shall find me shall find life, and shall have salvation from the Lord" (Proverbs: 8:32-35). Our Lady is called the Gate of Heaven because Jesus came to us through her and because she obtains for us the friendship of God, without which we cannot obtain salvation.

APPLICATION. The purpose of man's life is to love and serve God in this world, and to be happy with Him in heaven (Catechism). The life we live in our home, our country, and among our associates, is directed along the pathway of serving God. By following the footsteps of Our Lady, we are guided to heaven because Mary is the Gate of Heaven.

Prayer

Gate of heaven, *pray for us.*

Litany of the Blessed Virgin

LORD, have mercy on us.
Christ, have mercy on us.
Lord, have mercy on us.
God the Son, Redeemer of the world, have mercy on us.
God, the Holy Ghost, have mercy on us.
Holy Trinity, one God, have mercy on us.
Christ, hear us.
Christ, graciously hear us.
God the Father of heaven, have mercy on us.
Holy Mary,[1]
Holy Mother of God,
Holy Virgin of virgins,
Mother of Christ,
Mother of divine grace,
Mother most pure,
Mother most chaste,
Mother inviolate,
Mother undefiled,
Mother most amiable,
Mother most admirable,
Mother of good counsel,
Mother of our Creator,
Mother of our Saviour,
Virgin most prudent,
Virgin most venerable,
Virgin most renowned,
 [1] Pray for us.

Virgin most powerful,
Virgin most merciful,
Virgin most faithful,
Mirror of justice,
Seat of wisdom,
Cause of our joy,
Spiritual vessel,
Vessel of honor,
Singular vessel of devotion,
Mystical Rose,
Tower of David,
Tower of ivory,
House of gold,
Gate of heaven,
Ark of the covenant,
Morning star,
Health of the sick,
Refuge of sinners,
Comforter of the afflicted,
Help of Christians,
Queen of angels,
Queen of patriarchs,
Queen of prophets,
Queen of apostles,
Queen of martyrs,
Queen of confessors,
Queen of virgins,
Queen of all saints,
Queen conceived without original sin,

Queen assumed into heaven,
Queen of the most holy Rosary,
Queen of peace.
Lamb of God, who takest away the sins of the world, spare us, O Lord.
Lamb of God, who takest away the sins of the world, graciously hear us, O Lord.
Lamb of God, who takest away the sins of the world, have mercy on us.
Christ, hear us. Christ, graciously hear us.
℣. Pray for us, O holy Mother of God. ℟. That we may be made worthy of the promises of Christ.
Let us pray
Grant, we beseech Thee, O Lord God, unto us Thy servants, that we may rejoice in continual health of mind and body; and, by the glorious intercession of blessed Mary ever Virgin, may be delivered from present sadness, and enter into the joy of Thine eternal gladness. Through Christ our Lord. Amen.

An indulgence of 7 years. A plenary indulgence once a month on the usual conditions for the daily devout recitation of this Litany with its versicle and prayer (See "The Raccolta," the official work of indulgenced prayers, page 216).

MARY AS A GUIDE THROUGH LIFE. The free will of man accepts the guidance of Mary in the way of life. This guidance of Mary is part of our religion. It affects our home life, our association with our fellow man, our civic obligations, our career in life, and our acceptance of life's problems.

Courtesy of Rev. J. B. Carol, O. F. M.

Land of Our Lady Series

Founders of Freedom
by
Sister M. Benedict Joseph, S.H.N.
Los Angeles, Calif.

Bearers of Freedom
by
Sister M. Veronica, S.P.B.V.
Central Falls, R. I.

Leaders of Freedom
by
Sister M. Clarita, O.P.
Watertown, Mass.

Challenge of Freedom
by
Sister M. Theresine, S.N.D.
Cleveland, Ohio

Guardian of Freedom
by
Sister M. Augusta, H.H.M.
Akron, Ohio

Land of Our Lady Series

Leaders
of
Freedom

by Sister M. Clarita, O.P.

EDITOR-IN-CHIEF:
Rev. Timothy F. O'Leary, Ph.D.
Assistant Superintendent of Schools
Archdiocese of Boston

ASSISTANT EDITOR-IN-CHIEF:
Sister M. Veronica, S.P.B.V.

CO-EDITORS:
Rt. Rev. Clarence E. Elwell, Ph.D.
Superintendent of Schools
Diocese of Cleveland

Rev. Patrick J. Roche, Ph.D.
Assistant Superintendent of Schools
Archdiocese of Los Angeles

REPUBLISHED BY
THE NEUMANN PRESS
LONG PRAIRIE, MINNESOTA

BY SPECIAL ARRANGEMENT WITH
BENZIGER PUBLISHING COMPANY
NEW YORK, CINCINNATI, CHICAGO, BOSTON, SAN FRANCISCO

ISBN 0-911845-55-0
THIS 1997 EDITION IS PUBLISHED THROUGH SPECIAL ARRANGEMENT WITH
BENZIGER PUBLISHING COMPANY BY
THE NEUMANN PRESS
LONG PRAIRIE, MINNESOTA

EDITORS' INTRODUCTION

WHEN the minutemen answered the call of Paul Revere in 1775, the struggle with England, the mother country, had begun. The outcome of that struggle was the birth of a new nation, independent and freed from all ties with England. During the years that followed, the fledgling democracy was tested and refined by the fire of political and economic troubles. The Christian principles of freedom and dignity, justice and equality, proved staunch bulwarks of solidarity and strength through the years of trial endured by the young nation.

The transition period of our country lasted through the period of Federalist power and the era known as Jeffersonian democracy. By degrees the United States emerged from its youthful difficulties, until about 1830 it commenced to breathe in an atmosphere of individuality all its own.

The content of this text deals with the eventful years mentioned above. It tells of the great documents of human liberty written during this period; namely, the Declaration of Independence, the Articles of Confederation, and the Constitution of the United States. It speaks of the noble minds and hearts that guided the pens and voices of our leading statesmen. Their inspiring influence is found in the pages of this text, fittingly named *Leaders of Freedom*.

The first Unit tells how the colonists won the fight for political freedom and emphasizes the principles found in the preamble of the Declaration of Independence. The circumstances surrounding the writing of the Articles of Confederation, and the Christian social principles upon which our Constitution is built, are given due consideration in the second Unit. The events connected with Washington's and John Adams' administrations are found in Unit Three. The fourth Unit narrates the important features of the administrations of subsequent Presidents Jefferson, Madison, Monroe, and John Quincy Adams. The extension of our land to the Mississippi is the subject of Unit Five. The development of early culture in America is portrayed in the last Unit of the text.

The contribution of Catholics during the period of American history covered by this text is given due emphasis in the pages of *Leaders of Freedom*. Catholics fought and died in both Wars for Independence along with their fellow men of other faiths. They brought with them the spiritual elements that enriched our land with their character, culture, and virtue. They labored courageously in the construction of roads, ships, and railroads. At the same time, they rose to positions of trust and honor in the United States. Although the record of early inventions and improvements is told in this text, the complete story of immigration is found in the text, *Challenge of Freedom*.

While the new government was still in its infancy, the Catholic Church was establishing its foundation in the United States. Along with the political, economic, social, and territorial development of the country there emerged the history of the Catholic Church in pioneer stage and growth.

The God-given rights and liberties found in our Constitution and Bill of Rights have been the teaching of the Catholic Church since its foundation by Christ Himself. Some of these Christian social principles are those of freedom and justice, the dignity and equality of every human being, the acknowledgment of God as the Supreme Being and Source of all authority, rights and duties common to all men, and the interdependence of people throughout the world.

In the twentieth-century world of today, we are faced with a serious challenge to our rights and liberties. Forces of evil are bent upon the destruction of moral principles and Christianity itself. All, then, who are engaged in the work of Catholic education should welcome every opportunity for the development of correct attitudes in our pupils in regard to Christian social principles. The content of this text is, therefore, of major significance.

A realization of the worth and importance of the Christian principles that guided our Founding Fathers in establishing our fundamental laws should inspire our pupils with gratitude to Almighty God for giving us this great land. May He continue to protect and safeguard our sacred rights and freedoms in this glorious country, the *Land of Our Lady!*

THE EDITORS

CONTENTS

UNIT ONE

1763—DISSATISFIED ENGLISHMEN. 1787 PATRIOTIC AMERICANS

UNIT TWO

LEADERS OF FREEDOM FORM A NEW GOVERNMENT

UNIT THREE

THE SUCCESS OF THE NEW PLAN OF GOVERNMENT

UNIT FOUR

JEFFERSONIAN DEMOCRACY IN ACTION

UNIT FIVE

WESTWARD TO THE MISSISSIPPI

UNIT SIX

CHANGES IN THE AMERICAN WAY OF LIFE

LIST OF MAPS

FOREWORD

THE publication of the "Land of Our Lady" Series marks a notable advancement in the field of history textbooks for Catholic elementary schools. The Series fulfills very effectively the need for history textbooks that are devoid of secularistic and materialistic tendencies and based on the sound principles of Christianity and therefore, a Christian philosophy of history.

This Series includes not only the factual data that comprise the history of America as a nation, but it incorporates also those elements of American Catholic history that can be assimilated by pupils of the elementary school level. The growth and development of the Catholic Church in the United States parallels the content of American history in each textbook of the Series.

The greatest contribution of these texts to the training and schooling of young American Catholic boys and girls is the manner in which Christian social principles are woven in the texts. As the various events of history are taken up for study, the textbooks point out the positive or negative correlation of the factual data to the principles of Christian social living.

We are grateful to the firm of Benziger Brothers, and to the competent Board of Editors and Authors for the task they have successfully accomplished in producing this American Catholic Series, "Land of Our Lady."

RT. REV. FREDERICK G. HOCHWALT, PH.D.
SECRETARY GENERAL, N.C.E.A.

Mary and Homes

MEANING. The angel told Mary: "The Holy Spirit shall come upon thee and the power of the most High shall overshadow thee" (Luke 1:35). Mary was like a beautiful golden house which became the dwelling place of the Holy Spirit, because she was the mother of God and was full of grace. The Catholic home should also be God's dwelling place. Through devotion to Jesus and Mary, through kindness to parents, brothers and sisters, a home can really become the "house of God."

APPLICATION. The family is the group in the community which sets an example of unity that is reflected among all other groups. A happy people passes on to others its spirit for the welfare of humanity. The family spirit of Nazareth, centering around Mary, the House of Gold, is a treasured example to all.

Prayer

House of gold, *pray for us.*

Litany of the Blessed Virgin

LORD, have mercy on us.
Christ, have mercy on us.
Lord, have mercy on us.
God the Son, Redeemer of the world, have mercy on us.
God, the Holy Ghost, have mercy on us.
Holy Trinity, one God, have mercy on us.
Christ, hear us.
Christ, graciously hear us.
God the Father of heaven, have mercy on us.
Holy Mary,[1]
Holy Mother of God,
Holy Virgin of virgins,
Mother of Christ,
Mother of divine grace,
Mother most pure,
Mother most chaste,
Mother inviolate,
Mother undefiled,
Mother most amiable,
Mother most admirable,
Mother of good counsel,
Mother of our Creator,
Mother of our Saviour,
Virgin most prudent,
Virgin most venerable,
Virgin most renowned,
  [1] Pray for us.

Virgin most powerful,
Virgin most merciful,
Virgin most faithful,
Mirror of justice,
Seat of wisdom,
Cause of our joy,
Spiritual vessel,
Vessel of honor,
Singular vessel of devotion,
Mystical Rose,
Tower of David,
Tower of ivory,
House of gold,
Ark of the covenant,
Gate of heaven,
Morning star,
Health of the sick,
Refuge of sinners,
Comforter of the afflicted,
Help of Christians,
Queen of angels,
Queen of patriarchs,
Queen of prophets,
Queen of apostles,
Queen of martyrs,
Queen of confessors,
Queen of virgins,
Queen of all saints,
Queen conceived without original sin,

Queen assumed into heaven,
Queen of the most holy Rosary,
Queen of peace.
Lamb of God, who takest away the sins of the world, spare us, O Lord.
Lamb of God, who takest away the sins of the world, graciously hear us, O Lord.
Lamb of God, who takest away the sins of the world, have mercy on us.
Christ, hear us. Christ, graciously hear us.
℣. Pray for us, O holy Mother of God. ℟. That we may be made worthy of the promises of Christ.
Let us pray
Grant, we beseech Thee, O Lord God, unto us Thy servants, that we may rejoice in continual health of mind and body; and, by the glorious intercession of blessed Mary ever Virgin, may be delivered from present sadness, and enter into the joy of Thine eternal gladness. Through Christ our Lord. Amen.

An indulgence of 7 years. A plenary indulgence once a month on the usual conditions for the daily devout recitation of this Litany with its versicle and prayer (See "The Raccolta," the official work of indulgenced prayers, page 216).

MARY AS A GUIDE THROUGH LIFE. The free will of man accepts the guidance of Mary in the way of life. This guidance of Mary is part of our religion. It affects our home life, our association with our fellow man, our civic obligations, our career in life, and our acceptance of life's problems.

Courtesy of Rev. J. B. Carol, O. F. M.

UNIT ONE

1763—DISSATISFIED ENGLISHMEN 1787—PATRIOTIC AMERICANS

CHAPTER I—MISUNDERSTANDINGS AND INJUSTICES LED TO SERIOUS QUARRELS

English and Colonial Ideas of Government
Troublesome Trade and Navigation Laws
Laws of King George III and English Parliament
Organized Protests by Colonists

CHAPTER II—DISAGREEMENT GROWS INTO REBELLION

Stamp Act—Resistance to It
Stamp Act Congress—First United Action against
   England
New Taxes—More Opposition—Colonies Punished
First Continental Congress—People United in Crisis
Warfare at Lexington, Massachusetts—Colonists
   Fighting for Rights

CHAPTER III—REVOLUTIONARY WAR—REBELLION FLARES INTO MILITARY CONFLICT

Second Continental Congress
Washington, Commander-in-Chief of Continental
   Army
American Declaration of Independence—Separation
   from England
War in Middle Colonies
Battle of Saratoga—Turning Point of War

CHAPTER IV—VICTORY AT LAST—INDEPENDENCE

Hardships at Valley Forge
Father Gibault's Work in Northwest Territory
Naval Heroes—Barry and Jones
War in the South
Burgoyne—Surrender at Yorktown
Treaty of Peace 1783

UNIT ONE

1763—DISSATISFIED ENGLISHMEN 1787—PATRIOTIC AMERICANS

BECAUSE of unjust laws, the people in England could no longer worship God as they wished. In order to regain this lost freedom, some of them left their homes in England to come to the New World. Another reason why these English people came to America was the hope of becoming rich by farming and by trading with the Indians.

You have learned that the same land was often claimed by more than one country and that the French and Indian War was fought to settle these claims. The Treaty of 1763 gave the largest share of land to England.

England became the greatest colonial power in the world of that day and the undisputed "mistress of the seas."

King George III and his Parliament (par'-li-ment) decided to tax the colonists to help pay the large war debt. The colonists objected to these laws because the colonies were not represented in the English Parliament and thus had nothing to say in the making of these laws.

One quarrel led to another until the colonies openly rebelled against England and declared their independence. Before this independence was gained, it was necessary to fight the long, hard war of the American Revolution.

In this Unit you will study: (1) the causes that led to rebellion; (2) the acts of armed resistance; (3) the fight for freedom which gained for the colonies their independence.

CHAPTER I

MISUNDERSTANDINGS AND INJUSTICES LEAD TO SERIOUS QUARRELS

Anything worth having is worth struggling for. The early Americans had many reasons to struggle for freedom. As good Americans, we want to learn the reasons why our forefathers rebelled against England. She insisted on taxing the people of the thirteen colonies unjustly. They resisted secretly at first but were finally forced to fight openly to protect their liberty and secure independence.

In this chapter we shall study the causes which led colonial America to rebel openly against British authority.

1. English and Colonial Ideas of Government

England had one idea of a colony: the colonists another. England, like all European countries, founded colonies to increase her wealth. The colonists could supply the mother country with food and raw materials while goods made in England could be sold in colonial markets.

England claimed the right to appoint colonial governors and to pass laws which would regulate trade and business in the colonies. She claimed the right to tax the colonies any time money was needed to run the home government. The English colonists had trouble with the French fur traders, and England sent troops and supplies to help the colonists. England wanted the colonists to pay for this help, so she decided to tax the colonists. England had been at war also and so she was in debt.

The colonists believed that they should choose their own governors, have their own form of government, and control their own trade. They did not wish England to interfere with their business. They believed they should be taxed only by a government in which they had representatives. Perhaps they were selfish. Perhaps England was selfish. Perhaps each should have tried to understand the other's ideas.

Suppose you had lived in one of the colonies during the eighteenth century. Would you think that your father had the right to elect the man who was to pass the tax laws which would pay the nation's bills? Or, would you feel that the English Parliament should write the laws for him and for all the other colonists without their consent?

Misunderstanding. Has it ever happened that you said or did something which offended even your best friends? You said, "I really did not mean it that way; you just misunderstood me." The people in the colonies and the people in England misunderstood each other.

They lived far apart, separated by three thousand miles of ocean. It took weeks for letters to come and go between England and America. Besides, a new way of life had begun in the colonies. It was the "American Way." The English could not understand any way but an English way of government.

For more than a century and a half, the people in America had been governing themselves in their own assemblies. They had been deciding many important matters in their town meetings also. This home rule made them more independent than the citizens of England. The English rulers did not realize that this change had taken place. They could not understand what the colonists meant when they used the word "representation."

In America, representation was based on population. The colonial legislatures were made up of men elected to represent the people in all sections of the colony. Each man elected went to the colonial assembly to safeguard the interests of the people by whom he was chosen. Towns or settlements were called burghs (burgs) or boroughs (bur'-owes), and representatives from the burghs were called burgesses (bur'-jes-es). The burgesses were elected by the people to represent them in the colonial legislatures, or assemblies.

In England, Parliament was the lawmaking body of the government. The authority of Parliament could not be questioned. Representation in Parliament was not based on population because no census had been taken for more than a hun-

The House of Commons, the lower house of Parliament, where tax laws were passed for the colonies

dred years. The people in the large cities had the same number of representatives as the people in the small villages.

The colonists could not understand why Parliament should claim the right to pass tax laws for them. Neither the English government nor the English people could understand what the colonists meant by "Taxation without Representation." Were they not British subjects? As such were they not represented in Parliament, even though they did not vote for their representatives?

The Trade and Navigation Acts. Another cause of misunderstanding was the trade and navigation acts which the English Parliament had passed in 1660 and 1663. Most of these acts were either broken or simply not enforced until after the French and Indian War in 1763. Then they were strictly enforced; so the colonists strongly protested.

The Navigation Acts were not new laws. They were laws passed to protect English trade. Many members of Parliament were merchants who were jealous of the large fortunes made by Dutch traders in the colonies. These merchants demanded that Parliament pass laws which would stop competition from merchants of foreign countries.

The first trade law passed by Parliament ruled that all goods brought to England or to the American colonies must be carried in English- or colonial-owned ships. This trade law actually helped the colonies. It encouraged the shipbuilding industry in New England. It also gave profit to the merchants of the ports of Boston, New York and Philadelphia. However, the British merchants feared that American ship owners were taking profit from them. They demanded other trade laws to limit this profit.

Disturbing news. Colonial ship owners and sea captains learned that England had passed another trade act. This time the colonists were still more displeased. The new law forbade them to carry products to any foreign country unless they first stopped at a British port and paid a tax.

An American harbor was a busy place in Colonial times. Why would Americans resent the Navigation Laws?

Many bitter words were spoken against the mother country as the old ship captains sat in the inns discussing their problems. The inn, in colonial days, was the place for exchanging news, since there were no daily newspapers. The news was carried from inn to inn by post riders.

The colonists could not understand why Parliament passed these trade laws. There was no reason for forbidding colonial trade with other nations. Many of the colonists would not pay the taxes because they believed the laws were unjust. They planned to trade secretly with the forbidden countries.

King George III

Culver

Secret trading to avoid the payment of taxes is called smuggling.

New trade law is ignored. For over a hundred years this secret trade continued. The British government, busy with war and other troubles at home, had little time to learn what was happening in America. Colonial legislatures were passing laws which the colonists believed necessary for peace and order. They passed tax laws to collect money for necessary colonial expenses. This showed that they did not object to taxation if they could decide the taxes for themselves. Any interference on the part of England which would take away their right to govern themselves was quickly resented. England watched the colonies grow rich and powerful.

2. A New King—Trouble Begins

George III. The colonists did not approve of the young King of England, George III. They believed he would not be a just king. George was the son of a German Princess. His mother had determined that her son should be a forceful ruler. She kept repeating to him: "George, be king!" When George became king he resolved that his American subjects must be made to accept the laws of Parliament. Perhaps trouble would not have started so soon if George III had understood his colonial subjects.

Disagreement. In 1763, Lord Grenville became Prime Minister, or the chief officer in the British government. He and King George III decided to enforce the old trade and navigation laws. But the colonists refused to obey the new laws because they had ignored the old trade and navigation laws. Besides, their trade with other countries was old and well established.

Soon a fleet was ordered to patrol the coast to stop the smuggling. Troops were landed in America to see that all taxes ordered by Parliament were paid. The colonists believed that these soldiers were their enemies. They made fun of them and nick-named them "red-coats" because of the color of their uniforms. These soldiers did not want to be in America. They were not happy when they had to search the homes of the colonists, for they too believed that "An Englishman's home is his castle."

Writs of Assistance. Even the fleet sent by England did not stop the smuggling. Parliament now passed a law which allowed the use of papers called "Writs of Assistance." These writs permitted English soldiers to enter the home or the store of any colonist to search for smuggled goods.

Colonists protest the Writs of Assistance. Meetings of protest were held in every colony. Leaders of the colonists criticized the government for daring to issue these writs. They questioned the right of Parliament to allow searches of private homes in the colonies. These leaders demanded that something be done and urged the colonists to resist such unfair treatment.

From the balcony of the Old State House in Boston, James Otis (owe'-tis) addressed a gathering of cheering townspeople. In a fiery speech, he declared that England was making the colonists almost slaves. He said that England was taking from them the rights to live, to be free, to be happy, and to enjoy the privacy of home.

These are sacred, God-given rights which every good government must protect. Every citizen must safeguard them by knowing and appreciating their value.

Words you should know

burgesses   competition   interference
enforce   representation   census
legislature   representatives   assemblies

Things to talk about

1. It is 1765. Your Father, a Catholic merchant in the colonies, is losing business because of the Trade Laws. What should he do?

2. James Otis, a lawyer in Massachusetts, defended the colonists against the Writs of Assistance. Was he justified? What did he have to say?

Match Column A with Column B

Column A

1. Parliament
2. Writs of Assistance
3. smuggling
4. James Otis
5. George III
6. rebellion

Column B

a. fight against the government
b. lawmaking body in England
c. stirred the people against injustices
d. our way of governing
e. trading secretly to avoid taxes
f. a heavy tax
g. an unreasonable ruler of England
h. papers permitting English soldiers to search colonial property at any time.

Who's Who in Chapter I

Number lines on a paper from 1 to 8. After each number write the correct answers. There are two answers for each number.

1. In what two ways were colonies valuable to the mother country?

2. A conflict arose between two ways of life. What were these two ways?

3. Its members believed it was unjust to make the British people at home pay all the war debt. Name this body. Its ruler believed the same. Who was he?

4. People who believed they should be taxed only by a government in which they had representatives. Name the people. What were their representatives called?

Select the word or words which best complete the sentence.

1. James Otis defended the colonists against
    a. smuggling
    b. Writs of Assistance
    c. George III
    d. Indians

2. The English taxed the _____ in order to pay for the French and Indian war.
    a. Indians
    b. Canadian fur traders
    c. American colonies
    d. red-coats

3. _____ claimed the right to appoint colonial governor for the colonists
    a. England
    b. French missionaries
    c. Colonial merchants
    d. Judges

4. In early America, representation was based on _____.
    a. competition
    b. census
    c. representation
    d. wealth

5. One big cause of misunderstanding between the English government and the colonies was __.
    a. the townspeople
    b. Lafayette
    c. Trade and Navigation Laws
    d. Benjamin Franklin

6. George III was the son of ____.
    a. a German Princess
    b. a French King
    c. an English nobleman
    d. a Canadian governor

7. From the balcony of _____, Otis declared England was making the colonists almost slaves
    a. a private home
    b. the State House
    c. an English auditorium
    d. a town hall

8. England and the colonies were separated by _____ of ocean.
    a. 80 leagues
    b. 300,000 sq. yards
    c. 3,000 miles
    d. 100 miles

9. _____ was made up of men elected to represent the people in the colonies.
    a. the English Parliament
    b. the British Navy
    c. the red-coats
    d. the colonial legislature

10. An English fleet patrolled the Atlantic Coast in order to stop _____.
    a. American leaders
    b. the smuggling
    c. fur traders
    d. Spanish explorers

DISAGREEMENT GROWS INTO REBELLION

Actions speak louder than words. After 1763, serious quarrels began between the thirteen colonies and England. Disputes arose over taxes, trade, and colonial forms of government. George III had not tried to understand the difficulties. If he tried, new laws would not have been forced upon the colonists at this time. The American colonists were liberty-loving people. They had left the Old World in search of freedom—freedom of religion, freedom from want, and freedom to rule themselves.

England made unfair demands upon the people of America. These demands united the colonists to work together for the good of all.

In this chapter you will learn that the resentment over taxation increased as time went on. Finally, there was nothing for the colonists to do but to fight against Great Britain for their rights.

1. Stamp Act—Trouble Begins

The hated Stamp Act. Parliament did not try to understand why the colonists opposed the Navigation Acts and the Writs of Assistance. Instead it passed more tax laws in 1765. One of these laws was the Stamp Act. This act required that all newspapers, calendars, and official papers bear a stamp showing that a sum of money had been paid to the British government. This act was openly opposed.

The Stamp Act was not much different from our tax laws today. The sticker on the windshield of an automobile is a "stamp." You can find tax stamps on playing cards, tobacco, and many other articles. We feel that such taxes are necessary to pay the expenses of our government.

The colonists did not object to paying the tax; but they believed that the right to tax belonged to their representatives, not to the English Parliament in which they had no representation.

The colonists oppose taxation. Leaders in America persuaded the colonists to oppose the Stamp Act, for it took away their right to tax themselves. The Act affected every colony and every group of people. In Massachusetts, Samuel Adams roused the colonists to fight against this new law.

In Virginia, a young lawyer, Patrick Henry, had been elected by the Virginians to represent them in the House of Burgesses. He urged the burgesses to pass a resolution against the Stamp Act and declared that "the local legislature was the only government which had a right to tax the people of Virginia." Upon hearing this, several members of the House shouted, "Treason!" Patrick Henry retorted, "If this be treason, make the most of it!" A vote was taken, and Patrick Henry's resolution was adopted.

The Sons of Liberty. Many others, like Patrick Henry, believed that the Stamp Act should be abolished.

In almost every colony, clubs called "Sons of Liberty" were formed to prevent the sale and use of stamps. Members of

Brown Brothers

A document with a stamp as required by English law

these clubs compelled the stamp agents to resign and destroyed all the stamps they could get. In Boston, the home of Thomas Hutchinson, the Chief Justice, was burned down.

The Stamp Act of Congress. The members of the Massachusetts Legislature, among whom were James Otis and Samuel Adams, planned a Stamp Act Congress to be held in New York on October 7, 1765. They invited the other colonies to send delegates.

Patrick Henry delivers his Speech against unjust taxation

Nine colonies accepted the invitation. At this congress the delegates decided that the colonies should be taxed only by a legislature in which they were represented.

A message was sent to King George III and to the English Parliament. The message explained that the delegates considered themselves loyal British subjects. However, they felt deprived of their rights as Englishmen. They reminded the King that they could not, and would not, accept the Stamp Act because it meant "taxation without representation."

Parliament repeals the Stamp Act. Soon "taxation without representation" became a battle cry. The Sons of Liberty, led by Samuel Adams, the "Father of the Revolution," encouraged the colonists to boycott the British merchants. To boycott means to refuse to buy or to use certain goods.

American colonists agreed not to buy any manufactured articles or goods from English merchants until the tax was discontinued. When Americans refused to buy English goods, the British merchants lost money. They complained about the Stamp Act and asked Parliament for help. The Stamp Act was repealed in 1766. This action was taken, not because the British were following God's law of justice, but rather because of the selfishness of the British merchants. They were losing money; so they demanded that the law be changed.

2. The Spirit of Rebellion Continues

Townshend Acts. For a while the bitter feeling between England and the American colonies died down because most of the tax laws had been repealed.

In 1767 discontent again became evident. The new Prime Minister, Charles Townshend, caused much of this bitter feeling to grow. Through his efforts taxes were placed on items like lead, tea, glass, paint, and paper. These were things the colonists needed. Parliament hoped to collect a great deal of money through these new taxes. England planned to use the tax money to pay the

Gatherings of angry colonists discussed the evils of taxation without representation

salaries of the governors and other English officers in the colonies. Again, it was not the tax which angered the colonists, but the reason for the tax. The colonists did not want these "hired" Englishmen. Why should they pay their salaries?

The colonists became so troublesome that Parliament soon saw that England was gaining nothing by the Townshend Acts. All taxes were removed except a small tax on tea. This tax was to show that England had the power to make laws for the colonies when she so desired. For a few years there was peace in the colonies.

The Committees of Correspondence. Although the colonies were enjoying this period of peace, many patriots in the colonies were watching every movement of the British government. In 1772, at a town meeting in Boston, Samuel Adams suggested the forming of "Committees of Correspondence" in each town of Massachusetts. This suggestion was accepted and committees met to discuss the action of the British. These committees exchanged letters. They wrote reports of activities and conditions in their own towns and sent copies of the reports to every other town. Before long Committees of Correspondence were established in the other colonies. Through letters a spirit of unity was developed among all colonists who opposed British rule.

Why the tea tax? Many of the colonists were still angry about the tax on tea, which they refused to buy, even though it was much cheaper than the tea smuggled in from Holland. Tea had for long been the favorite drink of English people. Yet these Englishmen would rather do without their tea than pay a single penny tax on a pound of tea.

Everywhere in the colonies plans were made to keep the taxed tea from being sold. In Charleston, South Carolina, the tea was stored in damp cellars and left to spoil. Ships carrying tea were not allowed to unload in New York or in Philadelphia. The people of Boston determined to prevent the unloading of a shipment of tea which was soon to arrive there.

One cold December night in 1773, three ships were in Boston harbor. The colonists had warned the captains to leave the harbor and not to unload the tea. But Governor Hutchinson would not permit the ships to leave until the tea had been unloaded and the taxes paid.

Boston Tea Party. This was a very unusual tea party. The guests were not welcome. Dressed as Indian braves, carrying hatchets and tomahawks, they went aboard the three British ships. They dumped all the tea overboard. The teapot was Boston Harbor. The cup of tea they made was worth about seventy-five thousand dollars ($75,000). We can understand why the colonists were angry, but we cannot excuse the unjust destruction of property. The merchants who owned the tea were not to blame for the tax. Yet it was their tea that was destroyed. It was their loss.

Boston is punished. King George and his advisors were stunned at the unruly action of the Bostonians. The English government passed very severe laws to punish the people of Massachusetts. The patriots called these new laws "Intolerable Acts" because they could not stand them.

These laws provided that: (1) The port of Boston was to be closed until the East India Company was paid for the destroyed tea; (2) Self-government was to be taken from the colony. The governor was to permit no town meetings; (3) The colonists were to feed and house English soldiers in their homes when the barracks were filled; (4) British officials charged with serious crimes were to be sent to England for trial. They were not to be tried in colonial courts.

Quebec Act. Another act passed at this time was the Quebec (quee-bek') Act. This act is sometimes included among the "Intolerable Acts." By it all the land north of the Ohio River and east of the Mississippi River was made part of Canada.

The colonists of Massachusetts, New York, and Connecticut bitterly resented this act because it took away their western lands, which had been given to them by their charters.

The act also granted freedom of religion to the Canadians living in this region. Most of these Canadians were Catholics. The colonists resented this part of the act. They were not in favor of religious freedom for Catholics. Some of the colonists even claimed that the King was favoring Catholics.

Although most of the colonists had come to America to enjoy freedom of worship, yet

The Boston Tea Party

they wished to deny that right to others. Remember the hardships the early colonists suffered for their religious beliefs.

3. The Spirit of Rebellion Grows

Colonies aid Boston. The Committees of Correspondence spread the news of what had happened in Boston. Secret and open meetings were held in towns and cities throughout the colonies. The colonists were angry at the way England had treated Boston. They knew the people of Boston would have a hard time getting supplies because the port of Boston had been closed. The other colonies sent the Bostonians food, clothing, and other necessary supplies by land. As a result of the Intolerable Acts a stronger spirit of friendliness and understanding developed among the thirteen colonies.

A plan for united action again was made. The Virginia House of Burgesses sent out a call asking all the colonies to meet and talk over the dangers facing America.

Samuel Adams suggested

that the colonies send delegates to a colonial congress in Philadelphia. All responded except Georgia.

First Continental Congress. On September 5, 1774, more than fifty American leaders met at Carpenter's Hall in Philadelphia. George Washington and Patrick Henry from Virginia were there, and John Hancock and Samuel Adams from Massachusetts. Charles Carroll was sent from Maryland. This meeting was known as the "First Continental Congress." The members discussed the problems which faced the colonists. They talked especially of the way England had treated Boston. They felt that an attack on one colony was an attack on all.

After weeks of discussion, the Congress decided to send to England a long letter called the "Declaration of Rights." In it the colonists protested againt the Intolerable Acts, the Quebec Act, and the other laws passed by the English Parliament.

The colonists said they would not buy any British goods or sell any American goods to England until the objectionable laws were repealed. They promised their loyalty to King George III but said nothing

Brown Brothers

Carpenter's Hall, Philadelphia

about independence or breaking away from England.

The members of this Congress also planned to hold another meeting in Philadelphia during the following May, unless they received a favorable reply to their letter.

Both sides act. The danger of war was becoming more real. General Gage had been appointed Governor of Massachusetts. He brought English troops to Boston to protect people who favored English rule. Such people were called Tories.

The colonists felt that Gage's soldiers were a threat to their freedom. In every colony, troops began drilling. Military supplies were being gathered and hidden for an emergency.

Minutemen. The patriots around Boston had collected gunpowder, bullets, and guns and stored them in a barn near the town of Concord. Some of the colonists drilled together on their village greens. They formed a militia ready to fight the British the minute they were called to action. These soldiers came to be known as "minutemen."

General Gage was watching very closely the actions of the men around Boston. The "Sons of Liberty" also learned that Gage planned to send troops to Lexington to arrest Adams and Hancock, who had fled there for safety.

When would the British troops begin to march, and which route would they take? Sentries were stationed in the tower of the Old North Church in Boston. They were ready to give the signal, if the British troops should move.

A flash of a lantern, and then another! This was the signal

Paul Revere rides through the night to warn the Colonists of the British attack

agreed upon to signify that the British were beginning to march to Lexington. Paul Revere and William Dawes, who had been watching for the signal, rode on fast horses in different directions to Lexington to tell the minutemen to get ready to fight.

All through the night of April 18, 1775, Paul Revere galloped towards Lexington. He was the first messenger to arrive and he warned John Hancock and Samuel Adams that the British were coming to arrest them. Before the "red-coats" arrived, Hancock and Adams slipped away and were on the road to Philadelphia to attend the Second Continental Congress.

The shot heard 'round the world. Long before daybreak, the sharp, quick steps of the marching British could be heard as they moved towards Lexington. They did not realize that the minutemen were ready. As the British came near Lexington Green, they were met by about fifty minutemen.

"Disperse, ye rebels!" shouted Major Pitcairn, the British leader. "Disperse, ye rebels! Lay down your arms and disperse!"

Yet "disperse" they would not. These brave patriots obeyed their leader, Captain Parker, who ordered: "Don't fire unless fired upon; but if they mean to have war, let it begin here!"

A shot rang out! No one knew who fired it. The fighting had begun. Eight of the minutemen lay dead or injured on Lexington Green.

The British column then turned and marched towards Concord, where another battle took place. The British destroyed the minutemen's small store of ammunition and then prepared to return to Boston. As they marched along, the entire countryside, angered by the reports from Lexington and Concord, came out armed with guns and pitchforks. The weary "red-coats" were no match for these angry patriots who fought Indian-fashion from behind stone walls, rocks, trees, or barns. Before the British soldiers reached Boston, almost three hundred of their men were missing.

The news of the attack at Lexington and Concord spread far and wide. It reached all the colonies. It also reached King George III and his ministers in England.

Soon the whole world knew

The Battle of Lexington. Why was this battle important in the Revolutionary War?

that the American colonies were rebelling against England. As an American poet wrote, the shot fired at Concord was "heard 'round the world." The fight for freedom had begun.

Words and phrases you should know

taxation without representation
Sons of Liberty
boycott of British merchants
rights of Englishmen
Committees of Correspondence

Intolerable Acts
Lexington Green
Tories
minutemen
sentries

Things to talk about

1. Most of the colonists came to America for freedom of religious worship. Why did they deny that right to Catholics?

2. Today, Americans pay more money in taxes than the American colonists were asked to pay England. Why do we not refuse to pay these taxes as the colonists did?

Test your memory for facts

1. The British government passed the Stamp Act in the year _____.

2. The Virginian patriot who opposed taxation was _____.

3. On April 18, _____, the first battle of the Revolutionary War took place at _____, Massachusetts.

4. The _____ Acts were passed to punish _____.

5. The Townshend Acts placed a tax on _____, _____ and _____.

6. The "Sons of Liberty" were formed to _____ the sale and use of stamps.

7. The Stamp Act was repealed in the year _____.

8. At a town meeting in Boston, Samuel Adams suggested the forming of _____ _____ _____ to discuss the action of the British.

9. Because Parliament passed the _____ _____ colonists were forced to support British soldiers in their homes.

10. On September 5, 1774, the _____ _____ _____ was held at Carpenter's Hall in Philadelphia.

A Reason Test - Choose the one that is correct

1. The colonists opposed taxation because
   a. they had no money.
   b. it took away their right to tax themselves.
   c. they hated England.
   d. they could boycott English merchants no longer.

2. The Boston Tea Party was a very unusual party because
   a. the guests were all welcome.
   b. everyone drank tea.
   c. Governor Hutchinson was there.
   d. the party cost $75,000.

3. All of the land north of the Ohio River and east of the Mississippi River was made part of Canada because of
   a. the Navigation Acts.
   b. the Townshend Acts.
   c. the Quebec Act.
   d. all acts of Parliament.

4. One reason the minutemen are famous is because
   a. the British came to arrest them.
   b. they were expertly trained over a long period.
   c. they fought the British the minute they were called to action.
   d. they had no guns.

35

CHAPTER III

REBELLION FLARES INTO WAR

Submit or fight. The right to govern themselves is one which Americans have always considered sacred. You recall that the colonial charters gave the colonists in America this right. The laws which governed them were passed in their Assemblies by local representatives. The people themselves elected these men.

England was heavily in debt after the French and Indian War. In order to raise money and to pay these war expenses, Parliament passed new tax laws. The American colonies resented these taxes and refused to pay them. They declared it was their right as Englishmen to tax themselves. They requested Parliament to withdraw all tax laws.

The colonial leaders claimed the colonists in America were taxed by a government in which they had no representatives.

How could the members of Parliament know or understand the Americans' problems? Besides, some of these members had little or no interest in the colonies in the New World. Thus, when England tried to take away certain rights, the colonies rebelled.

In this chapter you will study: (1) the earlier part of the Revolutionary War; (2) the Declaration of Independence, which announced our freedom to the people of the United States and to the rest of the world.

1. Colonists Fight for Rights

The Second Continental Congress. You will remember that when the Stamp Act was in effect the colonists met at Philadelphia to discuss what might be done to repeal it. Now, for the second time, the colonists were about to hold a meeting to plan united action. Shortly after the fight-

36

ing at Concord and Lexington, their leaders met at the State House in Philadelphia, May 10, 1775. This meeting is known as the Second Continental Congress.

The members of Congress desired to work out a way for settling the trouble between the colonists and Parliament. Most of them hoped that peace might be made. Yet they knew they had to prepare to defend the colonists' rights.

At the beginning of the Congress, John Adams asked that the minutemen form a Colonial Army. Immediately every member agreed that an army was necessary for the defense of the rights of Americans. These rights were sacred to them. All were determined to safeguard them.

Washington in command of the Continental Army. George Washington, who had won glory as a soldier during the French and Indian War, was appointed the first commander-in-chief of this army. He firmly believed in the claims of the colonists. All recognized him as a man of ability, courage, and honor.

George Washington is appointed Commander-in-chief of the Continental Army

Culver

Not long after his appointment, General Washington left for Massachusetts to take command of the army at Cambridge. On his way to take command of the army, Washington received news that a fight had taken place at Bunker Hill.

"Did the militia fight?" he asked. When Washington was told that they had fought bravely, he exclaimed: "Then the liberties of the country are safe."

Colonel Prescott at Bunker Hill. At the time Washington was on his way to take command of the army, a large band of English soldiers was in Boston. The colonists were determined to drive them out.

On the night of June 16, 1775, fifteen hundred volunteers commanded by Colonel William Prescott secretly fortified Breed's Hill which overlooked the British camp. On the morning of June 17, 1775, General Howe, the British commander, ordered his soldiers to drive the rebels out.

The colonial troops had only a small supply of ammunition. So the men were ordered to

The Americans prepare to repulse the British, at the Battle of Bunker Hill

shoot "only when you see the white of their eyes."

The British were twice driven down the hill. On the third charge the Americans were forced to leave because they had no more gunpowder.

This battle, later called the Battle of Bunker Hill, was a victory for the British. The battle was very important for it showed that the colonists had courage to fight, and because it made the people very proud of the men who had done so much with so little.

The gateway to Canada. Meanwhile in May, 1775, Ethan Allen, with a group of "Green Mountain Boys" from Vermont, surprised the British at Fort Ticonderoga (tie-con-der-owe'-ga) in northern New York. These patriots captured the fort and much ammunition.

This victory gave the Americans control of the easiest route to Canada. The ammunition and cannon captured at Ticonderoga were sent to Boston, and the following winter they were used against the British.

Attempt to gain Canada. Since the Vermont patriots had been successful at Ticonderoga, Congress planned an invasion of Canada.

With the consent of General Washington, Richard Montgomery led a patriot army into Canada and succeeded in capturing Montreal. With a group of soldiers from New England, Benedict Arnold was sent to join Montgomery. In December, 1775, during a terrific blizzard, the two forces attacked Quebec.

The French people of Quebec refused to assist the Americans because they remembered that the Americans strongly opposed the Quebec Act ten years before. The Canadians were so grateful to England for giving them freedom of religion that they remained loyal to her.

The Americans fought hard and well at Quebec, but they lost the battle. They also lost their general, Richard Montgomery, and Benedict Arnold was wounded.

An effort to win the help of Canada. The military attack on Canada failed because the colonists did not get the support of the Canadian people. In the spring of 1776 the Second Continental Congress sent a delegation to ask the Canadians to help them in their fight for freedom.

Benjamin Franklin, Samuel Chase, and Charles Carroll were appointed by Congress to go to Canada. Charles Carroll

Washington takes command of the
Continental Army

July 3, 1775. What a sight he beheld! An armed mob, not trained soldiers, waited to greet him under a great elm tree, known since then as the "Washington Elm." Only a few had blue-and-buff uniforms; the others wore everyday clothes, and many of them were rather ragged. How different from the well-trained and well-dressed United States Army today!

Washington's first task was to get supplies and to train these New England farmers and laborers to be soldiers. This training was difficult, for the men had enlisted for only a few months or a year. They wanted to return to their homes and farms as soon as their period of service had ended.

The Second Continental Congress, which was acting as the war government, had no power either to draft these men or to keep them in the regular army. It could neither pay these soldiers a salary nor buy them supplies. If they had not had a strong spirit of liberty, these patriotic people would never have had the courage to go on. They were convinced their cause was a noble one. Inspired by the example of their great leader, George Washington, these soldiers became the back-

was probably chosen because he was the leading American Catholic in the colonies. He took with him his cousin, Father John Carroll. It was thought these men might use their influence to win over the French Catholics to the American side.

The French could not be swayed, and again refused to help the American colonists. In this refusal, they were encouraged by their Catholic leader, Bishop Briand (bree-an').

The Continental Army. Washington did not take command of the Continental Army until bone of the Continental Army. **The British leave Boston.** Washington's army was fairly well-drilled by the early part of 1776. But it could not attack the the British at Boston, for it did not have enough guns and ammunition. As soon as the cannon and ammunition captured at Ticonderoga reached Boston, Washington's army camped on Dorchester Heights, a hill overlooking Boston Harbor. There strong defenses were built. From this location the army threatened the British fleet anchored in the harbor.

On March 17, 1776, General Howe, who had replaced General Gage as the commander of the British forces, ordered the fleet to sail for Nova Scotia. The small British garrison from Boston and more than a thousand Loyalists, who remained faithful to England, went with the fleet. War in New England was ended.

2. Colonists Move Towards Independence

Yield — or separate. Colonial leaders realized that the King considered them disloyal subjects. They had organized an army. They had captured British forts. They had driven the British army from New England. The colonists had committed acts of war. The King could not now believe they wanted to be loyal to him. But he himself had treated the colonies unjustly. He had even hired thirty thousand German soldiers to fight the American colonists. By such actions he had done more than Samuel Adams, Patrick Henry, or James Otis to stir up the American people to revolt.

Other colonists also spoke and wrote against English rule. Thomas Paine distributed his booklet called *Common Sense*. In this booklet he urged the colonies to keep the freedom they had, and to break away from England. He convinced thousands of Americans to fight for independence.

Samuel Adams began begging Congress to declare America independent. This was a very new idea and the Congress did not believe it could be done. However, by the middle of 1776, most of the Americans had decided that they must choose between independence or service to an unjust government. The delegates from North Carolina were the first to vote for independence. Gradually the other colonies followed. **The Declaration of Independence.** On June 7, 1776, Richard Henry

41

Brown Brothers
Independence Hall, Philadelphia, where the Declaration of Independence was signed

Lee of Virginia said in a resolution, "These united colonies are, and of right ought to be free and independent states." John Adams seconded this resolution. Then for many weeks the question of independence was debated. At last, five leaders, John Adams, Benjamin Franklin, Robert Livingston, Roger Sherman, and Thomas Jefferson were appointed to draw up a statement declaring independence. Adams asked Thomas Jefferson to write the final form of the "Declaration of Independence."

The Declaration of Independence was officially accepted by the Congress on July 4, 1776. Then and there a new nation was born.

The bell in Independence Hall, in Philadelphia, proclaimed this joyful news to the assembled patriots. The people shouted, cannon roared, and bonfires were lighted.

Messengers on swift horses carried copies of the declaration from town to town. Before long, everyone in the thirteen colonies heard the news and was delighted. There were celebrations everywhere.

The Declaration of Independence tells us that God created all men equal and gave them certain rights, among which are the rights to life, liberty, and happiness. It tells us that governments receive their rights from the consent of the people, and that if a government does not protect the people's rights it may be changed, or a new government may be formed.

In this remarkable document, Jefferson listed the unjust things King George III and his government were doing to the colonists in America.

The declaration ends with the statement that the English colonies are and ought to be free and independent states.

Drafting the Declaration of Independence

Relying on the Providence of God, the members pledged their lives, their fortunes, and their honor to make America free.

Signers of the Declaration of Independence. John Hancock, the president of the Second Continental Congress, was the first to sign the document. He wrote his name very large and said: "There, King George can read that without his spectacles."

After signing the Declaration, Benjamin Franklin said, "From now on, citizens, we must all hang together or most assuredly we shall all hang separately." Charles Carroll of Carrollton, one of the richest men in the colonies, was the only Catholic to sign this document. By signing the declaration he showed his trust in God and his love of country. By August 2, 1776, all the delegates had signed this famous document.

Although the men who drew up the Declaration of Independence were not Catholics, the document expresses truths which the Catholic Church taught then and is still teaching. In the Declaration of Independence, our dependence upon God is shown to be a necessary part of American life. The document tells us that life itself and all human rights are given to us by God. The signers of this great work built our nation on religion. They showed that true Americanism has nothing in common with atheism.

3. The American Flag

Colonists adopt a national flag. Each colony had its own flag. During the early part of the Revolutionary War many different flags could be seen on the same battlefield. As soon as the Declaration of Independence was signed, the colonists saw the need of a national banner. Congress arranged to have one made.

The new flag would have thirteen stripes, alternating red and white, and thirteen white stars arranged in a circle on a blue field. The thirteen stripes and stars represented the thirteen colonies and showed that all were equal. The unbroken circle of stars on the blue field signified that the people were united by the Christian ideals expressed in the Declaration of Independence. On June 14, 1777, this flag was adopted as the national emblem.

In 1791 and 1792, Vermont and Kentucky were admitted to the Union. Their admission changed the number of stars and stripes from thirteen to fifteen. But as other sections asked for admission, it became impossible to add a star for each.

In 1818, it was decided to have thirteen stripes to represent the original colonies and to add a star as each new state was admitted to the Union.

Betsy Ross' flag. There is an interesting story connected with our flag. It is one of our favorite American legends. George Washington, Colonel Ross, and Robert Morris visited the home of Bety Ross on Arch Street in Philadelphia. They asked Betsy to make a flag. When George Washington gave her the sketch he had drawn for the new flag she suggested that the stars have five points instead of six. The flag which Betsy Ross made had thirteen stripes with thirteen five-pointed stars.

Some say that this flag was the one hoisted over Fort Stanwix, now Rome, New York. Others say that it was the one flown from the mast of Captain John Paul Jones' ship in which he sailed to France in 1777.

Red, White, and Blue. "Old

Betsy Ross is said to have made the first American flag

Glory" stirs the spirit of patriotism in every American heart. It makes us proud to be American citizens. We should thank God for the freedom of which the American flag is a symbol, that freedom for which the colonial patriots fought so bravely to keep and which we now enjoy.

The colors in our flag speak a language. The red means courage and daring; the white represents purity and liberty; and the blue stands for reverence to God, loyalty, and justice. The future of America depends on how wisely Americans treasure their blessings and how carefully they guard them!

4. Colonists Fight for Independence

The British capture New York. Soon after the British left Boston, Washington moved his forces from Boston to New York. He knew that the British would soon try to capture it because of its fine harbor.

Early in the summer of 1776, Admiral Howe, with a large fleet, and the Admiral's brother, Genral Howe, with thirty thousand soldiers landed

The British prepare to execute Nathan Hale

on Staten Island in New York harbor. They hoped to capture Washington's army and cut off New England from the rest of the colonies.

In August, 1776, the British force attacked and defeated the small force of Americans on Long Island. Washington ordered a retreat across the East River to Manhattan. A heavy fog during the night protected the Americans from enemy fire. When the British attacked the next day, the Americans had gone! Washington retreated north, and the British took New York, which they held until the end of the war.

Nathan Hale—an American hero. General Washington did not intend to remain defeated. He must know the British plans. Calling his soldiers together, he asked for a volunteer to go behind the enemy lines to get this information. Many responded. Nathan Hale, a young school teacher from Connecticut, was chosen for this dangerous work. He disguised himself as a Dutch schoolmaster and entered the enemy territory. There he obtained the needed information.

On his way back to Washington's headquarters, a Loyalist recognized and reported him.

On the following day the British hanged him as a spy. Hale's last words were "I regret that I have but one life to lose for my country."

The retreat across New Jersey. The enemy controlled New York City and the lower Hudson. The Americans were forced to retreat through New Jersey. As soon as Washington and his army had crossed the Delaware, he ordered his men to destroy all boats along the shore.

The British followed but could not cross the river. General Howe thought it unnecessary to follow Washington immediately and ordered his men back to New York to wait until the river should freeze.

Trenton and Princeton—renewed hope. General Washington did not wait until the British attacked him. As soon as he could, he courageously led his army across the river again. After marching nine miles in a blinding snow storm, they reached Trenton, New Jersey.

Three regiments of Hessians,

Washington crosses the Delaware

the German troops hired by England, were celebrating Christmas. On the following morning at daybreak, Washington made a sudden attack. After hours of fighting, a thousand prisoners were taken, as well as a great quantity of powder and food supplies.

This victory encouraged the Americans and angered the British. An army under Lord Cornwallis was sent to retake Trenton. Cornwallis did not attack at once but gave his soldiers time to rest. He said: "At last we have run down the 'old fox' and we will bag him in the morning."

But the "old fox" did not wait to be "bagged." In the night, Washington moved his men to Princeton at the rear of the enemy. Cornwallis did not suspect that the Americans had left camp. The American camp fires were burning and some soldiers pretended to be working on defenses for the planned battle of the next day. What a surprise when a cannon roar told Cornwallis that the Americans were attacking his rear guard at Princeton miles away.

Cornwallis sent his army some aid, but it was too late. The Americans soon were on Morristown Heights, where they were protected from the enemy.

Howe's army returned to New York. The British commanders realized that it would not be easy to defeat the rebels.

Robert Morris. General Washington knew that victory alone would not keep his army together. Money was needed to supply the men with food, clothing, and ammunition. Washington appealed to his friend, Robert Morris, a banker in Philadelphia. This man went from house to house in his city and raised fifty thousand dollars for the American cause. Without this help, the war could not have been carried on.

5. British Attempt to Divide the Colonies
The British Plan for 1777. The victories at Trenton and Princeton raised the spirits of the Americans. When the British saw that the Americans could not be easily defeated, they made a new plan for the year 1777. The plan depended upon the action of three armies:

1. Colonel St. Leger (saint lej'-er) was to sail to Fort Oswego on Lake Ontario. Then he was to march through the Mohawk Valley to join the other armies at Albany.

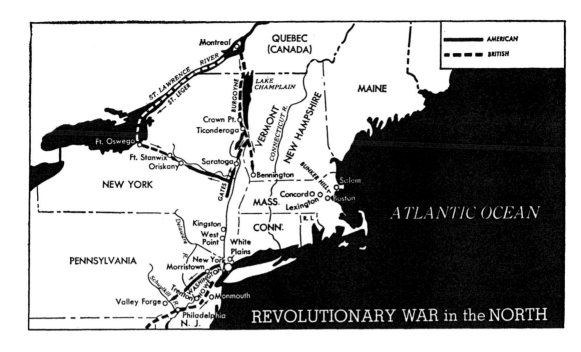

REVOLUTIONARY WAR in the NORTH

2. General Burgoyne (burgoin') was to lead his army from Montreal by way of Lake Champlain and then across the Hudson River at Albany.

3. General Howe was to advance up the Hudson River from New York City and meet the other armies at Albany.

The British hoped to capture the State of New York and to cut off New England from the other colonies. General Washington sent some of his best troops to the New York area because he knew that the state must be held.

Stars and Stripes fly over Fort Stanwix. Following the British plan for 1777, Colonel St. Leger marched down the Mohawk Valley. His troops attacked the Americans at Fort Stanwix. The British were defeated there by the people who lived nearby and some troops under Benedict Arnold. It was here that the "Stars and Stripes" waved for the first time over an American battlefield. The patriots hoisted the American flag above the British flag. The British flag was turned upside down as a sign of the British defeat.

Saratoga, an important American victory. General Burgoyne started from Montreal along Lake Champlain and defeated some American colonists who held Fort Ticonderoga. Then he marched to Fort Edward which is located at the upper end of the Hudson River.

The deep forests made the marching difficult. Besides, his route was blocked by American troops under General Schuyler (sky'-ler). As Schuyler moved ahead of Burgoyne, his men burned bridges and cut down trees which they placed across the roads.

The delay caused the British supplies to run low. Burgoyne sent a troop of soldiers to Vermont to seize some food, but they were defeated at Bennington. After this American victory, thousands of men poured out from the farms of New York and New England and enlisted in the American army.

As Burgoyne neared Saratoga, he learned that St. Leger had returned to Canada and that Howe was still in Philadelphia. In desperation he attacked the American forces and fought two battles near Saratoga.

The combined forces of the American army began to surround the British soldiers at Saratoga. When Burgoyne saw that he was being trapped, he made a vigorous attack. But he suffered a crushing defeat. Burgoyne and his entire army surrendered to the Americans under General Gates. This victory took place on October 17, 1777.

Saratoga was the turning point of the war. Up to this time, France had been giving some help to the colonies. When she learned about the victory at Saratoga, she openly entered the war to fight on the American side.

General Howe at Philadelphia. General Howe did not march north to Albany as planned. Instead, he went south to capture Philadelphia, the capital of the Continental government. General Washington, who had sent many of his best soldiers to the defense of General Schuyler at Albany, immediately prepared to defend the capital. He attacked the British at Brandywine Creek and again at Germantown, a few miles from Philadelphia.

In all of his attempts to save Philadelphia, Washington was defeated. With his army he took up winter quarters at Valley Forge, not far from Philadelphia. Here the army spent a terrible winter because of cold and hunger.

Words you should know

national emblem	garrison	invasion
Providence of God	Loyalist	headquarters
Christian ideals	document	Hessian

Who's Who

1. He asked Congress that the minutemen form a colonial army.
2. This colonel, with 1200 volunteers fortified Breed's Hill—June 16, 1775.
3. A British officer ordered his men to drive the rebels from Breed's Hill on June 17, 1775.
4. A patriot army, led by this man, succeeded in capturing Montreal.
5. He was sent to join Montgomery to attack Quebec and was wounded.
6. These three famous men were appointed by Congress to go to Canada.
7. The final form of the Declaration of Independence was written by him.
8. The first signer of the Declaration of Independence wrote his name very large.
9. Washington's friend, a banker in Philadelphia, raised $50,000 for the American cause.
10. The British plan for 1777 depended upon the action of two generals and a colonel.

Choose the correct ending

1. The Second Continental Congress was held at
    a. Mount Vernon, Virginia.
    b. Fort Stanwix in New York.
    c. Faneuil Hall in Boston.
    d. Philadelphia.
2. The Battle of Bunker Hill was a victory for
    a. the Americans.
    b. the British.
    c. the Loyalists.
    d. the Hessians.
3. The attempt to win Canada failed because
    a. Montgomery's patriot army was weak.
    b. the Americans fought poorly.
    c. the colonists were not able to obtain the support of the Canadian people for their cause.
    d. Washington was not yet in command.
4. The Declaration of Independence tells us that
    a. George III could no longer rule England.
    b. God gave men certain rights, among which are the right to life, liberty, and happiness.
    c. war in New England would end.
    d. General Howe was to advance up the Hudson.

51

CHAPTER IV

VICTORY AT LAST—INDEPENDENCE

The goal is reached. In May, 1775, the Continental Congress met in Philadelphia. The delegates had assembled to decide what course must be taken. Discontentment had led to open rebellion in the colonies. Armed resistance began the actual war at Concord and Lexington.

The Declaration of Independence broke the ties between England and America. It was signed on July 4, 1776. From this date, the patriots fought for their independence. They hoped to prove they were able to rule themselves.

We have just seen how the American colonists were encouraged to fight under the leadership of their Commander-in-Chief, General George Washington. We have also seen that the victory at Saratoga won for them the open aid of the French government. By this aid and the sympathy of other European countries, final victory was won.

This chapter will tell you about: (1) the hardships of Washington and his soldiers at Valley Forge; (2) the Northwest lands which were taken from the British; (3) the battles on sea; (4) the surrender of the British at Yorktown.

1. The Darkest Hours of the Revolution

Valley Forge, 1777-1778. After the English had taken over Philadelphia, General Howe and his troops stationed there enjoyed every comfort. Since Washington was unable to recapture Philadelphia, he led his forces into winter quarters at Valley Forge, about twenty miles away.

The winter was very severe, and the soldiers suffered greatly. Those who were able, built log huts to sleep in. Many soldiers, too sick to work, lay on the frozen ground without

52

Washington's Headquarters at Valley Forge today is in the midst of a beautiful park where the sufferings of the men are a revered memory

blankets or even straw. Food was so scarce that the men were hungry for days at a time. Hundreds of soldiers were without shoes, and often blood from their feet stained the snow-covered ground.

George Washington shared the hardships of his men. By his kindness and example, the soldiers were encouraged to bear their sufferings. Again and again he urged the Continental Congress to relieve them, but in vain.

Most of the suffering was not necessary. The country had food and clothing, but the Continental Congress had neither the money nor the power to raise it to buy supplies for Washington's army. Moreover, some of the members of Congress disliked what Washington was doing. They thought he and his men should be attacking the enemy.

However, in spite of these sufferings, the Continental Army at Valley Forge improved. Baron von Steuben (stoo'-ben), a Prussian general, arrived from Europe while the army was encamped at Valley Forge. He drilled those soldiers who were strong enough to march. He taught them how to fight and how to obey orders. Under his direction the discouraged fighters became excellent soldiers. Washington's courage and loyalty and Von Steuben's training strengthened the soldiers' morale. The fight for liberty showed promise of success.

Aid from Europe. We often hear of the aid we are now sending to the countries of Europe which are still suffering from two World Wars. This aid should be gladly given in gratitude to the people whose forefathers gave so much help to our country in its fight for freedom.

Before the surrender of Burgoyne at Saratoga, the King and the nobles of France had given secret aid to the American patriots. After the victory, open aid was secured by Benjamin Franklin, who went to France as a representative of the American colonies. A fleet of warships, many troops, and large sums of money were sent to America from Catholic France.

One of the greatest friends of the American cause was the young Marquis de Lafayette

Lafayette

Culver

De Kalb

Culver

(mar-kee' de la-fay-et'). This French nobleman had chartered a vessel to come to America with a large supply of food, clothing, and ammunition for the soldiers. Baron de Kalb (de-kalb), a German soldier, came with Lafayette to assist in training the American troops. Rochambeau (roe-sham-boe'), another Frenchman, helped at Yorktown.

From another Catholic country, Poland, came two famous generals, Casimir Pulaski (cas'-i-mir poo-las'-key), who gave his life at Savannah, and Thad-deus Kosciusko (thad-dee'us kos-i-oos'-koe), who planned the fortifications at West Point. He also built many forts, and served as an engineer until the end of the Revolution. He then went back to Poland.

The British leave Philadelphia. General Clinton, who had succeeded Howe in Philadelphia, ordered his troops to New York because he had heard that a French fleet was on its way from the West Indies.

Washington's army, now strong and well-trained after the terrible winter at Valley

The Capture of Major André

COUNT PULASKI.

Culver

Pulaski

Forge, pursued the British. The two armies met at Monmouth, New Jersey. Just as the Americans were winning, their commander, General Charles Lee, ordered a retreat. Because of this retreat, the British were able to reach New York, and Washington was defeated.

A hero turns traitor. After the British had left Philadelphia, Washington placed Benedict Arnold in command of that city. Arnold, a brave leader, had served his country well both at Quebec and Saratoga. He became very angry because he did not receive an expected promotion. Washington, to please him, placed him in command of

West Point. However, Arnold determined, out of revenge, to turn his country over to the British. He planned with an Englishman, General Clinton, to surrender West Point. In return, General Clinton promised Arnold a large sum of money and an important position in the British Army.

Clinton sent Major André (and-ray') to Arnold to get the plans for capturing West Point. As André was returning to the British lines, he was stopped by three American soldiers and searched. The plans of West Point and other important papers, given by Arnold, were found in his boots. André was tried and hanged as a spy. Arnold escaped and joined the British.

2. War in the Northwest

The struggle moves to the frontier. Not every battle of the Revolution was fought in the original thirteen states. Many successful battles took place beyond the Ohio River. Territory there had been given to Canada by the British when the Quebec Act was passed. Most of the settlers were French-speaking Canadians who loved and practiced their Catholic religion.

The English controlled this western land from their forts at Detroit, Vincennes (vin-sens'), and Kaskaskia (kas-kas'-kee-a). From these strongholds Indian attacks were made against the pioneers along the Appalachian frontier. Colonel George Rogers Clark of the Virginia militia, with the permission of Governor Patrick Henry, grouped together a force of soldiers to take the western lands from England.

Kaskaskia. In 1778, Colonel Clark led his small force through the woods to Kaskaskia, the British fort. The Americans surrounded the fort, seized the guards, and took the fort without firing a shot.

Everything was in the Americans' favor. A dance was going on at the fort when Clark slipped in. Suddenly an Indian recognized him, and confusion followed. Clark calmly said: "Go on with your dance. Only remember that you are now dancing under the American flag." What courage this young soldier had!

Clark made friends with the French settlers in this region, and with their priest, Father Gibault (zhee-boe'). Clark told the priest that France had signed a treaty with the Americans.

The treaty said that France would help the Americans fight until they won independence from Great Britain. Clark promised Father Gibault that the Americans would allow his people religious freedom. On hearing this, the priest advised the settlers to support Clark. They took the oath of allegiance and formed a company of volunteers in the American cause.

Vincennes. Clark now wished to move against Vincennes. Father Gibault offered to take a letter to the commander of the Vincennes fort. This letter demanded surrender in the name of Clark and the Continental Congress. Father Gibault persuaded the commander to surrender the fort without bloodshed. Father Gibault was happy to bring back the joyful news that the American flag was waving over old Vincennes.

Lost and regained. General Hamilton, who commanded the British forces at Detroit, was determined to recapture Vincennes. He attacked and took the town on December 17, 1778, while Clark was still at Kaskaskia. Clark did not intend to let the British retake this territory so easily. Colonel Francis Vigo (vee'-go), a patriotic Italian, acted as a spy and reported to

Clark and his men on the rugged march to Vincennes

Clark that the fort at Vincennes was not well protected.

Once again, Father Gibault helped Colonel Clark. He asked the men of Kaskaskia to join Clark's army in the attack on Vincennes. Before they went to battle, Father Gibault gave them absolution and his priestly blessing. It was a long and bitter march to Vincennes in the dead of winter. Imagine the surprise of the British when the Americans attacked! After fighting for several hours, the British surrendered Fort Vincennes to Clark on February 24, 1779. General Hamilton was taken prisoner and sent to Virginia.

This victory gave the American patriots control in the Ohio Valley, the section known later as the Northwest Territory.

Trusted friends. The French Canadians who helped Colonel Clark were not the only Catholics who fought for liberty. Others also played their part in supporting the cause of American independence. From the very beginning of the Revolutionary War, Catholics, although few in number, played a very important part in the American cause. They fought for freedom side by side with other American colonists who had persecuted them.

Patriotic Catholics could be found among the trusted friends of General Washington. Stephen Moylan, an Irish Catholic, was one of his assistants and later became Washington's secretary. Moylan and his brother John did much in organizing the forces.

Stephen Moylan's ability was recognized by Washington. He assigned him to many important posts. Moylan organized the first army and navy of the United States. He had charge of the distribution of supplies.

Although Colonel Stephen Moylan was doing splendid work for the cause, he desired active service. In the army Colonel Moylan and his Dragoons became famous for their bravery under fire. They fought in almost every important battle. When Pulaski resigned, Moylan succeeded him in command of the cavalry. General Washington promoted Moylan to the rank of brigadier-general.

Another Catholic soldier was John Fitzgerald. Enlisting with him were eight others, the en-

tire Catholic population of Alexandria, Virginia. Colonel Fitzgerald was made an assistant secretary to Washington. He discovered a plot to remove Washington from the head of the army. His loyalty to the general made them close friends.

Thomas Fitzsimons, a wealthy Catholic patriot from Pennsylvania, fought in the war and gave Washington large sums of money to buy food and clothing for the soldiers. He also fitted out ships.

There are many unknown Catholics who fought and died that we might have the "blessings of justice, peace, and civil

John Barry

Culver

59

and religious liberty." The blood of Catholics "flowed as freely as that of any of their fellow citizens." We should appreciate our American Catholic heritage.

3. War on the Sea

Captain John Barry—Father of the American Navy. At the beginning of the Revolutionary War the colonies had no warships. They had a number of merchant ships and fishing vessels. Congress allowed these ships to be armed and used to capture English merchant ships. These privateers, as they were called, made war on English ships. When they captured a ship and its cargo, they brought it into port to be sold. John Barry, a Catholic from Ireland, was the captain of one of these privateers.

In 1775, Congress provided some ships and fitted them with guns and ammunition. Congress named John Barry captain of one these ships.

It was under his command that the *Lexington* captured the English warship, *Edward*. This was the first naval victory for the Americans.

Commodore Barry was successful in his naval warfare against the English. Lord Howe urged him to desert the American cause. He offered Barry a large sum of money and a commission in the English Navy. Barry refused to accept the bribe.

When the United States established a navy in 1794, Barry was made its first officer. His commission was signed by President Washington. Barry's work won for him the title, "Father of the American Navy."

Philadelphia has honored Commodore John Barry by placing his picture in Independence Hall and his statue in Independence Square. Washington, the nation's capital, also

John Paul Jones
Brown Brothers

pays him tribute by having a fine statue of him erected in the city.

Captain John Paul Jones — a daring sea fighter. After France had decided to help the Americans, the French King offered Benjamin Franklin the use of five warships. This fleet of ships was put under the command of Captain John Paul Jones, a Scotsman, who had come to America in 1773. The fleet was used to sink or capture English merchant vessels. Jones' own vessel, the *Bonhomme Richard* (bon-om' ree-shar'), did the most damage.

On September 23, 1779, Jones sighted English ships escorted by two warships. In a fierce battle with the British vessel *Serapis* (se-rap'-is), off the coast of England, the *Bonhomme Richard* burst into flames.

When the English Commander on the *Serapis* asked Jones to surrender, the latter shouted, "I have not yet begun to fight!" Jones lashed the two vessels together. He and his men climbed over the sides onto the deck of the *Serapis* and bravely fought the enemy in a hand-to-hand battle. The English commander was forced to surrender, and the *Bonhomme Richard* sank shortly after.

4. War in the South

British Victories. After failing in the North, the British hoped to

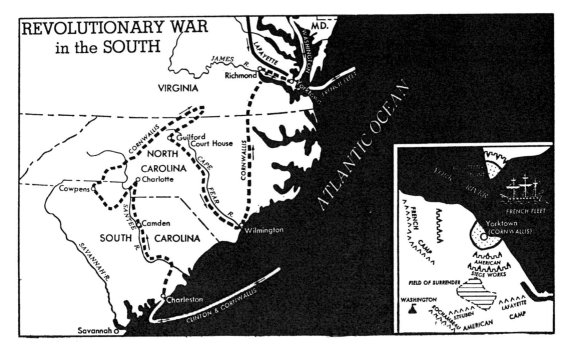

REVOLUTIONARY WAR in the SOUTH

General Greene

instead of remaining at his post!

A new commander. Nathaniel Greene took Gates' place. Next to Washington, General Greene was the most able commander in the Continental Army. He won success by small victories, by orderly retreats, and even by defeats.

A group of backswoodsmen had checked the northward march of the British at King's Mountain before Greene took command. It was now up to Greene to drive the British farther south or towards the sea.

win in the South with the help of the Loyalists there. British soldiers attacked and captured Savannah, Georgia, in December, 1778. Charleston, South Carolina, surrendered in May, 1780. General Cornwallis was left in charge of this section.

The few American soldiers in the South were led by Francis Marion, who was known as the "Swamp Fox." The men fought in small bands and annoyed the British in surprise attacks made from swamps and forests.

General Gates, in command of the patriots in the South, was badly defeated by Cornwallis at Camden, South Caroline. He saved himself by flight

Greene's army was not ready to attack the English army under Cornwallis. Instead, Greene planned to wear out the enemy by a series of skirmishes which would make Cornwallis follow him from Charleston. Thus the English would be led from their supplies and into the enemy territory.

Cowpens. Events in the South began to favor the American cause. At the Battle of Cowpens, South Carolina, the Americans defeated the British under Colonel Tarleton.

Guilford Courthouse. Then Greene lured Cornwallis about two hundred miles away from his supplies and attacked him at Guilford Courthouse. It was a British victory, but it so weakened the British that Cornwallis began a retreat towards Virginia.

The patriots suffered small losses but gained the courage to continue their war in the South. In thirteen months, General Greene had driven the English from every section in Georgia and the Carolinas, except from the city of Charleston.

Yorktown. As Cornwallis marched northward into Virginia, he met Lafayette and about three thousand French troops. Cornwallis did not fear Lafayette, whom he called the "little boy."

However, the "little boy" was too clever for Cornwallis. Lafayette and his men would dart from the hills in Virginia, engage in a skirmish, and then dart back again. Cornwallis' troops kept chasing Lafayette and his men from place to place. Finally, the English were worn out and Cornwallis led his troops into Yorktown in August, 1781. Here he had unknowingly put himself into a trap.

Lafayette sent word to Washington in New Jersey that Cornwallis had been cornered at Yorktown. Lafayette and his men were blocking the British escape by land. The French Admiral de Grasse (de gras'), having defeated the British fleet off Chesapeake Bay, moved in and surrounded Yorktown, making it impossible for Cornwallis to receive any help by sea.

Meanwhile, Washington with his American troops, and Rochambeau with the French soldiers, arrived at Yorktown to join Lafayette. Escape for the British was impossible.

British surrender. After several days of firing from American and French guns, Cornwallis and his army surrendered at

Cornwallis surrenders at Yorktown
Brown Brothers

Yorktown on October 19, 1781. The war was over!

There was great rejoicing in all the colonies. A Mass of thanksgiving was celebrated in Saint Mary's Church in Philadelphia.

Both Catholics and Protestants thanked God for victory. How often He had helped them during the dark days of the Revolution! There were times when everything seemed hopeless, when only trust in Almighty God gave these patriots the courage to keep on fighting. God rewarded their confidence in Him by giving them victory. **Peace and independence.** The British surrender at Yorktown ended six and a half years of war between the American colonies and Great Britain. However, it took two years more to get the peace treaty written and signed. Benjamin Franklin, John Jay, and John Adams signed this treaty in 1783.

By this treaty England: (1) Acknowledged the independence of the United States of America; (2) England lost all her lands south of Canada, north of Florida, west of the Atlantic, and east of the Mississippi; (3) She also had to give back Florida to Spain; (4) American fishermen were given the right to use the Canadian fishing grounds near Newfoundland.

In November, 1783, the last British troops set sail for England from New York Harbor. At their departure, Washington and his troops moved into New York City. The Stars and Stripes, the symbol of American freedom, was unfurled by the general. There was great rejoicing.

Soon afterwards, George Washington, the "Father of our Country," sent his soldiers to their homes. He himself went to Annapolis where the Congress was in session. There he resigned his position as Commander-in-Chief of the Army, and returned to his home at Mount Vernon, Virginia.

The independence declared by the patriots on July 4, 1776, was won in 1783. Then colonial America ended, and the American nation was born.

Freedom. You have read how this nation owed its life to many brave men. Some of these men were great statesmen. Some of them were great soldiers. Then there were many ordinary men and women who worked and sacrificed that America might be free.

Freedom does not mean that we can all do just as we please. Freedom means that we have an opportunity to do what is right. We must therefore try to do what is right. We must therefore try to be kind and just to our neighbors. We must never have hatred in our hearts for anyone whose skin is a different color from ours. We must never hate anyone because he has a different religion from ours. We must never hate anyone because he has customs or a language different from ours.

Real freedom can only come from loving God, and loving all men because they too are God's children.

God wants us to be good citizens. That means that we should do our part to help our country, our state, and the city or community in which we live. Can you tell some of the ways boys and girls can be good citizens?

We have many advantages that the people of early America did not have. We have many schools. We have such things as radios and television and automobiles and comfortable homes. We should use all these things to help us become better Americans. Then we will show that we are worthy of the great heritage of freedom that has been given to us in this great land of ours.

Words you should know

organized	skirmish	lured
fortification	strongholds	dragoons
frontier	allegiance	wintered

Things to talk about

1. Pretend you are one of Washington's soldiers at Valley Forge. In the bitter cold you have no blanket, the ice cuts through your thin shoes, you are tired and hungry. But you will not leave the army. Why?

2. Since England was better prepared for war than the colonists, why were the colonists able to defeat England and win the Revolutionary War?

Can you place these events in the order in which they happened?

1. The Colonial Army wintered Valley Forge.
2. Cornwallis surrendered at Yorktown.
3. Fort Kaskaskia surrendered to the Americans.
4. Vincennes surrendered to the Americans.

5. Battle of Guilford Courthouse.
6. Peace Treaty of Paris written and signed.
7. Naval battle between the *Serapis* and the *Bonhomme Richard*.

Find the incorrect sentence

1. Valley Forge was the last battle of the Revolution.

   Valley Forge was one of the darkest hours of the Revolution.

   Valley Forge made more secure the fight for liberty.

   Valley Forge improved the training of American soldiers.

2. Lafayette was a young Marquis who helped train American troops.

   Lafayette was an American spy.

   Lafayette was a good friend of the American cause.

   Lafayette was assisted by Baron de Kalb, a German soldier.

3. Pulaski and Kosciusko came from a Catholic country.

   Pulaski and Kosciusko brought ammunition from France.

   Pulaski and Kosciusko were Polish.

   Pulaski and Kosciusko were famous generals.

4. Major André was sent to Arnold to get plans for capturing West Point.

   Major André was an American spy.

   Major André carried important papers in his boots.

   Major André was an Englishman tried and hanged as a spy.

Making connections

Give the topic which each of the following suggests to you.

1. Washington led his forces into winter quarters. The soldiers suffered greatly.

2. One of the greatest friends of the American cause chartered a vessel to come to America with large supplies of food, clothing, and ammunition for the soldiers.

3. A brave leader who served America well both at Quebec and Saratoga turned traitor.

4. *The Lexington* was commanded by the "Father of the American Navy."

5. A British surrender ended the war betwen the American Colonies and Great Britain.

6. In 1783 a great nation was born.

Checking your knowledge of Unit One

I. Connect an important event with each of the following.

Baron von Steuben	James Otis	Father Gibault
Colonel George Rogers Clark	Nathaniel Greene	Casimir Pulaski
George Washington	Baron de Kalb	Lord Cornwallis
Marquis de Lafayette	Thaddeus Kosciusko	General Gates

II. Find on a map each place listed below and connect an event with it.

Boston, Massachusetts	Yorktown	Saratoga
Carpenter's Hall, Philadelphia	Trenton, New Jersey	Bunker Hill
Lexington and Concord	Fort Stanwix	Quebec
Cambridge, Massashusetts	Old North Church	Valley Forge

III. Who said it?

"I have not yet begun to fight."

"I regret I have but one life to lose for my country."

"There, King George can read that without his spectacles."

IV. Who was called?   What was?

"Swamp Fox"	A patriot
"Little Boy"	A loyalist
"Old Fox"	A colonist
"minuteman"	A red-coat

V. Make a time line. (A time line is arranging events in the order in which they happened.)

1. Second Continental Congress
2. Surrender of Cornwallis at Yorktown
3. First Continental Congress
4. Battle of Saratoga
5. Battle of Lexington and Concord
6. Treaty of Paris, 1783
7. Boston Tea Party
8. Stamp Act Passed by Parliament
9. Declaration of Independence
10. Battle of Bunker Hill

VI. Do you know where these places are? Find them on a map.

Boston	Philadelphia	New York
Cambridge	Bunker Hill	Trenton
Ticonderoga	Yorktown	Albany
Saratoga	Concord	Kaskaskia

VII. Find in this Unit, examples which show:

1. Loyalty to a cause
2. Self-forgetfulness
3. Courage under great difficulties
4. God's care over us

67

VIII. How did it happen?

1. How did the life lived by the colonists help to make them so freedom-loving and self-reliant?

2. How was it possible for the American colonies to win their independence from a nation that was as strong as England?

3. Why did England and her colonies misunderstand each other so much?

IX. Some activities to help you master this Unit.

1. Make a cartoon showing how George III punished Bostonians.

2. Show how Cornwallis was trapped.
   Make a sketch or map showing Yorktown's situation between the two rivers, the York and the James.
   Then show on the map where the French fleet anchored, and what were the positions of the French and American armies on land.

3. Classroom Scrap Book—
   UNIT ONE IN PICTURES
   Get a large loose-leaf scrap book.
   Who can find the most suitable and greatest number of pictures showing people, places, and events which are studied in this Unit? The pictures should be well trimmed, labeled, and placed in the book in the order of their occurrence in this Unit.

X. Copy on paper the *number* before each statement.
   Choose the *letter* which best completes each statement and write it beside the number.

1. The first battle of the Revolutionary War was fought at
   a. Bunker Hill
   b. Lexington
   c. Boston
   d. Revere

2. A priest who helped George Rogers Clark was
   a. Father Briand
   b. Father Gibault
   c. Father Jogues
   d. Father Carroll

3. Burgoyne surrendered his army at
   a. Saratoga
   b. Ticonderoga
   c. Yorktown
   d. New York

4. Ethan Allen captured the English forces at
   a. Trenton
   b. Boston
   c. Saratoga
   d. Ticonderoga

5. A Catholic signer of the Declaration of Independence was
    a. Nathan Hale
    b. John Barry
    c. Charles Carroll
    d. Charles Moylan

6. Benjamin Franklin, to get aid for the Americans, went to
    a. France
    b. Spain
    c. England
    d. Poland

7. The Declaration of Independence was written by
    a. James Otis
    b. John Hancock
    c. Thomas Jefferson
    d. Roger Sherman

8. The Quebec Act was favorable to the
    a. colonists
    b. Canadian Catholics
    c. Hessians
    d. English soldiers

XI. Class Quiz on the highlights of Unit One

1. Name three events that happened before the Revolution which made the colonists very angry.

2. Do you think it was right for the colonists to rebel against England?

3. Why did the American colonists declare their independence from Great Britain?

4. When was the first American flag adopted by the Continental Congress?

5. Why did the British hire German soldiers?

6. How did the Revolution help unite the people of the thirteen colonies?

7. Name three foreign soldiers who fought on the American side.

8. Which of Washington's character traits do you like best?

9. Show how Robert Morris helped win the war.

10. Why was the work of George Rogers Clark so important?

11. What assistance did Father Gibault give to George Rogers Clark?

12. In what ways did France help us win the war?

13. Why were the battles at Lexington, Saratoga, and Yorktown so important?

14. Name three results of the Treaty of Peace of 1783.

15. Who is often called the "Father of the American Navy?"

16. Name three Catholics who greatly aided General Washington and the Continental Army.

17. Tell in what way each helped.

18. What are the rights of all men stated in the Declaration of Independence?

19. Why do we celebrate July Fourth?

20. Why were the English sailors afraid of John Paul Jones?

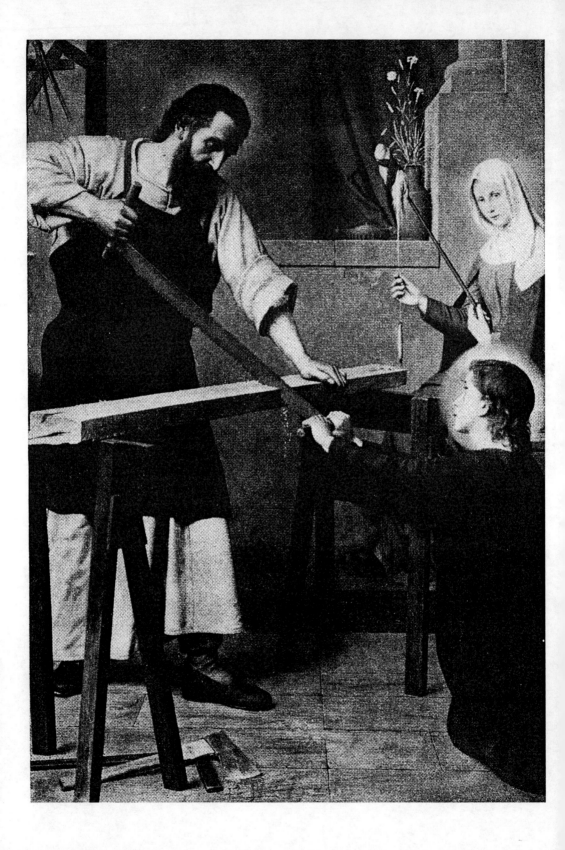

Mary and Vocations

MEANING. The Church gives us Our Lady as a wise adviser who should be consulted before making any serious decisions in life, for "Her thoughts are more vast than the sea, and her counsels more deep than the great ocean" (Ecclesiasticus 24:39). It is especially important to consult her before selecting a vocation. Our Lady is the patroness of all who work for a livelihood. She herself knew what it was to work hard. Through her and her divine Son, work has been made noble, for it is a way to heaven.

APPLICATION. The right to work is part of the national heritage. The obligation to work for a living affects all mature persons. In youth, study and environment lead to future careers. Mary's Son worked as a carpenter. As Mother of Good Counsel, Mary guides all who are shaping their careers.

Prayer

Mother of good counsel, *pray for us.*

Litany of the Blessed Virgin

LORD, have mercy on us.
Christ, have mercy on us.
Lord, have mercy on us.
God the Son, Redeemer of the world, have mercy on us.
God, the Holy Ghost, have mercy on us.
Holy Trinity, one God, have mercy on us.
Christ, hear us.
Christ, graciously hear us.
God the Father of heaven, have mercy on us.
Holy Mary,[1]
Holy Mother of God,
Holy Virgin of virgins,
Mother of Christ,
Mother of divine grace,
Mother most pure,
Mother most chaste,
Mother inviolate,
Mother undefiled,
Mother most amiable,
Mother most admirable,
Mother of good counsel,
Mother of our Creator,
Mother of our Saviour,
Virgin most prudent,
Virgin most venerable,
Virgin most renowned,
  [1] Pray for us.

Virgin most powerful,
Virgin most merciful,
Virgin most faithful,
Mirror of justice,
Seat of wisdom,
Cause of our joy,
Spiritual vessel,
Vessel of honor,
Singular vessel of devotion,
Mystical Rose,
Tower of David,
Tower of ivory,
House of gold,
Ark of the covenant,
Gate of heaven,
Morning star,
Health of the sick,
Refuge of sinners,
Comforter of the afflicted,
Help of Christians,
Queen of angels,
Queen of patriarchs,
Queen of prophets,
Queen of apostles,
Queen of martyrs,
Queen of confessors,
Queen of virgins,
Queen of all saints,
Queen conceived without original sin,

Queen assumed into heaven,
Queen of the most holy Rosary,
Queen of peace.
Lamb of God, who takest away the sins of the world, spare us, O Lord.
Lamb of God, who takest away the sins of the world, graciously hear us, O Lord.
Lamb of God, who takest away the sins of the world, have mercy on us.
Christ, hear us. Christ, graciously hear us.
℣. Pray for us, O holy Mother of God. ℟. That we may be made worthy of the promises of Christ.
  Let us pray
Grant, we beseech Thee, O Lord God, unto us Thy servants, that we may rejoice in continual health of mind and body; and, by the glorious intercession of blessed Mary ever Virgin, may be delivered from present sadness, and enter into the joy of Thine eternal gladness. Through Christ our Lord. Amen.

An indulgence of 7 years. A plenary indulgence once a month on the usual conditions for the daily devout recitation of this Litany with its versicle and prayer (See "The Raccolta," the official work of indulgenced prayers, page 216).

MARY AS A GUIDE THROUGH LIFE. The free will of man accepts the guidance of Mary in the way of life. This guidance of Mary is part of our religion. It affects our home life, our association with our fellow man, our civic obligations, our career in life, and our acceptance of life's problems.

Courtesy of Rev. J. B. Carol, O.F.M.

UNIT TWO

LEADERS OF FREEDOM FORM A NEW GOVERNMENT

CHAPTER I—GOVERNMENT OF THE CONFEDERATION

Union or Disunion—Attempts at Union
Articles of Confederation—Weaknesses
Northwest Ordinance—Principal Work of Government
Hard Times—Shays' Rebellion—Quarrels
Annapolis Convention

CHAPTER II—A NEW PLAN OF GOVERNMENT IS MADE

Constitutional Convention Meets at Philadelphia, 1787
Members Decide on New Plan of Government
Three Important Compromises
New Constitution Is Completed
The States Approve Constitution in 1788

CHAPTER III—THE CONSTITUTION OF THE UNITED STATES

Constitution Provides for a More Perfect Union
Constitution Provides for Three Government Branches
Bill of Rights Is Added to the Constitution

LEADERS OF FREEDOM FORM A NEW GOVERNMENT

EVERYONE wishes to be happy. When God created man, He placed in him the desire for happiness. The English began to take away the rights and liberties of the colonists. To safeguard these rights and liberties, the fearless patriots of America openly rebelled. They declared that if necessary they would even fight to safeguard their God-given rights.

In 1776 the American colonists adopted the Declaration of Independence. To make this decision took courage, for by this act the rebellious colonists broke all connections with England.

You have seen in the first Unit how the thirteen colonies had to struggle to win independence and to become a new nation.

In this Unit you will study a great deal about our national government. You will see how it worked under the Articles of Confederation. You will learn that it was necessary to make a new and strong form of government, if the nation were to last.

However, before it was too late the leaders of the nation got together. They laid aside their differences and agreed upon a set of laws to hold the nation together.

After much debating the people in the different states approved and accepted the Constitution. This was the name given to the new set of laws. In a short time a Bill of Rights was added. The Constitution has proven itself to be an excellent plan of government.

CHAPTER I

GOVERNMENT OF THE CONFEDERATION

Union or disunion. A crisis arose when war broke out in Massachusetts in 1775. It was the signal for all the colonies to join in the fight. Who would direct the colonies and take over the responsibilities of war? The Second Continental Congress faced the task of carrying on the war, though its members knew it had no authority to do so.

When independence was declared in 1776, the people knew they would need some form of central government. The Second Continental Congress agreed upon a set of rules known as the "Articles of Confederation." These rules became the law by which the colonies were governed.

1. The New Nation Needs a Central Government

Attempts at union. Whenever danger threatened the colonies, attempts were made to unite for protection. When the English colonies were young the colonists had to defend themselves against attacks of Indians and of Dutch and French settlers and traders. In 1643 the four English colonies, Massachusetts Bay, Plymouth, Connecticut, and New Haven formed a confederation or league. As members of the same league or confederation, they promised to help one another in time of trouble. This union of colonies was called the New England Confederation.

Over one hundred years later, the English colonies held a congress or meeting to work out another plan for union. They called it the Albany Plan of Union. Benjamin Franklin organized this plan of union to defend English settlements from the French.

In 1765, when England tried to tax the colonists, another meeting or congress was called. It was the Stamp Act Congress. Nine years later, in 1774, the First Continental Congress met. This Congress of colonial patriots was a meeting to protest against the unfair treatment given by England.

Although these attempts failed to unite the colonists they helped to plant the idea of union in the minds of the colonists.

Plans for a central government. The Second Continental Congress met in Philadelphia in 1775. Even before the Declaration of Independence was written, patriotic leaders like Patrick Henry, John Hancock, and Benjamin Franklin realized that the colonies must unite and work together if they were to win the war for independence. But the colonists were not ready for complete separation from England. However, once the Declaration was signed, the colonists realized that they would have to unite for safety. Since they had declared their freedom from England, they were now no longer English colonies, but separate states of a new nation.

Each state sent representatives to Philadelphia. There, under the leadership of a famous lawyer, John Dickinson, a plan of government was drawn up for the new nation. In November, 1777, Congress approved this plan. It was called

Benjamin Franklin   *Culver*

John Dickinson
                                 Culver

the "Articles of Confederation."

The thirteen states adopt the plan. Before the Articles of Confederation could become law, all the states would have to adopt them. It would be difficult to get all of the states to do so. Some people were afraid that a central government might take away some authority from the individual states. These people remembered too well the injustices they had suffered from the English Parliament.

Gradually the states accepted the new plan of government. At first, a few states like Maryland refused for a very just reason. Some states had claims on western lands; others, including Maryland, had none. She claimed that all the states had an equal right to these lands because all had fought for them. Maryland said that when all these lands were given up to the nation, she would accept the Articles of Confederation. New York and Virginia agreed to give up their western lands. Then the Maryland delegates signed the Articles. The others soon followed, and in March, 1781, the Articles of Confederation became the law of the new nation.

Articles of Confederation. Although the United States now had a definite form of government, it was very weak. Under the Articles of Confederation the states did not agree to a national government but only to a "league of friendship" with each other. Each state still regarded itself as free, separate, and independent. These Articles provided for a Congress of one house. This house was to be made up of representatives chosen each year by the separate states. Regardless of how many people represented a state, it had only one vote. The votes of nine states were necessary before a law could be passed. The consent of every state was required before any change could be made in the Articles of Confederation.

Congress was given some powers by the Articles of Confederation. It could make laws and treaties. It could declare war and keep an army and navy. It could coin money and establish post offices. Nevertheless, it had no authority to enforce whatever laws it might make. It had no court to try anyone who broke the law.

2. The New Government was too Weak to Secure Law and Order

Why articles of Confederation were weak. It was not long before the leaders of the nation discovered the weaknesses of their government. Each state wished to be independent. Everyone's first thought was loyalty to his own state. The country, instead of being one strong nation, was a group of thirteen small nations.

Congress powerless to collect taxes. Unfortunately, right from the start the government of the Confederation did not work well. The main trouble was that the central government had not enough power. Congress was not permitted to collect taxes. Therefore, it did not have sufficient money to do its work.

To carry on the Revolutionary War, Congress was forced to borrow large sums of money from loyal patriots and friendly nations. It could not force the citizens of the states to pay taxes. It could ask the states for money. Seldom did they contribute the amount requested. For example, at the end of the Revolutionary War Congress was millions of dollars in debt. It asked all the states to give as much money as possible. The sum received was far below the amount needed. Congress did not even receive enough money to pay the men serving in the army. Even though actual fighting had stopped in 1781 these soldiers had to remain in camps until the peace treaty was signed in 1783.

Congress unable to pay soldiers. The soldiers were complaining because they were not being paid. In June, 1783, a group of about eighty men left camp and marched to Philadelphia. Armed with bayonets, these soldiers lined up before the building in which Congress was meeting. They demanded their back pay. So frightened were the members of Congress, that as soon as it grew dark, they left Philadelphia and went to Princeton, New Jersey.

Congress needed money to do its work. The money situation became worse after the war. More than ever Congress needed money to pay the war debt, and to manage the national government. When Congress asked the states to pay taxes to raise this money, most of them refused. They had fought a long, hard war with England because of taxation. They resented being taxed by the national government.

Every state, in defense of its own right to tax, would not yield to the national government. The people did not recognize their duty to share the cost and burdens of liberty as well as their privilege to enjoy its benefits. Americans had not yet learned how necessary it was to unite in order to become a strong nation.

Congress had no power to regulate trade. Other difficulties arose over trade and commerce. Congress had no power to control the trade carried on between the states. Each state regulated its trade to suit its own interest. This led to disputes and bitterness among the people of the various states. European countries, watching the quarrels among the states, wondered how long such a form of government could last.

Congress not able to settle disputes. Many of the states were jealous of each other. A group of people moved from Connecticut to Pennsylvania. The newcomers were treated as enemies or foreigners, not as fellow Americans. The Indians nearby were encouraged to attack them. Other states fought over boundary lines. Serious trouble started over the territory now known as the State of Vermont. New York, New Hampshire and Massachusetts claimed this territory.

In these and many other instances, each state was preferring its own interest and advantage to the good of its neighbor. God's law of charity was too often set aside. Congress was unable to step in and settle these troubles between the states.

The country needed a President and court. The Articles of Confederation made no provision for a President nor for a national or supreme court. A President and judges were needed to make the government more competent. Americans interested in freedom and order were disturbed about the quarrellings and discontent among the people.

The Northwest Ordinance. A very important law, the "Law of 1787," was passed by the central government. This law was called the Northwest Ordinance. It set up rules for governing the Northwest Territory. It provided that not less than three nor more than five states should be formed from the territory north of the Ohio and east of the Mississippi Rivers.

The members of Congress who made the Law of 1787 showed great wisdom by granting freedoms which were denied in many of the states. Con-

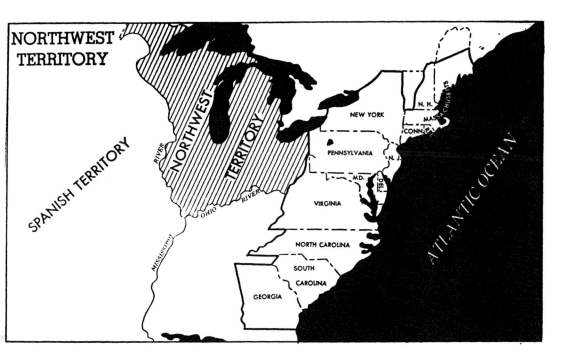

NORTHWEST TERRITORY

SPANISH TERRITORY

NORTHWEST TERRITORY

RIVER

OHIO RIVER

MISSISSIPPI

NEW YORK

N. H.

MASSACHUSETTS

CONN.

PENNSYLVANIA

N. J.

MD.

DEL.

VIRGINIA

NORTH CAROLINA

SOUTH CAROLINA

GEORGIA

ATLANTIC OCEAN

gress declared that the people in the Northwest Territory were to have freedom of religion, freedom of education, and trial by jury. Slavery was to be forbidden. Education was to be encouraged. The dignity of man was to be recognized and respected. The people were to be allowed to practice their religion.

A governor and three judges were appointed by Congress to govern the territory. As soon as any section contained 60,000 inhabitants it could take steps to become a state. The government officials would then prepare a state constitution and ask Congress to admit the district as a state.

The Ordinance provided for a democratic form of government in this territory. It permitted all men to vote and hold office. It laid the foundation of many of our American political ideals. Today, territories of the United States are governed much as the Northwest Territory was in the eighteenth century.

Americans living in this territory valued the rights and privileges granted to them by the Northwest Ordinance. Do United States citizens today appreciate these same rights? Each voter should consider it his duty to cast a ballot at every election. People should choose for leaders unselfish Americans

Bettmann Archive
Continental Money

to work for God and country. Those capable of leadership should imitate the early pioneer Americans who held key positions. More Catholics should engage in governmental work and be more conscious of their duties of service to the United States government.

Money problems. The time between 1781 and 1787 is called the "Critical Period" because there were so many problems to be solved. The regulation of money was one of them. All paper money has to have gold or silver in the treasury to give it any value. At this time America had many debts in Europe which had to be paid in silver and gold. The payment of these debts left very little real money in this country.

The government of the Confederation printed so much paper money that it became en-tirely worthless. This money had so little value that some people even papered their rooms with it. How would you like to wake up in your room some morning and look at the walls covered with worthless dollar bills?

To make things worse, many states printed their own paper money. Money that was valuable in one state was worth little or nothing in another. Spanish, Dutch, French, and British coins were often used. This caused even more confusion.

Hard times. The soldiers who had fought in the Revolutionary War returned discouraged to their homes. The government had been unable to pay these veterans their salaries. The cost of everything was high and there was very little work to be had. As a result, many soldiers had to sell their farms and shops in order to pay their debts.

People who owed money and could not pay were often thrown into prison. The people became so enraged at these conditions that quarrels and riots occurred in many states.

Shays' Rebellion. In Massachusetts, money troubles were at their worst. Prices were high; taxes were high. Some of the farmers in the western part of the state had lost their farms. Others were put in jail because they could not pay what they owed.

Many were worried because the state laws were so severe regarding debts. A plea was made to stop collecting money for a while and to delay imprisoning the debtors. Nothing was done to relieve the situation.

In 1786, the people in Massachusetts rebelled. Daniel Shays, a veteran of the Revolutionary War, led an armed group of farmers and traders who marched on the courthouse in Worcester. They were determined to prevent the court from jailing any more debtors.

From Worcester the mob marched to Springfield. There, in order to get arms and ammunition, Shays and his followers attacked the United States Arsenal. The rebellion was broken up by the state troops, and Shays escaped to another state.

The leaders of the country were alarmed about this revolt in Massachusetts. It was further proof that the government under the Articles of Confederation was not succeeding.

Quarrels between the states. Another cause of serious trouble

Bettmann Archive

A scene during Shays' Rebellion. Here a tax collector is being ducked by one of the rebels

was the question of trade between the states. Congress had no power to regulate commerce, so the states did. Taxes were placed on goods carried from one state to another. A Connecticut farmer wishing to sell his produce in New York had to pay a tax as he crossed the state line. The people of Connecticut resented this tax. They resolved to boycott the goods of the New York merchants.

Maryland and Virginia quarrelled over their trade rights on the Potomac River. To settle the dispute, delegates from both states agreed to meet at Washington's home at Mount

Vernon in 1786. A satisfactory settlement was reached.

Annapolis Convention. Another meeting was held at Annapolis in September, 1786.

This meeting was very important, for as a result, the delegates decided to hold a third meeting at Philadelphia in order to change the Articles of Confederation.

Do you remember why?

1. Maryland would not accept the Articles of Confederation until 1781?
2. Representatives from Maryland and Virginia met at Mount Vernon?
3. The thirteen states were more concerned about their own welfare than that of the nation?
4. The plan of government under the Articles of Confederation failed?

Multiple Choice Test

Choose the correct answer in each of these statements.

1. Provisions for the Northwest Territory were contained in
   a. the Articles of Confederation
   b. the Constitution
   c. the Declaration of Independence
   d. the Ordinance of 1787
2. The Articles of Confederation did not permit Congress
   a. to collect taxes
   b. to regulate trade
   c. to declare war
   d. to settle disputes
3. Shays' rebellion in Massachusetts was put down by
   a. the United States Army
   b. the state troops
   c. the Navy
   d. the police
4. The "Critical Period" of American History was the period between
   a. 1781-1789   c. 1776-1783
   b. 1763-1776   d. 1783-1785

Select the date in Column B which tells when each event listed in Column A happened.

Column A	Column B
1. Second Continental Congress	a. 1781
2. Declaration of Independence	b. 1787
3. Articles of Confederation adopted	c. 1763
4. Annapolis Convention	d. 1775
5. Northwest Ordinance	e. 1786
	f. 1790
	g. 1776

CHAPTER II

A NEW PLAN OF GOVERNMENT IS MADE

Working for a better union. People all over the country were much distressed over the uprisings and quarrelings between the states. They were wondering if the struggle for freedom had been in vain. Even George Washington was fearful lest the United States might not remain an independent nation. In a letter to a friend he wrote that the country would never be a success if the nation continued to depend upon "a half-starving, limping government, tottering at every step."

It had become clear to almost everyone that changes had to be made in the Articles of Confederation. Plans were formed for a meeting to discuss changes. This meeting was to be held at Philadelphia in 1787. Before the time came, however, many of the states realized how foolish it was to be jealous of the other states. They saw the weaknesses of the Articles of Confederation and the need of change. All but Rhode Island sent delegates to Philadelphia in 1787.

In this chapter we shall see what the Convention accomplished. We shall study the difficulties which faced the great Americans who assisted in solving our country's problems at this meeting.

1. American Statesmen Meet Again in Independence Hall

Constitutional Convention, May-September, 1787. Early in 1787, Congress invited the states to send delegates to a meeting in Philadelphia. These delegates were to revise the Articles of Confederation. Fifty-five representatives came. All the states except Rhode Island were represented. The Convention was held at the Old State House, now known as Independence Hall. This was one of the most important meetings ever held in America. The delegates were

83

determined to do their best to work out a more satisfactory plan of government. These men worked untiringly from May to September, 1787. During this time they wrote a new set of rules for government.

Leading Members of the Convention. Most of America's great men were present at this meeting. These delegates were a remarkable group of Americans. Chief among them was the beloved George Washington from Virginia. He was chosen chairman of the Convention because no other man in the United States was so well known or so highly respected. All could be expected to listen to him and to respect his opinions.

Alexander Hamilton *Culver*

Washington appreciated this honor of being made chairman but he also realized its responsibility. He begged the blessing of Almighty God on the delegates and on their work. He then began his difficult task of directing the meeting.

James Madison, too, was from Virginia. This man had studied and read a great deal about government. His notes on the Convention, written day by day, give an excellent picture of the important events discussed at the meetings. Madison played so important a part in the Convention that he is called "the Father of the Constitution."

Benjamin Franklin, then over eighty years of age, was the leader of the delegates from Pennsylvania. It was his suggestion that in order to obtain the assistance of God each day's work begin with a prayer. "God governs in the affairs of men," he said, "and if a sparrow cannot fall to the ground without His notice, is it possible that an empire can rise without His aid?" Franklin with his wit and common sense settled many disputes.

Gouverneur Morris of Pennsylvania helped to convince the others of the need for a new plan of government, not simply a revision of the old one. Morris was largely responsible for the wording of the Constitution. Even though he was a cripple he worked untiringly for a stronger plan of union for the thirteen states.

Alexander Hamilton of New York also urged a strong central government. He thought that our country would be safer if run by a few able leaders. The plan which he offered failed to satisfy many of the delegates, who thought he wanted the wealthy to rule the poor.

Two of the delegates were Catholics. These men were Daniel Carroll of Maryland and Thomas Fitzsimons of Pennsylvania. They knew that their fellow-Catholics wanted a government which would protect not only their rights, but the rights of others.

Nearly all the members of the Constitutional Convention had worked for the government at some time. Many were good lawyers. All had been in business and had property of their own. They were aware of the need for better laws to regulate money, taxes, and trade. These capable, unselfish leaders were God-fearing men. They would pass only such laws as would

Culver

Daniel Carroll

foster the right of every human being to "life, liberty, and the pursuit of happiness." These men were ready to give up some of their opinions in order to obtain the blessings of peace and happiness for America.

Only four well-known leaders were absent from the Philadelphia Convention. Thomas Jefferson was in France and John Adams in England. Samuel Adams was not chosen to represent Massachusetts. Patrick Henry was chosen by Virginia, but refused to go to the meeting.

Religious ideas of government. Although only two delegates were Catholics, the convention

Brown Brothers

St. Thomas Aquinas

used ideas of government that St. Thomas Aquinas, St. Robert Bellarmine (bell'-are-min), and other great Catholics had taught.

The delegates agreed that the government must have authority to require the citizens to obey the law. The delegates knew that all authority comes from God. They also knew that the people who make just laws are God's representatives. Therefore, the laws and rules they make should be obeyed. Obedience to just laws is required by God. Such obedience brings peace and happiness to all within the country.

It is necessary to have good laws for our own good and for the welfare of our country. Each day we should pray that God will help the lawmakers of our great land to make good and just laws. We should ask Him to guide our lawmakers as He guided the men who formed our Constitution. We can say the prayer which Archbishop Carroll wrote asking God's assistance for those holding positions in the United States government.

2. Problems of the Convention Settled by Compromise

A wise decision. As soon as the Convention had chosen its officers, it adopted some rules. The meetings would be held in secret. Only members could attend. No reports would be given out until the end of the Convention. The delegates feared undue pressure would be put upon them if the meetings were open to the public.

Everyone of the thirty-five delegates knew that the Articles of Confederation had failed to give peace and order to the country. They realized that the country needed a government that could act at all times and in all emergencies. Must they revise the Articles of Confederation or draw up a new plan? Congress had given them power only to change the Articles of Confederation.

Finally, a majority of the delegates decided it was necessary to write an entirely new set of laws. These laws would give powers to the national government. The delegates knew that if this were done, each state would have to give up some of its powers.

The "Great Compromise." During the first two months the Constitutional Convention accomplished very little. Problems arose which seemed impossible to solve. Perhaps the most difficult of these was the question of representatives in Congress.

Wishing to please the large states, Governor Randolph of Virginia called for representation based on population. William Paterson of New Jersey, who favored the smaller states, wanted equal representation for all states.

This difficult problem was settled by the "Great Compromise." A compromise is an agreement by which each side gives up something and each side gains something. In this way both sides are satisfied.

The delegates finally agreed that Congress should consist of two houses or assemblies. The first house, or Senate, was to be made up of two senators from each state. The second house, or House of Representatives, was to consist of members chosen according to the number of people living in each state.

The "Three-fifths Compromise." Representation by population provoked another question. Should the slaves be counted in the population? The southern states wanted slaves counted so that these states would have more representatives. These states, however, did not want to pay taxes on the slaves. The northern states said that since slaves were considered as property they should be taxed as such. The northern states did not want the slaves counted for representation.

The two groups made another compromise. Five slaves were to be counted as equal to three white persons for both taxation and representation. This was called the "Three-fifths Compromise."

The commerce compromise. A dispute over commerce led to a third compromise. The North and the South disagreed over the right of Congress to control trade. The North was the commercial and ship-owning center of the nation. Northerners wanted Congress to have the power to control trade. The The South did not wish Congress to have such power because it might forbid the importation of slaves. Southern planters believed slavery necessary for the success of their plantations.

An agreement was reached. Congress was allowed to regulate foreign commerce and commerce between states, but it was forbidden to interfere with the slave trade before 1808. Many other problems, too, were settled by compromises.

The Constitution is drawn up. As soon as the delegates of the Convention came to satisfactory agreements over the problems discussed, the laws were written. These laws became our great Constitution. A constitution is a written form of government. Our Constitution is one of the most important written laws in the history of the world.

The Constitution is signed. The members at the Constitutional Convention believed they had worked out a good plan of government. The powers between

The signing of the Constitution

Bettmann Archive

the states and the central government had been divided as fairly as possible.

On the morning of September 17, 1787, they met to sign the newly written Constitution. A few members refused to sign their names.

George Washington, president of the Convention, was the first to sign. Names were called according to states. One by one each man wrote his name below that of Washington. Thirty-nine delegates, representing twelve states, signed the Constitution. Among these were two prominent Catholics, Thomas Fitzsimons from Pennsylvania and Daniel Carroll from Maryland.

The Convention had finished its work. All the members said good-by to each other. Each one returned home to explain the Constitution to his fellow Americans and to urge them to accept it. They tried to convince the people that the new plan of government was much better than the old one.

3. The Constitution Becomes the Law of Our Nation

Will the states accept the Constitution? The Constitution was written and signed. Copies of it were sent to the states for ratification. Nine of the thirteen states would have to ratify it before it could become the law for all. During the fall and winter of 1787 and 1788, elections were held in all the states. The purpose of these elections was to choose representatives for their state conventions.

When these state conventions met, some of the delegates favored the Constitution and others disapproved of it. The chief objection was that it did not state the rights of the people. The opposing delegates demanded that before they would accept the Constitution it should state exactly what rights the citizens had. They said that the powers of government were stated plainly.

The people in all the states were just as excited as those at the state conventions. Everywhere, men were talking about the new laws of government. The main topic of conversation was the Constitution.

People were divided in their thinking about the Constitution. Some people did not like it. They feared that such a strong central government might take away their rights. They asked, "What is to prevent a President and Congress from becoming as unjust as King George III and Parliament?"

Many others favored the Constitution. These people had confidence in the judgment of delegates like Washington and Franklin, who would never draft unfair laws. Had not most of the members of the Convention fought for freedom in the Revolutionary War?

For nine months the states argued over the acceptance of the Constitution. People were divided into two parties. Those who approved of the Constitution were called Federalists. Those who opposed it were called Anti-Federalists. These argued that the rights of the people were not safeguarded by the Constitution.

The Constitution is ratified. By June, 1788, nine states had ratified the Constitution. It was now the law of the United States.

Delaware had the honor of being the first state to approve the Constitution. Pennsylvania was the next. New Jersey, Georgia, Connecticut, Massachusetts, Maryland, and South Carolina followed. Finally New Hampshire cast the vote necessary to put the new government under the Constitution into effect.

Virginia was the next state to ratify the Constitution. The votes of New York, Rhode Island, and North Carolina were still missing. In New York a bitter struggle was going on among the delegates at the state convention. Opposition was so strong that it looked as if New York would never adopt the Constitution.

Alexander Hamilton, James Madison, and John Jay wrote letters to the New York newspapers explaining the Constitution. In these letters they urged the New Yorkers to persuade their delegates to vote for the Constitution. Later these articles were reprinted in several papers of other states. These letters were put into a booklet called the *Federalist*. At last, the members of the state convention voted for the Constitution. Its approval was decided by just three votes.

New York had finally adopted the Constitution, but only with the understanding that a Bill of Rights would be added. This would protect the individual rights of all.

North Carolina and Rhode Island did not accept the Constitution until the government was set up. North Carolina came into the Union in November, 1789, and Rhode Island in May, 1790.

What do these words mean?

Constitution   Federalist   Anti-Federalists
Convention   compromise   House of Representatives
revision   adopted   Senate
ratify   safeguarded   Bill of Rights

How well can you discuss these topics?

1. A good way to settle disputes is by compromise.
2. The Constitution is built upon Catholic truths.
3. All lawful authority comes from Almighty God and for this reason it should be obeyed.
4. Many states refused to adopt the Constitution until they were assured that a Bill of Rights would be added to it.

Write these sentences and fill in the blanks correctly

1. The Constitutional Convention met at _____ in 1787.
2. Congress is made up of the House of Representatives and the _____.
3. A constitution is a _____ form of government.
4. The first state to approve the Constitution was _____.
5. The Constitution was adopted when _____ states voted for its approval.
6. The number of delegates who went to the Constitutional Convention was _____.
7. The state not represented at the Constitutional Convention was _____.
8. The Constitution was adopted in _____.
9. Rules adopted for the good of people are called _____.
10. Benjamin Franklin recommended that the meetings be opened with a _____.

Making connections

Tell what each of the following suggests.

1. The sessions at the meeting were not peaceful.
2. It decided that the number of representatives in the House of Representatives would depend upon the population.
3. A booklet which gave reasons for adopting the Constitution.
4. Members used common sense and great wisdom when they decided not to revise the Articles of Confederation.

CHAPTER III

THE CONSTITUTION OF THE UNITED STATES

Points to remember. The country was fortunate to have such able and experienced delegates to send to the Constitutional Convention. These men wisely formed a new plan of government instead of trying to patch up the old Articles of Confederation.

During the meetings many arguments came up. It was only natural that these men should hold different opinions on such important matters as those discussed at the Convention. Some delegates had little faith in the ability of people to govern themselves. Others felt that the people in the colonies had proved themselves capable of self-government. The interests of the larger states clashed with those of the smaller ones.

Time after time during heated arguments, it looked as if the Convention were going to break up. This would mean the delegates would go home without accomplishing anything. During such exciting meetings, Franklin or Washington would urge the members to stop arguing and drop the discussions for a few days. During that time, the men whose opinions had clashed would talk over the disagreement with their friends. They always found a way to solve the problems.

At the next meeting, the members settled the disagreement by compromise. Each one gave in a little in order to come to an agreement. In this way nobody got just what he wanted, but everyone won some points. The spirit of willingness to compromise proved what great statesmen these men were. They were working for the good of all the states. How does your patriotism compare with theirs? Are you a loyal, unselfish American?

In September, 1787, the Constitution was completed. Copies of it were sent to the states. Many Americans did not favor the Constitution because they thought it made the central government too strong. After a hard fight, nine states adopted the Constitution.

This chapter will give you much more information about the Constitution. It will show you how the powers of the government were divided. You will learn also about the Bill of Rights.

1. Constitution Provides for a More Perfect Union

The federal government. The Constitution was to be used instead of the Articles of Confederation. However, it was not to take the place of the constitutions of the states. The national or federal government was to work with the governments of the states.

Much power was given the federal government, but much was also left to the states. All powers not given to the national government were reserved for the states. States could control their own schools. They could pass laws to meet the needs of their people. State governments could take care of all local affairs.

The states were to share

The Constitution and the Declaration of Independence are preserved in Washington

their authority with the central government. This sharing of powers between the central government and the state government is sometimes called the federal system.

An important document. Our Constitution is not a long document, but it is a thorough one. With the exception of the Declaration of Independence, it has proved to be the most important paper ever written in the United States.

The Constitution is made up of three parts. First comes the Preamble or introduction, then the Articles, and finally the Bill of Rights with the Amendments or changes. The Bill of Rights and the Amendments were not in the original Constitution.

In the Preamble, the writers tell clearly who was responsible for making of the Constitution and why it was made.

We, the people of the United States, in order to form a more perfect union, establish justice, insure domestic tranquility, provide for the common defense, promote the general welfare, and secure the blessings of liberty to ourselves and our posterity, do ordain and establish this Constitution for the United States of America.

WE, THE PEOPLE OF THE UNITED STATES . . . ESTABLISH THIS CONSTITUTION. This is a sentence full of meaning. It tells us that the new government gets its power directly from the people, not from the states. The people now will make their own government and govern themselves.

TO FORM A MORE PERFECT UNION. This means that an improved plan of government was to be set up. This plan would be better than the one the nation had.

ESTABLISH JUSTICE. Americans would be treated fairly and protected by just laws. They would have trial by jury.

INSURE DOMESTIC TRANQUILITY. The government promises to keep peace between the states. The people are assured of being able to live peacefully and orderly with their neighbors.

PROVIDE FOR THE COMMON DEFENSE. The new government would protect the people from foreign enemies and, if necessary, from troubles within the country.

PROMOTE THE GENERAL WELFARE. Whatever possible would be done to improve the American way of life.

AND SECURE THE BLESSINGS OF LIBERTY TO OURSELVES AND OUR POSTERITY. The authors of the Constitution wanted to make sure that the rights and privileges of every American would always be protected.

DO ORDAIN AND ESTABLISH THIS CONSTITUTION FOR THE UNITED STATES OF AMERICA. The framers of the Constitution planned that the new government would be strong. They hoped that under it, American freedom would always be secure.

2. The Constitution Provides for Three Government Branches

Articles of the Constitution. The Articles are really the framework of the Constitution. The plan of government described

A joint Session of the Senate and House of Representatives of the United States
in session

in them is in many ways different from any plan of government established elsewhere at that time. The Articles provide for a central government that gets its power from the people.

By the new Constitution the powers of the government are divided into three independent parts. The legislative branch makes the laws. The executive branch sees that the laws are carried out. The judicial branch explains the laws and passes judgment on them. **The legislative branch.** This branch is more often called the Congress of the United States. It consists of two houses, the Senate and the House of Representatives. At the present time, the members of both houses are elected by the people.

The Senate has two senators from each state. These men serve for six years. In the House of Representatives, the number of members from each state depends on the state population. There is one representative for about every 300,000 people in a state. A census is taken every ten years.

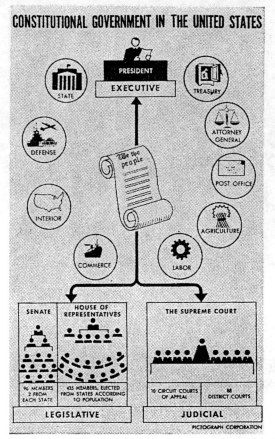

CONSTITUTIONAL GOVERNMENT IN THE UNITED STATES

PRESIDENT
EXECUTIVE

STATE
TREASURY
DEFENSE
ATTORNEY GENERAL
POST OFFICE
INTERIOR
AGRICULTURE
COMMERCE
LABOR

We the people

SENATE	HOUSE OF REPRESENTATIVES	THE SUPREME COURT
96 MEMBERS 2 FROM EACH STATE	435 MEMBERS, ELECTED FROM STATES ACCORDING TO POPULATION	10 CIRCUIT COURTS OF APPEAL	88 DISTRICT COURTS
LEGISLATIVE		JUDICIAL

PICTOGRAPH CORPORATION

Pictograph Corp.

No matter how small the population is, however, each state has at least one representative. The Congressmen, as they are called, are elected for two years.

The Constitution gives Congress the right to make laws which will protect the people and allow them to enjoy their God-given liberties. Congress has the right to collect taxes and to borrow money. By this means the government can pay its expenses. Lack of power to raise money was one of the great weaknesses in the Articles of Confederation.

Congress has other powers such as regulating commerce, coining money, and establishing post offices. Besides, it may maintain both an army and navy which are large enough to protect the nation. Congress may declare war and draft men to serve in the armed forces.

The executive branch. The President is the head of the executive branch as well as of the nation. Both he and the Vice President serve for a term of four years and may be elected again. If the President should die or anything prevent him from carrying on his work, the Vice President becomes the President until the next election. Both men must take an oath to protect, preserve, and defend the Constitution.

The chief duty of the President is to see that the laws of the nation are carried out. He appoints the judges of the Supreme Court and many assistants to help him with his duties. The President is the commander-in-chief of both the army and navy. He takes care of business with foreign nations. His position is the most important in the country. This is why we should ask God to guide him, for much depends on his decisions.

The judicial branch. This branch consists of the United States Supreme Court and the lower federal courts. The Supreme Court is composed of a Chief Justice and eight other justices. All the judges of these courts are appointed by the President and approved by the Senate.

The Supreme Court decides what the laws of our nation mean. It determines whether or not laws passed by Congress agree with the Constitution. All laws passed by Congress and by the states must agree with the Constitution. The Supreme Court is the highest court in the land. It has the final decision on all legal matters.

Checks and Balances. In order to be sure that no branch of the government take over the powers of another branch, there is a system called checks and balances. An example will show what is meant by this.

Congress passes a bill. Before it can become a law, it goes to the President of the United States to be signed. If the President does not want the bill to become a law, he may refuse to sign it. This refusal is called a veto. However, the bill may still become a law over the President's veto if two-thirds of the members of Congress vote for it. In this way the President and Congress act as a check on one another. This system of checks and balances protects the rights of the people.

The framers of the Constitution used good judgment in separating the branches of the government. It took experience and wisdom to think out ways and means of placing limits on the powers of each branch. By so doing the Constitution was made a law for the government as well as for the people. Everyone, from the highest to the lowest, is bound to obey it.

The Constitution is of such importance that each year millions of people study it. There is a copy of the Constitution in the back of this book. In the Archives of the United States in Washington, D. C., the Constitution of the United States and the Declaration of Independence are kept in large glass cases. Every day, visitors from everywhere go to see these documents.

3. The Bill of Rights Protects Our Liberties

The Bill of Rights. At the Constitutional Convention, George Mason of Virginia proposed that a Bill of Rights be included

97

in the Constitution. A bill of rights is a statement of those rights which are guaranteed to all citizens of a country. If the members had acted on Mason's advice, much trouble would have been avoided.

The chief complaint against the adoption of the Constitution was that it did not safeguard the individual liberties of the people. Freedom-loving Americans insisted that a bill of rights be added. They wanted to be protected from cruel and unjust treatment by their government and by their fellow citizens.

Many of the states refused to accept the Constitution unless it contained a bill of rights. Washington and Madison promised to work for such a bill as soon as the first Congress met.

When Congress met at New York in 1789, Madison suggested several Amendments. Ten of them were accepted and later approved by the states. In December, 1791, these ten Amendments were added to the Constitution. These Amendments are generally spoken of as the Bill of Rights. Since then only twelve Amendments have been added to the Constitution, although tremendous changes have taken place in the United States.

In the first eight Amendments you will find a list of rights and freedoms which are guaranteed to every person living in the United States. These are the precious liberties which you possess and so often take for granted. You may not grasp the whole meaning of these Amendments when you read them. However, after class discussion with your teacher, you should understand more clearly the Bill of Rights. The illustration on the next page will help fix the main ideas in your mind.

In 1791, the Bill of Rights assured the people of the United States the right to worship God in accordance with their consciences. Nevertheless, complete religious freedom was not given in all the states until a much later date. Some people were still being deprived of the right to property, to vote, and to hold offices in the government because of their religious beliefs. As time went on, all the states amended their laws to grant freedom of religion.

Personal liberty charter. Americans are justly proud of their government. People have privileges here in the United States that others elsewhere do not enjoy. They have the right to worship God in their own churches. They have the right to speak and write frankly, provided it does not interfere with other people's rights. People are free to express opinions in newspapers, books, magazines, on the radio, and on television. Citizens can meet to discuss public affairs. No one can be imprisoned without a trial. Americans have a right to a trial by jury. No cruel or unjust punishment can be imposed. Homes cannot be searched unless an officer of the law has a legal warrant. These and other privileges are guaranteed in the Bill of Rights and in our Constitution.

Since Americans have such rights, they also have many duties to their government and to their country. They should always obey and respect its laws. People living in this Land of Our Lady should make every effort to preserve freedom and liberty. They should be constantly on the alert to keep America "the land of the free and the home of the brave."

As Catholics, we are obliged to perform our duties as citizens. We must also be aware of our responsibilities and of our

Important Provisions of the Bill of Rights

Freedom of Speech and Press

Freedom of Religion

Right to Assemble

Freedom from Unreasonable Search

Right to Trial by Jury

Just Compensation for Private Property

Diagram of Bill of Rights

neighbor's welfare. God's law commands us to do these things. Our duties, rights, and responsibilities are explained clearly in the Commandments of God and the Commandments of the Church. If you are a good Catholic, it must follow that you will be a good American.

The Constitution can be changed. One of the finest things about our Constitution is that it can be amended or changed to suit the needs of the growing nation. If the people want to add a new law or change an old one, they must petition Congress to vote on it. When Congress approves of the change, then the states vote on it. An Amendment can be added to the Constitution only when three-fourths of the states consent.

The highest law of the land. In our country, which is a democracy, the Constitution is the supreme law of the land. It is the foundation of our government. For more than a century and a half, it has guided the nation through many difficulties. It has achieved the high ideals set forth in the Preamble.

America has proved to the world that a democratic form of government can succeed—"a government of the people, by the people, and for the people." Many countries, particularly those of Latin America, have modeled their governments on our Constitution.

May the United States government under the Constitution continue its great work of preserving our American way of living. May it continue to be an inspiration for those nations which do not have these blessings of freedom and which are still fighting for their rights.

Word Game

Put list of words on blackboard. Divide the class into teams. The captain of each team will give each pupil in his group a word or expression to look up. The following day, have each student explain the word or expression without naming it. Another student will give the word pertaining to the explanation.

legislative branch	Articles of the Constitution	guaranteed
executive branch	Bill of Rights	petition
judicial branch	federal system	Amendments
checks and balances	Preamble	charter

Interesting topics to talk about

1. Good Catholics are always good Americans.
2. The Constitution of the United States plays an important part in the life of every American.
3. The Bill of Rights is the guardian of our liberties.
4. The people of the United States have duties as well as rights.
5. "Sweet land of liberty."

Are you ready to work?

1. Memorize the Preamble to the Constitution.
2. The Preamble tells who made the Constitution and gives six reasons why it was made. Do you know these six reasons, and who made the Constitution?

3. Radio and television afford opportunities for freedom of speech. Why must these means of communication be used in the true American way?

Checking your knowledge of Unit Two

I. List the numbers 1-20 on your answer paper. Beside each number write the letter in Column B which matches each item in Column A.

Column A	*Column B*
1. James Madison	a. Catholic signer of the Constitution
2. ratify	b. to forbid
3. executive department	c. first ten Amendments
4. judicial department	d. to approve
5. legislative department	e. government from 1781-1789
6. Benjamin Franklin	f. bitter opponent of the Constitution
7. Preamble	g. makes laws
8. Bill of Rights	h. two-thirds of the states must approve
9. Patrick Henry	i. to change
10. Thomas Fitzsimons	j. chairman of the Convention
11. amend	k. Constitution adopted
12. "Three-fifths Compromise"	l. opposed the Constitution
13. Articles of Confederation	m. supreme law of our land
14. Federalists	n. a conclusion
15. June, 1788	o. three-fourths of the states must approve
16. George Washington	p. oldest member at the Convention
17. September 17, 1787	q. Samuel Adams
18. Constitution	r. enforce laws
19. Anti-Federalists	s. North and South divided over slaves
20. To make a new Amendment	t. favored the Constitution
	u. Father of the Constitution
	v. an introduction
	w. explain laws
	x. Constitution signed

II. Arrange these events in the order in which they happened.

1. Constitutional Convention
2. Declaration of Independence
3. Annapolis Convention
4. Bill of Rights
5. Articles of Confederation adopted
6. Albany Plan of Union
7. Shays' Rebellion
8. Approval of the Constitution

III. Find the incorrect word or group of words in each of the following:

1. The United States courts
   a. settle quarrels
   b. make laws
   c. punish law-breakers
   d. protect people from unfair punishment

2. Delegates to the Constitutional Convention were
   a. Thomas Jefferson
   b. Benjamin Franklin
   c. George Morris
   d. Edmund Randolph

3. Among the first nine states that ratified the Constitution were
   a. Delaware
   b. Massachusetts
   c. New Hampshire
   d. New York

4. The Constitution provided
   a. for a President
   b. for a Congress
   c. for a Cabinet
   d. for a Supreme Court

5. The Bill of Rights gives
   a. the right of trial by jury
   b. the right to raise money by lottery
   c. the right to practice one's religion
   d. the right to speak freely

6. The state governments could
   a. control their schools
   b. take care of local affairs
   c. keep their state bills of rights
   d. coin money

7. These states sent representatives to the Constitutional Convention:
   a. Rhode Island
   b. Virginia
   c. New Jersey
   d. Maryland

8. The First Amendment to the Constitution provides for
   c. freedom of religion
   b. freedom of speech
   c. freedom of press
   d. freedom from want

9. In a democracy, people can differ with
   a. the governor of the state
   b. the President of the United States
   c. the laws of God
   d. their friends

10. At the Constitutional Convention, disputes were settled by the
    a. Missouri Compromise
    b. "Great Compromise"
    c. Commerce Compromise
    d. "Three-Fifths Compromise"

IV. Answer yes or no.

1. The delegates to the Constitutional Convention were wise, experienced, and capable leaders.
2. The government under the Articles of Confederation provided a strong central government.
3. Large and small states disagreed on representation.
4. The Constitution is the foundation of our government.
5. To prevent any one branch of government from becoming too powerful, the Constitution provides for a system of checks and balances.
6. The national government has four branches.
7. A government has no authority to take away from people the rights that God has given them.
8. Americans have always been freedom-loving people.
9. The Constitution gave more rights to the state than to the national government.
10. American democracy is based upon the teachings of Christ.
11. The members of the Constitutional Convention had great great trust in God.
12. The Northwest Ordinance was passed by Congress under the Articles of Confederation.
13. A bill goes to the President of the United States before it becomes a law.
14. In 1791, complete religious freedom was given to all the people in all the states.
15. The delegates at the Constitutional Convention made a new plan of government.
16. The Constitution guaranteed some personal liberties even before the Bill of Rights was added.
17. The President of the United States may veto a bill passed by Congress.
18. Thomas Jefferson wrote the Constitution.
19. Differences of opinion are settled by compromise.
20. The Constitution contains many Christian truths.

V. Divide the class into five groups. Each group will choose a speaker to report on one of the topics listed below. Get additional information from other books. Each group will help his speaker collect interesting material. Class will vote on the best speaker.

1. Government under the Articles of Confederation
2. The Constitutional Convention
3. The Approval of the Constitution
4. The Constitution of the United States
5. The Bill of Rights

Mary and Society

MEANING. The Church shows us Mary as our kind Mother in the words of the Bible: "She hath opened her hand to the needy, and stretched out her hands to the poor" (Proverbs: 31:20). Mary teaches us to be kind to others. Her Son Jesus has told us: "Thou shalt love thy neighbor as thyself" (Matthew: 19:19). Mary helped others at the marriage feast at Cana, when, at her request, Jesus turned the water into wine. By following Mary, we can learn to love and help others.

APPLICATION. World order demands fellowship among all people. Friends, schoolmates, neighbors, and strangers deserve respect, honor, and tolerance. All mankind forms a society that calls for cooperation on the part of each individual. Mary and Jesus showed great love for humanity, and as Help of Christians, Mary guides all mankind.

Prayer

Help of Christians, *pray for us.*

Litany of the Blessed Virgin

LORD, have mercy on us.
Christ, have mercy on us.
Lord, have mercy on us.
God the Son, Redeemer of the world, have mercy on us.
God, the Holy Ghost, have mercy on us.
Holy Trinity, one God, have mercy on us.
Christ, hear us.
Christ, graciously hear us.
God the Father of heaven, have mercy on us.
Holy Mary,[1]
Holy Mother of God,
Holy Virgin of virgins,
Mother of Christ,
Mother of divine grace,
Mother most pure,
Mother most chaste,
Mother inviolate,
Mother undefiled,
Mother most amiable,
Mother most admirable,
Mother of good counsel,
Mother of our Creator,
Mother of our Saviour,
Virgin most prudent,
Virgin most venerable,
Virgin most renowned,

[1] Pray for us.

Virgin most powerful,
Virgin most merciful,
Virgin most faithful,
Mirror of justice,
Seat of wisdom,
Cause of our joy,
Spiritual vessel,
Vessel of honor,
Singular vessel of devotion,
Mystical Rose,
Tower of David,
Tower of ivory,
House of gold,
Ark of the covenant,
Gate of heaven,
Morning star,
Health of the sick,
Refuge of sinners,
Comforter of the afflicted,
Help of Christians,
Queen of angels,
Queen of patriarchs,
Queen of prophets,
Queen of apostles,
Queen of martyrs,
Queen of confessors,
Queen of virgins,
Queen of all saints,
Queen conceived without original sin,

Queen assumed into heaven,
Queen of the most holy Rosary,
Queen of peace.
Lamb of God, who takest away the sins of the world, spare us, O Lord.
Lamb of God, who takest away the sins of the world, graciously hear us, O Lord.
Lamb of God, who takest away the sins of the world, have mercy on us.
Christ, hear us. Christ, graciously hear us.
℣. Pray for us, O holy Mother of God. ℟. That we may be made worthy of the promises of Christ.

Let us pray

Grant, we beseech Thee, O Lord God, unto us Thy servants, that we may rejoice in continual health of mind and body; and, by the glorious intercession of blessed Mary ever Virgin, may be delivered from present sadness, and enter into the joy of Thine eternal gladness. Through Christ our Lord. Amen.

An indulgence of 7 years. A plenary indulgence once a month on the usual conditions for the daily devout recitation of this Litany with its versicle and prayer (See "The Raccolta," the official work of indulgenced prayers, page 216).

MARY AS A GUIDE THROUGH LIFE. The free will of man accepts the guidance of Mary in the way of life. This guidance of Mary is part of our religion. It affects our home life, our association with our fellow man, our civic obligations, our career in life, and our acceptance of life's problems.

Courtesy of Rev. J. B. Carol, O. F. M.

UNIT THREE

THE SUCCESS OF THE NEW PLAN OF GOVERNMENT

CHAPTER I—THE NEW GOVERNMENT IN ACTION

Washington—First President of the United States

Washington's Cabinet

Hamilton's Financial Plan—Settles Payment of Public Debt

Raising Revenue—Leads to Whiskey Rebellion

First Bank of United States Established

Political Parties — Federalists — Anti-Federalists

CHAPTER II—FOREIGN AFFAIRS DISTURB UNITED STATES

France Expects Aid—Washington Proclaims Neutrality

England and America Disagree—Jay's Treaty

Spain Causes Trouble—Pinckney Treaty

Washington Retires

CHAPTER III—ESTABLISHING OUR FOREIGN POLICY

Election of 1796—John Adams Elected

Troubles with France Continue—XYZ Affair

Unpopular Laws—Downfall of Federalists

Alien and Sedition Laws — Virginia and Kentucky Resolutions

UNIT THREE

THE SUCCESS OF THE NEW PLAN OF GOVERNMENT

THE AMERICAN COLONISTS had united against England and won their freedom in 1783. Independence brought many problems to this Land of Our Lady. Men like Washington and Franklin feared that the nation would not hold together. The states would have to be more united. The people would have to agree upon a form of government that would protect the states and form one nation.

Most Americans wanted a national government that could be run by the people and for the people. The first plan under the Articles of Confederation was not successful. The central government was not given enough power. The nation was unable to pay its debts. Thus it was not respected by European countries. There was no uniform system of money. Conditions became so bad that it was agreed to make some changes in the laws.

In May, 1787, leaders of our nation met in Philadelphia to change the Articles of Confederation. Instead, they drew up a new plan of government, the Constitution, which has served our nation well for more than a century and a half.

In this Unit, we shall see how successful the statesmen were in establishing a new government under the Constitution. We shall learn how the money problem was taken care of. We shall see how political parties began and how difficult problems with European nations were satisfactorily settled.

CHAPTER I

THE NEW GOVERNMENT

Success in affairs at home. The Constitution was adopted by nine of the thirteen states. Now it was ready to be tested. People began inquiring, "Who will be the first President?" Everyone wanted someone whom they could trust to govern the nation wisely. Most Americans believed that George Washington was the only one capable of getting all people to work together. That is why the electors chose him to be first President.

In this chapter, you will study about George Washington and other great Americans who helped to build up our country in its early years.

1. Steps in the Right Direction

Washington—our first President. We know that after the Revolution was won, General Washington was happy to return to his home at Mount Vernon, in Virginia, to live a quiet life. Yet he did not refuse to go to the Philadelphia Convention. Through his able leadership, this Convention formed our great Constitution.

The Constitution provided for the selection of a President, and the people wanted no one but Washington. He had been their leader through war and national difficulties. Now, in peace, they wanted him as their leader.

New York City had been selected for the capital of the nation and Congress was to meet there March 4, 1789. The weather was so bad and travel so slow that many members did not get there until early in April. Congress then met in Federal Hall on Wall Street to count the votes for the President and Vice President.

Every vote for President was cast for George Washington. No President since has received all the votes. John Adams of Massachusetts, having received the second highest number of ballots, was elected Vice President. Congress sent messengers to tell these men of their election. Washington did not want the office. However, he was too good a citizen not to accept this call to duty.

Once again, Washington left his home at Mount Vernon to serve his country. He traveled through Pennsylvania and New Jersey over the routes where he had led armies. Along the way, Washington was greeted by cheering crowds of people. Everywhere, to honor him, villages and towns were decorated. Men paraded and bands played. Little children scattered flowers in front of his carriage. Washington knew before he reached New York that the people admired and trusted him.

Washington was taken from the New Jersey shore of the Hudson River to New York City in a special boat decorated with red curtains and satin awnings. The barge was rowed by thirteen captains, wearing white uniforms trimmed with blue. Several boats filled with people were waiting in the bay.

When the boat carrying Washington landed at New York, Governor Clinton of New York State was there to welcome him. Members of Congress were also present. Thousands of people were waiting on the wharves and along the streets. To honor him, bells were ringing and cannons were firing as he arrived.

The inauguration. On April 30, 1789, Washington took the oath of office, and became the first President of the United States.

New York planned a big celebration and a holiday for everyone. Every place was decorated with bunting and flags. There was a large float called the Ship of State which represented the Constitution. Soldiers were lined up in front of public buildings. From the streets, men, women, and children were looking on. In the morning, the church bells rang and many went to church to pray for Washington and the success of the new government.

At noon, Washington arrived at Federal Hall where Congress had assembled. Accompanied by John Adams, he stepped out on the balcony overlooking the street. There, before a large crowd, he reverently took the oath of office required by the Constitution. An oath of office is a solemn promise made to

God. Washington placed his right hand on a Bible and slowly repeated the words of the oath after Robert Livingston, the chief law officer of New York. By this oath, Washington promised to be a good President and to do his work faithfully.

As the new President finished speaking, Livingston stepped forward and shouted, "Long live George Washington, President of the United States." The crowds from below yelled, "God bless our Washington! Long live our beloved President." The flag of the United States was proudly raised over the balcony.

Then Washington stepped back, went into the room where the Senate was meeting and read a short speech to Congress. From there, he and the Congress went to Saint Paul's Church to thank God for the new nation and to pray for His help in their work. These leaders knew how difficult a job it would be to organize the new government.

The inauguration of the President of the United States

Washington takes the oath of office as President, New York, 1789

Bettmann Archive

The inauguration of President Eisenhower. Note the microphones.
Compare this picture with that of Washington's inauguration

is always a public ceremony. Today, television has made it possible for millions to watch the ceremony.

Work of the first Congress. Washington and Congress began at once to set up the new government. One of the first things Congress did was to establish four departments to help the President. With the consent of Congress, President Washington appointed four men who he thought best fitted to be his helpers and advisers.

Another big job that President Washington and the Congress had to do was to plan for a Supreme Court and for lower courts. Perhaps the biggest problem that faced them was how to get money to pay the war debts and how to pay the men working for the government.

Washington's Cabinet. Washington appointed wise and capable men to help him. To regulate money problems, he chose Alexander Hamilton as Secretary of the Treasury. Thomas Jefferson was selected as Secretary of State to take charge of foreign affairs. Henry Knox was

John Jay

Culver

learned and most honest Americans of his day, was appointed by Washington as first Chief Justice. This is one of the most important offices in the government of the United States. Today the Supreme Court has a Chief Justice and eight associate justices.

2. Making the National Credit Good

Hamilton's financial plan. Among the many problems President Washington's government had to solve, the most difficult was the raising of money to pay the national debt and run the government. The colonists had borrowed fifty-four million dollars ($54,000,000) to carry on the Revolution. Now there was no money in the treasury. Unless it paid this war debt no country would respect this nation and no citizen would trust it. Washington had to build up a reputation for fairness and honesty.

Alexander Hamilton was well able for this task. He was industrious, intelligent, and shrewd about money matters. As Secretary of the Treasury he would take care of the nation's money and all the money affairs connected with his office.

Hamilton spent long hours making plans to solve the

chosen as Secretary of War, in charge of the Army and Navy. As Attorney General, Washington picked Edmund Randolph to advise him in matters of law and to act as lawyer for the government.

Washington talked over all important business with these four men. This group of assistants formed the first Cabinet. Who are the members of the President's Cabinet today?

Federal Courts. In time, Congress established a system of national courts. The Supreme Court was the highest of all courts. It was to have a Chief Justice and five associate justices. John Jay, one of the most money problems of the nation. He planned for the government to take over the national debt and also to pay the states' debts. Hamilton worked out a way to raise money by taxes. He helped to establish a national bank and also started a mint to coin money.

Settling the public debt. Every war costs a nation many millions of dollars. Hamilton made plans to pay every cent of the debts resulting from the Revolution. No one was unwilling to pay the national debt, but trouble arose when Hamilton said that the national government should also pay the state debts. All were sharing the freedom won by the war. Should not all share the cost of the war which brought this freedom? Some states had already paid their own debts and could not understand why they should have to help pay the debts of other states. The Southern states were against Hamilton's plan, but the Northern states favored it.

A bargain is made. At this time Congress was trying to decide where the capital of the United States should be located. There was great rivalry between the states for this honor. Five states offered large grants of land and large sums of money for the construction of the buildings. President Washington had taken the oath of office at New York City. Shortly afterwards Congress moved to Philadelphia. Virginia and some of the Southern states wanted the capital somewhere on the banks of the Potomac River.

Hamilton and Jefferson made an agreement. Hamilton promised to persuade the Northern representatives to vote that after ten years the capital would be moved from Philadelphia to a place on the Potomac River. Jefferson promised to persuade the Southern representatives to agree to have the nation pay the states' debts. In this way Congress came to pay the states' debts, and the national capital came to be located at Washington on the Potomac.

Raising revenue. To raise money for the payment of the debts, Hamilton suggested a tax on all manufactured goods brought or imported into the United States. Such a tax is called a tariff. It would not affect the people directly, for it would be included in the price of the article when sold by the merchants. A tariff would encourage the home manufac-

A scene during the Whiskey Rebellion. The mob has tarred and feathered a tax collector who is being ridden on a rail

turer, because it would raise the price of foreign goods. Thus, it would help build up industry in the states by increasing the demand for American-made goods.

Whiskey Rebellion. When the taxing of foreign goods failed to raise enough money, the Secretary of the Treasury recommended that another tax be placed on goods made and sold within the country. This is called an excise tax.

The farmers of Pennsylvania thought this tax was unjust. Their chief occupation was raising corn, and since they lived far from the markets they found it hard to carry the corn to the markets in order to sell it. It was easier to carry the whiskey which they could make from the corn, and for which they could get higher prices.

When the farmers learned that their whiskey was to be taxed, beginning in 1794, they refused to pay it. Their refusal to pay the tax was called the "Whiskey Rebellion."

Both Washington and Hamilton knew this refusal was a test of the strength of the new government. The President sent a force of soldiers into Pennsylvania. The farmers soon gave in and paid the tax. This action proved to the people that the government had the power not only to make laws, but also to see that the laws were obeyed.

The United States Bank. The Constitution had given Congress the right to raise money by taxes. Hamilton suggested that a national bank system would be a safe way to manage government funds. Such a bank could regulate money so that it would have the same value everywhere in the country. People would put their money into the banks and this money could be put to use by the government, which would pay interest on it. Hamilton's chief aim was to establish the nation's credit.

Not all the people of the United States agreed with him. Jefferson and his followers believed that Hamilton's plan gave Congress too much power. They said that since the Constitution did not mention a national bank, Congress had no right to establish one.

Hamilton saw things in a different way. In the Constitution there is a paragraph called the "elastic clause." This clause gives Congress the right to make any law necessary to carry out the powers given to it by the Constitution. It is found in Article I, Section 8, no. 18 of the Constitution. Hamilton claimed that if Congress has the right to collect taxes and coin money, it should have

a safe place to keep such funds. A National Bank would be the safest place.

With the support of President Washington, Hamilton finally won. Congress voted to allow a National Bank to conduct business for twenty years. When the bank was opened on July 4, 1791, at Philadelphia the people showed their trust in their new government by depositing large sums of money.

3. Political Parties

The Federalists. Differences of opinion about the National Bank led to the formation of political parties in our country. A political party is an organization of people working together to carry out certain policies in government. Those who approved Hamilton's ideas of a strong central government called themselves "Federalists." Most of them were bankers, merchants, or manufacturers. They claimed that the Constitution gave Congress many general powers which were not stated definitely in the law. This view is called a "broad construction" of the Constitution. It was the policy encouraged by the Federalists.

Anti-Federalists. Those who did not want a strong central government formed the Democratic-Republican Party. This party was led by Thomas Jefferson. Democratic-Republicans believed that Congress should have only those powers stated definitely in the Constitution. According to this party, the states had certain powers that were greater than those of the national government. This view is called a "strict construction" of the Constitution. The common people, the farmers, and the workingmen were the principal members of this party.

In the next book of this series, you shall read more about these ideas of "strict construction" and "broad construction." We shall see how a conflict over these two ideas led to war. This war divided our country for a time. But after it was over, the nation was reunited. Our country has remained a union. It has become one of the great nations of the world.

New words to use

electors	political parties	ceremony
oath	"elastic clause"	tariff
inauguration	President's Cabinet	treasury
financial	national debt	depositing
barge	excise tax	reputation

For you to talk about

1. Many people in America and Europe did not believe that a government built upon the principle that all men are created equal would succeed. How did President Washington and his helpers meet this challenge?

2. Alexander Hamilton believed that the national government should pay the debts made by the states during the Revolutionary War. Was he justified?

3. Have you noticed what is stamped on a cent? On the front is a picture of an American. The word liberty, which stands for freedom, is there too, and the words, "In God we trust." On the back is the United States motto, "E Pluribus Unum," which means "out of many one." This tells us that one nation has been formed from many states. Why do you think these things were put on the cent?

Recall Test

Place answers in the blanks.

1. Who was the first President of the United States?

   _____

2. What party favored increasing the power of the national government? _____

3. Who was the Secretary of the Treasury in George Washington's Cabinet?

   _____

4. Who were the leaders of the first two political parties in the United States?

5. Who was the first Chief Justice of the Supreme Court?

   _____

6. Where was the first capital of the United States?

   _____

7. Why did some of the states object to the nation's paying state debts? _____

8. What lesson did the Whiskey Rebellion teach the people of the United States?

   _____

9. Why did the followers of Thomas Jefferson object to a National Bank? _____

10. Who were the principal members of the Anti-Federalist party? _____

Choose the correct ending to complete these statements

1. The First Bank of the United States was established through influence of

   a. George Washington
   b. John Adams
   c. John Jay
   d. Alexander Hamilton

2. George Washington was inaugurated President

   a. April 30, 1789
   b. July 4, 1791
   c. May 5, 1787
   d. March 4, 1789

3. The Whiskey Rebellion took place in

   a. Massachusetts
   b. Pennsylvania
   c. New York
   d. Kentucky

4. For Attorney General, Washington chose

   a. Edmund Randolph
   b. Alexander Hamilton
   c. Henry Knox
   d. Thomas Jefferson

FOREIGN AFFAIRS DISTURB THE UNITED STATES

PRESIDENT WASHINGTON, with the help of Congress and the Cabinet, managed the government of our nation successfully. America soon gained the respect and trust of people at home and abroad. Through Hamilton's skill in handling the money problems of the country, the old war debts were being paid and the government was being supported. Jefferson and other leaders opposed Hamilton's plans for raising money. The result was that two political parties were formed. Those favoring Hamilton's program were called Federalists. Those opposing it were named Anti-Federalists, but later were known as Democratic-Republicans.

In the preceding chapter, you saw some of the problems that Washington and his co-workers had to meet at home. In this chapter you will study about the serious troubles that faced our leaders in their dealings with France, England, and Spain.

1. France Looks to the United States for Aid

The French Revolution. In 1789, shortly after George Washington became President, the French were fighting a far more terrible revolution than the one we had fought.

It was a war called the French Revolution. The French people revolted because for a long time they had been suffering injustices from their Kings and from the nobles. People like princes and dukes and other rulers were called nobles. The success of the American Revolution gave the French people courage to fight for their rights. The King who ruled France at the time of the Revolution was good and kind, but the revolutionists took away his power, as well as that of the nobles. The rebels started to set

Culver

The French Revolution was led by cruel, bloodthirsty men

up a new government called a republic.

Unfortunately, the French revolutionists were not blessed with such honest and God-fearing leaders as the American colonists had. The French leaders were cruel, selfish men, who committed many thefts and murders.

Washington proclaims American neutrality. In 1793, Americans became alarmed. In order to help the French King regain his throne, England declared war on France. France was looking to us for aid because she had helped us in 1778. Should we help those fighting for the French King, or help the French people, who had rebelled?

Opinions in the country differed about aid to France. The Democratic-Republicans thought aid should be sent to the French people bcause they were seeking freedom to govern themselves. The Federalists, on the other hand, wanted to help England, who was fighting for the French King and not for the French revolutionists. The Federalists said it was the

King, and not the people of France, who had sent men, ships, and money to America during the Revolutionary War.

To help either side would soon lead America into war. Washington and the members of his Cabinet realized that America was not prepared for war. On April 22, 1793, Washington publicly proclaimed neutrality. Neutrality means that the country would aid neither of the warring nations. By this Proclamation of Neutrality, the leaders of our country hoped to keep the United States friendly with both England and France.

Citizen Genet. The French revolutionists killed the King and Queen of France and set up the new republic. They wanted the United States to recognize this republic as a lawful government. In order to gain this recognition, the French sent us their representative, Citizen Edmond Genêt (zhe-nay').

Genêt came to America to get help for the French who were now fighting England. He landed at Charleston, South Carolina, shortly before Washington announced the message of neutrality. Many Americans gave Genêt a hearty welcome as he traveled from place to place. When Genet discovered that the President had warned the American people to keep out of the trouble in Europe, he became enraged. Citizen Genêt kept on stirring up ill-feeling against England and the other countries fighting against France. He even went so far as to arm merchant ships to attack English ships. He enlisted men to fight for France.

President Washington and the government officials did not like Genêt's actions and speeches. When Washington told the French representative that the United States would help neither warring nation, Genêt was bold and rude enough to insult the President. He even dared to say that he was going to ask the American people to choose between his ideas and those of Washington. Because of his conduct Genêt was very much disliked.

The government asked France to call Genêt home. Everyone agreed that he should be sent back to France. Another group of revolutionists had now come into power in France. Because these men were his enemies, Genêt pleaded with Washington for permission to remain in America. Permission was granted. America, which Gênet had treated so badly, was willing to give him refuge and to permit him to enjoy its freedom. He became an American citizen and later married the daughter of Governor Clinton of New York.

2. War Claims Lead to Trouble with England

England and America disagree. Although the Revolutionary War had ended in England's defeat, she had not given up the trading posts along the Great Lakes, because the fur trade was valuable. The United States minister to England complained about this. England, in turn, claimed that certain British debts had not been paid.

The British were still at war with France and they needed a large navy. English sailors were so poorly paid and fed that they refused to serve. British captains stopped American merchant vessels to search for English sailors who had deserted British warships. They often removed men who were American citizens. England also captured a ship carrying goods to France. Besides, the English government would not allow American merchants to carry on trade with the British West Indies.

Causes for war existed. Many in the country were demanding

Culver
The English search an American ship to find deserters from the British Navy

war with England. Others wondered how America could keep out of war. President Washington and other leaders, knowing how unprepared the country was for war, determined to keep peace. In 1794, the President sent the Chief Justice, John Jay, to England to try to settle these disputes so that war could be prevented.

Jay's treaty. Jay had a difficult task. Finally, in 1795, a treaty was made. England promised to withdraw her troops from our western boundaries within two years. She agreed to give up the forts along the Great Lakes if Americans paid their debts. England did not promise to stop searching our vessels, nor did she guarantee to respect American neutrality.

War is avoided. Americans were indignant at Jay for accepting such terms. Washington realized that the treaty was not satisfactory. Yet it was all that could be expected from England at the time. In order to prevent war, Washington worked hard to have the Senate approve the treaty. The people soon saw the wisdom of their President in accepting this treaty, for it put off war with England for almost twenty years. When war did come, we were better prepared to win.

3. Washington's Term of Office Comes to an End

Trouble with Spain. The troubles with France and England were not the only ones the American government had. The coast along the Gulf of Mexico belonged to Spain. She controlled all shipping through the port of New Orleans near the mouth of the Mississippi River.

In order to ship their products to the eastern states or to Europe, western farmers had to use the Mississippi to New Orleans. At that city the products were transferred to ocean-going vessels. Spain charged such high tariff there that the farmers made very little profit.

The Pinckney Treaty. The people of the West sent letters to Congress begging lower tariffs. In 1795, Washington sent Thomas Pinckney to Spain. When Spain learned that the Jay Treaty had been signed, she became alarmed. She feared that England and the United States might work together to attack the Spanish colonies in America. To prevent a war she signed a treaty giving many privileges to America.

This treaty settled the boundary line of Florida and gave the United States additional land along that boundary. It made it cheaper for the people of the West to ship goods down the Mississippi. It made New Orleans a free port. Americans could land and keep goods there without paying a tax. As a result of this treaty, many new settlers flocked to lands along the Mississippi and Ohio Rivers.

Washington retires. The American people hoped that Washington would be willing to govern his country for a third term. Washington believed that he should not hold office any longer. He announced to a disappointed people that he would not seek reelection in 1796, and began to prepare his farewell address.

In the speech he warned the

After his years of public service, Washington retired to his home in Mount Vernon, where he managed his farm

people of the dangers of mixing in the affairs of other countries. He advised Americans to give all their attention to building up a strong nation at home. He also advised them against quarrels between political parties, because he felt that such quarrels would weaken the government. He asked the people to respect each other's religious beliefs and to lead good, clean Christian lives.

Washington was a great President and a great man. He had guided the nation and formed it according to the principles of justice and charity. His hope was that the American people would always be united. It was his wish that America would be just and fair to all nations and live in peace and harmony with them. His greatest wish was that Americans would be devoted to their country and faithful to God.

On March 4, 1797, Washington retired to his home at Mount Vernon where he lived until his death in 1799. The whole nation was saddened by his death. Washington was "first in war, first in peace, and first in the hearts of his countrymen."

Most Reverend John Carroll—our first bishop. The year 1789 was an important year for the Church as well as for the nation. Pope Pius VI made Father Carroll the bishop of Baltimore in 1789. He had charge of the Catholic Church in the whole United States. Bishop Carroll was a great religious leader and a great American.

I. Do you know these words and expressions?

co-workers
proclaimed
republic
neutral

Proclamation of Neutrality
government officials
French revolutionists
United States ministers

reelection
nobles
principles
guarantee

II. Fill the blanks with the correct word or words

1. The success of the American Revolution gave the people of _____ courage to overthrow the government of their country.
2. The Democratic-Republicans thought aid should be sent to _____
3. The Federalists wanted to help _____
4. On April 22, 1793, Washington issued a Proclamation of _____
5. Citizen Genêt planned to hire ships and to arm them to fight against _____

6. Captains of British ships stopped American vessels to search for _____
7. In 1794 John Jay was sent to England to _____
8. Trouble with England arose in Washington's term of office because the British refused to give up _____
9. _____ Treaty settled the boundary between the United States and Florida.
10. In his farewell address, Washington warned the people against _____ and _____

III. Who am I?

1. I signed a treaty with England in 1795.
2. I refused to serve a third term as President of the United States.
3. I came to America to get help for France.
4. I secured a treaty with Spain which gave the United States the right to use the Mississippi River for navigation and trade.

CHAPTER III

ESTABLISHING OUR FOREIGN POLICY

WAR IN EUROPE was a real danger to the United States. Washington, by declaring neutrality, warned the people not to take sides with either France or England. This caused trouble with both of these countries. Although President Washington succeeded in keeping the nation at peace with France and England, war was still possible.

From the study of this chapter, you will see some reasons why the Federalists were becoming unpopular. The people did not want them to govern the nation any longer.

1. The Federalists Continue to Guide the Nation

In 1796, President Washington announced that he would not accept a third term as President. In spite of Washington's warning about political quarrels, in 1796 great rivalry arose between the Federalist Party and the Democratic-Republican Party. Each party wanted to gain control of the government.

The election of 1796. The Federalists selected John Adams of Massachusetts as their candidate for President. Adams was a very capable, honest man. He had done much for his country as a member of the First and Second Continental Congresses and as Vice President during both of Washington's terms.

Thomas Jefferson, the leader of the Democratic-Republican Party, was the rival candidate. He was the author of the Declaration of Independence and had served as Secretary of State under President Washington.

The results of the election were unusual. John Adams, the Federalist, was selcted President and Thomas Jefferson, the Democratic-Republican, won the Vice Presidency. It was to

Culver

Charles Pinckney

Brown Brothers

Elbridge Gerry

be expected that disagreements should arise between them. These political differences soon threatened to destroy the peace and unity of the country.

2. Threats of War Disturb the Federalists

Troubles with France continue. France was very angry about the Jay treaty because she felt that it broke a previous treaty America had made with her. Then France began delaying shipments to countries at war with her. French warships were capturing American vessels bound for England. To make things worse, the French government refused to receive Charles Pinckney, the new American minister. He was ordered to leave France.

Americans were furious because France had so badly treated our representative, Charles Pinckney. They wanted to break all connections with France. President Adams asked Congress to prepare for war, yet he still hoped to secure peace.

The X Y Z Affair. Adams sent John Marshall of Virginia and Elbridge Gerry of Massachusetts to France to join Charles Pinckney. This was done in an attempt to make a treaty.

The French Minister of Foreign Affairs refused to meet the Americans. He sent three agents to represent him. The Americans referred to these men as X, Y, and Z. The French agents asked that the United States loan a large amount of money to France. These agents demanded that the sum of $250,000 be given to certain French ministers as a bribe, before they would talk matters over. To this latter request the Americans replied that the United States was willing to pay "Millions for defense, but not one cent for tribute." The demand of a bribe was an insult to the honor of our country.

Undeclared war with France. War was not declared, but sea battles were fought when French warships attacked American vessels. These attacks stopped, and the captured vessels were returned to the United States when Napoleon became ruler of France. He had to give all his attention to his European wars. He did not have time to quarrel with America.

President Adams heard that France was willing to make an agreement with the United States. He sent a committee to France to discuss a peaceful settlement of the troubles. The men who formed this committee were well received by the French government. In 1800, a treaty was made with Napoleon.

3. The Power of the Federalist Party Lessens

The Naturalization Act. Some very unpopular laws were passed during Adams' term. One of these was the Naturalization Act of 1798. This act made it difficult for aliens or foreigners to become American citizens. The law required an alien to wait from five to fourteen years before he could become a citizen and enjoy the privileges and rights of American citizenship.

Due to the large number of immigrants from Europe, especially from Ireland, the Federalist Party became fearful of losing power. Large numbers of Irish immigrants were coming to America and settling in the large cities. When these people bcame citizens, most of them joined the Democratic-Republican party, thus threatening the Federalists' control of the government.

The Alien Act. This act gave the President the right to send out of the country any foreigner who was thought to be dangerous to the peace and safety of the United States.

The Sedition Act. Of all the acts passed during President

Adams' term the Sedition Act was the most unpopular. Sedition means disloyal conduct against the government. This law made it a crime to write or speak unfavorably about the government or government officials. The law would have prevented even just criticism of government measures. The editors of several newspapers were arrested for criticizing President Adams and other Federalists. These newspapermen had to pay a large fine or go to prison.

All over the country, Americans objected strongly and condemned the government for passing the Sedition Act. They said the act took away freedom of speech and fredom of the press, rights granted in the Bill of Rights. The Federalists were accused of attacking the liberties of the people, instead of protecting them.

There is no doubt that these laws were unjust and unreasonable. They were passed by Congress against the wishes of President Adams and Alexander Hamilton. In time all three laws were repealed.

Kentucky and Virginia Resolutions. Thomas Jefferson and James Madison protested against the Alien and Sedition Laws and wrote a set of resolutions against them. The legislators of Kentucky and Virginia accepted the resolutions and refused to abide by the Alien and Sedition Laws. In refusing to abide by these laws, Kentucky and Virginia were weakening the power of the central government.

The unpopular Alien and Sedition Acts were passed while the Federalists were in power. Since many of the people disliked these laws, they also came to mistrust the Federalists. In the election of 1800 the Federalists lost to the Democratic-Republicans.

Work of the Federalists. After twelve years of power, the work of the Federalists was finished. They had given great service to the new nation and left behind them the ideal of a strong central government. They established the government upon the solid foundations of justice, honesty, and freedom. They laid the foundation so well that the United States has prospered and grown.

Words and expressions you should know

bribe	solid foundation	immigrants
editors	rival candidate	foreigners

alien   Sedition Act   resolutions
tribute   political differences   repealed

Can you talk about these?

1. In 1796 many Americans were disappointed when George Washington refused to accept a third term of office. Do you think Washington should have followed their wishes and accepted office for a third term?

2. France demanded that a large sum of money be given to French ministers to secure their favor. The American agents said, "Millions for defense, but not one cent for tribute." What did this mean?

3. During John Adams' term of office, American citizens printed articles against the government for which they were punished. What rights of the people were denied by this punishment? Could such a thing happen today?

Choose the phrase that makes the statement right

1. The Federalist candidate for President in 1796 was
   a. Thomas Jefferson
   b. Edmund Randolph
   c. John Adams
   d. Alexander Hamilton

2. Washington issued the
   a. Bill of Rights
   b. Proclamation of Neutrality
   c. Alien Law
   d. Sedition Law

3. Washington thought the United States should keep out of European troubles because the United States was
   a. rich and powerful
   b. heavily in debt
   c. young and weak
   d. already at war with China

4. Washington served as President of the United States for
   a. four years
   b. six years
   c. eight years
   d. ten years

5. Citizens were forbidden to publish anything false against the government of the United States by the
   a. Naturalization Act
   b. Stamp Act
   c. Sedition Act
   d. Alien Act

6. The attempt of three Frenchmen to obtain a bribe from three United States representatives was known as
   a. Jay Treaty
   b. X Y Z Affair
   c. Bill of Rights
   d. Alien Law

7. The Kentucky and Virginia Resolutions declared that
   a. the Alien and Sedition Laws were not binding
   b. all states should obey national law

129

c. all men were created equal
d. American ports could be blockaded
8. In 1796, the Democratic-Republican who became Vice

President was
a. Thomas Jefferson
b. Alexander Hamilton
c. James Madison
d. Charles Pinckney

Checking your knowledge of Unit Three

I. Can you connect a person, an event, or a date with the following?

1. Mount Vernon
2. New York
3. Federal Hall, New York
4. State in which Whiskey Rebellion took place
5. Philadelphia
6. Spain
7. Port of New Orleans
8. John Jay
9. Thomas Jefferson
10. John Adams
11. Edmund Randolph
12. Henry Knox
13. Alexander Hamilton
14. Charles Pinckney

II. Write the dates on which each of following happened.

1. Washington took oath of office................................._____
2. First National Bank established................................._____
3. Whiskey Rebellion ...._____
4. Washington proclaimed neutrality............................._____

III. Match these correctly

1. George Washington
2. John Jay
3. excise tax
4. James Madison
5. Henry Knox
6. neutral
7. Alexander Hamilton
8. John Marshall
9. John Adams
10. Edmund Randolph

a. opposed the Alien and Sedition Laws
b. second President of the United States
c. tax on goods imported into a country
d. Atorney General
e. First United States Bank
f. being on both sides
g. Proclamation of Neutrality
h. tax on goods made or sold within a country
i. Secretary of War
j. famous Supreme Court Justice
k. being on neither side
l. unpopular treaty with England

130

IV. In this Unit find examples which show:

1. Respect for lawful authority.
2. Gratitude to God for wise decisions of our leaders.
3. Disregard for freedom of press.
4. Generosity in using talents to help others.

V. Some activities to help you master the information in this Unit.

1. Make a cartoon of the Whiskey Rebellion. Show how the farmers of Western Pennsylvania felt towards the excise tax.
2. Debate the question: Resolved: That the United States should have helped France in her war against England in 1793.
3. List the attempts made by the United States to keep out of the wars in Europe.
4. Try to write a play called "The New Government in Action." The following suggestions may be used for scenes of the play:
   Scene I   Compromise on nation paying state debts
   Scene II   Whiskey Rebellion
   Scene III Trouble caused by Jay Treaty
   Scene IV Citizen Genêt tries to secure aid for France
5. Show a film on George Washington or Alexander Hamilton.

VI. How well can you answer these?

1. Why did the success of the new government depend so much on George Washington?
2. How did Alexander Hamilton raise the money to pay the debts and to run the government?
3. In what way did the Whiskey Rebellion show that the national government had power to enforce its laws?
4. How was Washington, D. C., chosen for the capital of the United States?
5. In what cities have the Presidents of the United States taken their oath of office?
6. Why is John Marshall considered the greatest Chief Justice?
7. Why did Thomas Jefferson disagree with Alexander Hamilton on the question of establishing a bank?
8. How did political parties arise in the United States?
9. What advice did Washington give the people of America in his farewell address?
10. What is meant by the XYZ Affair?
11. Why did Napoleon want peace with the United States?
12. Who was the last Federalist to be elected President?

Mary and Civic Life

MEANING. Just as the Ark of the Covenant contained the tables of the law, the Ten Commandments, so Mary contained the law of God in her heart. Mary also helps those who love her to obey God's laws. God's laws also demand obedience to the laws of our country. Jesus said: "Render, therefore, to Cæsar, the things that are Cæsar's" (Matthew: 22:21).

APPLICATION. Obedience to the just laws of the state is an obligation. Laws are for the common good. Mary obeyed the laws of the state when she went to Bethlehem with Joseph to be enrolled. As Ark of the Covenant, Mary helps mankind to obey all just civil laws.

Prayer

Ark of the covenant, *pray for us.*

Litany of the Blessed Virgin

LORD, have mercy on us.
Christ, have mercy on us.
Lord, have mercy on us.
God the Son, Redeemer of the world, have mercy on us.
God, the Holy Ghost, have mercy on us.
Holy Trinity, one God, have mercy on us.
Christ, hear us.
Christ, graciously hear us.
God the Father of heaven, have mercy on us.
Holy Mary,[1]
Holy Mother of God,
Holy Virgin of virgins,
Mother of Christ,
Mother of divine grace,
Mother most pure,
Mother most chaste,
Mother inviolate,
Mother undefiled,
Mother most amiable,
Mother most admirable,
Mother of good counsel,
Mother of our Creator,
Mother of our Saviour,
Virgin most prudent,
Virgin most venerable,
Virgin most renowned,
  [1] Pray for us.

Virgin most powerful,
Virgin most merciful,
Virgin most faithful,
Mirror of justice,
Seat of wisdom,
Cause of our joy,
Spiritual vessel,
Vessel of honor,
Singular vessel of devotion,
Mystical Rose,
Tower of David,
Tower of ivory,
House of gold,
Ark of the Covenant,
Gate of heaven,
Morning star,
Health of the sick,
Refuge of sinners,
Comforter of the afflicted,
Help of Christians,
Queen of angels,
Queen of patriarchs,
Queen of prophets,
Queen of apostles,
Queen of martyrs,
Queen of confessors,
Queen of virgins,
Queen of all saints,
Queen conceived without original sin,

Queen assumed into heaven,
Queen of the most holy Rosary,
Queen of peace.
Lamb of God, who takest away the sins of the world, spare us, O Lord.
Lamb of God, who takest away the sins of the world, graciously hear us, O Lord.
Lamb of God, who takest away the sins of the world, have mercy on us.
Christ, hear us. Christ, graciously hear us.
℣. Pray for us, O holy Mother of God. ℟. That we may be made worthy of the promises of Christ.

Let us pray

Grant, we beseech Thee, O Lord God, unto us Thy servants, that we may rejoice in continual health of mind and body; and, by the glorious intercession of blessed Mary ever Virgin, may be delivered from present sadness, and enter into the joy of Thine eternal gladness. Through Christ our Lord. Amen.

An indulgence of 7 years. A plenary indulgence once a month on the usual conditions for the daily devout recitation of this Litany with its versicle and prayer (See "The Raccolta," the official work of indulgenced prayers, page 216).

MARY AS A GUIDE THROUGH LIFE. The free will of man accepts the guidance of Mary in the way of life. This guidance of Mary is part of our religion. It affects our home life, our association with our fellow man, our civic obligations, our career in life, and our acceptance of life's problems.

Courtesy of Rev. J. B. Carol, O. F. M.

UNIT FOUR

JEFFERSONIAN DEMOCRACY IN ACTION

CHAPTER I—DEMOCRATIC-REPUBLICANS GOVERN THE NATION

Election of 1800—Twelfth Amendment
Inauguration of Thomas Jefferson—Lover of Liberty
National Capital, Washington, D. C.
Louisiana Purchase—Our Territory Doubled
War with Tripoli—Rights of Americans Respected
Blockade of European Ports
Chesapeake Affair—Peace Threatened
Embargo Act and Non-Intercourse Act

CHAPTER II—A SECOND WAR FOR INDEPENDENCE

Causes of War
    Impressment of American sailors
    Indian attacks on Western frontier
America Unprepared for War
War on the Land—Invasion of Canada
War on Sea—British Blockade Atlantic Coast
War on Great Lakes—Perry's Victory
Battle of Lake Champlain
Jackson's Victory
Treaty of Ghent

CHAPTER III—EFFECTS OF WAR OF 1812

Results of War of 1812
Growth of American Industries
Era of Good Feeling
Western Expansion
Monroe Doctrine Warns Europe to Keep out of the
    Americas
Bishop John England
John Quincy Adams Becomes President
Adams' Plan for National Development

UNIT FOUR

JEFFERSONIAN DEMOCRACY IN ACTION

OUR FIRST TWO PRESIDENTS, George Washington and John Adams, were Federalists. These leaders guided the infant nation through its first difficult years. They worked constantly with the Cabinet members and Congress to keep peace at home and abroad. Through their efforts the nation won the confidence of the American people and of those in foreign countries.

Most of the people believed the Federalists favored the wealthy rather than the poor. For this reason, nearly everyone desired a change. Most people wanted to give men with different political opinions a chance to govern them. They realized the time had come for people to take a more active part in governing themselves.

In 1800, Thomas Jefferson, leader of the Democratic-Republican Party, was elected President. He believed in strong state governments and in giving power to the people. When France offered to sell the Louisiana Territory, Jefferson and Congress immediately seized the opportunity and bought it.

President Jefferson succeeded in keeping the country out of war. It was not until 1812 that the Second War of Independence was fought. For several years after this war there was a period of peace and prosperity. In this Unit, you will see how the United States became larger and more independent.

CHAPTER I

THE DEMOCRATIC-REPUBLICAN PARTY GOVERNS THE NATION

While Thomas Jefferson was President, the people were given a voice in the government and more leaders were chosen from among the common people. The size of the country was doubled. Our Navy was sent to Tripoli, and it stopped the raids of the Barbary Pirates on American merchant vessels in the Mediterranean Sea.

1. A New Party Comes to Power

The election of 1800. The campaign for the fourth Presidential election was very exciting. The feeling between the two political parties was bitter. People were afraid of the power of the Federalists, especially after they had passed the Alien and Sedition Acts. The majority of the voters were in favor of the Democratic-Republican Party. Its candidates promised to protect the rights of all and to give the common people more political opportunities.

The Federalists named John Adams again as their candidate for President and Charles Pinckney for Vice President. The Democratic-Republicans nominated Thomas Jefferson for President and Aaron Burr for Vice President.

To avoid the mistake of having a President from one party and a Vice President from the other, as in the last election, the Democratic-Republican electors agreed to vote for Jefferson and Burr on the same ballot. When the votes were counted both Jefferson and Burr had an equal number of electoral votes, seventy-three. Adams came out third. How was the new President to be chosen?

According to the Constitution, if the votes were tied, the election must be settled by the House of Representatives. Each state would have one vote. The names were given to the House of Representatives. Finally, after thirty-six ballots, Jefferson was elected President and Aaron Burr became Vice President.

Jefferson was chosen for President, chiefly through the influence of Hamilton. Although he was opposed to most of Jefferson's ideas, Hamilton persuaded many Federalists to vote for him. Hamilton believed Jefferson would make a better President than Burr. In doing this Hamilton proved that he had the welfare of his country at heart rather than the success of his party.

Burr never forgave Hamilton for his part in this election. As time went on, the ill-feeling between them grew stronger. Finally, Burr and Hamilton engaged in a duel. Hamilton was wounded so seriously that he died.

The Twelfth Amendment. To avoid future disputes over an election, the Twelfth Amendment was added to the Constitution in 1804. This Amendment provided that the electoral votes for President and the Vice President should be cast on separate ballots.

The Inauguration of Thomas Jefferson. Thomas Jefferson was the first President to take the

Culver

Thomas Jefferson

oath of office in the new Capitol Building at Washington. At that time, Washington was little more than a village, not the large city it is today.

On March 4, 1801, Thomas Jefferson, instead of riding in a coach drawn by horses, walked from his boarding-house to the Capitol to take the oath of office. His inauguration was very simple. It was in keeping with his democratic ideas. He wished to show the poorer people, who formed the greater part of the nation, that he was representing them as well as the wealthier classes.

In his inaugural address, Jefferson told the people of his

The Capitol Building at Washington at the time Jefferson was President

plans. He pleaded with the Federalists to forget their party differences and to unite with the Democratic-Republicans to work for the general welfare of the country. He told the people they were no longer Federalists nor Democratic-Republicans, but Americans.

The new President determined to give as much power as possible to the states. A wise and thrifty government was needed. He called the United States a "rising nation" whose future would be very great. The people must take an active part in governing themselves. This would require education for all and, therefore, schools should be provided. Since Jefferson believed in freedom of religion, freedom of speech, and freedom of the press, he guaranteed that these rights would be safeguarded. He would make every effort to put into practice the principles of the Declaration of Independence.

As we have seen before, these democratic principles were based upon the teachings of St. Thomas Aquinas and Cardinal

Bellarmine. The Catholic Church, ever since it was founded by Our Blessed Lord, has been teaching the principles of the rights of man and his duties to God, his neighbor, and himself.

Thomas Jefferson, a lover of liberty. Our third President was a man of strong character who loved liberty and his fellow men. He believed that man should use his intelligence to rule himself wisely. Jefferson could not understand how any form of unjust or cruel government could be permitted.

Although he owned slaves, Thomas Jefferson was against slavery and suggested means for freeing the slaves. He fought all his life for freedom and the rights of the people. He wished everyone to have equal opportunities. The University of Virginia was founded by him. The Military Academy at West Point was established while he was President.

Jefferson made use of his many talents. All his life Jefferson studied well and worked hard. He was interested in music, art, and literature and has left us

Monticello, the home which Jefferson himself designed

Brown Brothers

many valuable writings. Science and architecture also appealed to him. He invented the swivel chair, now used in offices, and an instrument to measure distances. His beautiful home in Monticello (mont-i-sel'-loe) and the University of Virginia were designed by him. Very few people use their God-given gifts to the extent that Jefferson made use of his.

Jefferson's appointments. President Jefferson, like President Washington, carefully chose his advisers. For Secretary of State he chose James Madison of Virginia, commonly known as the Father of the Constitution. He appointed Albert Gallatin (gal'-a-tin) of Pennsylvania as Secretary of the Treasury. Gallatin proved to be one of the most able Secretaries of the Treasury the country has had. The test that Jefferson used in selecting an official for a government position was, "Is he honest? Is he capable? Is he faithful to the Constitution?"

The National Capital. The capital city of any nation is an important city. The capital of the United States is not only important, but it is now one of the most beautiful cities in the world. In 1801, when Jefferson became President, the Capitol and the White House were unfinished and surrounded by forests. The land on the Potomac was given to the national government by Maryland and Virginia. Washington chose the location and he secured the services of a French Catholic, Major Pierre L'Enfant (pee-aire' lonfon'), to plan the city.

L'Enfant wanted the city to be "magnificent enough to grace a great nation." It was to be a city of beautiful parks, broad avenues, statues and monuments. A monument in honor of the first President, George Washington, was to be erected. After many years, these plans of L'Enfant were completed. Washington, D. C., honors in its name both Columbus and Washington.

John Marshall, the fourth Chief Justice. John Marshall, a Federalist, was appointed Chief Justice of the Supreme Court by John Adams. He became famous because of the many wise decisions he made during his thirty-five years as Chief Justice. One of the most important decisions he made was to insist that the Constitution was the Supreme Law of the Land. This means that a bill can not become a law unless it agrees with the Constitution.

Air view of Washington. L'Enfant's plan has been carried out

2. Jefferson Buys the Louisiana Territory from France

Port of New Orleans closed to Americans. You have learned that since 1763 Spain controlled all the land between the Mississippi River and the Rocky Mountains. This land was called the Louisiana Territory.

In 1795, Spain permitted the American farmers of the West to use New Orleans for shipping purposes. In 1802, Spain suddenly decided to withdraw this permission.

The farmers of the West were furious when Spain forbade them to use this river and port. They demanded that the government protect their trade. Jefferson realized that something must be done quickly, because the people were calling for war.

Spain gives Louisiana to France. About the same time, news reached the United States that Spain, through a secret agreement, had given back to France the Louisiana territory. This included the port of New Orleans. The Americans became alarmed because they knew that Napoleon had planned to

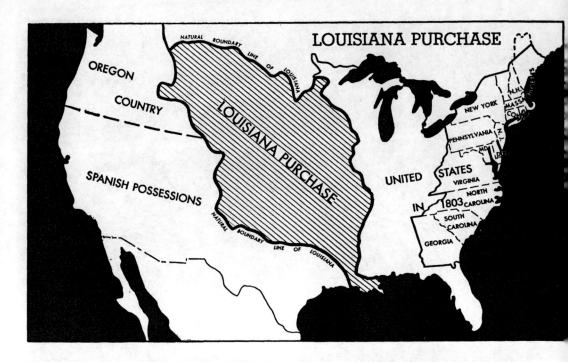

LOUISIANA PURCHASE

OREGON COUNTRY

SPANISH POSSESSIONS

NATURAL BOUNDARY LINE OF LOUISIANA

LOUISIANA PURCHASE

NATURAL BOUNDARY LINE OF LOUISIANA

UNITED STATES IN 1803

NEW YORK

PENNSYLVANIA

VIRGINIA

NORTH CAROLINA

SOUTH CAROLINA

GEORGIA

build a great French Empire in America. What would happen in the United States if such an ambitious and powerful leader controlled the Mississippi River and New Orleans?

Napoleon had determined to conquer the lands which had been taken from France. He began by sending an army to San Domingo in the West Indies. Napoleon was successful in conquering the natives, but most of the French soldiers died from yellow fever. At this time there was also the possibility that England would attack France. Because of this threat, Napoleon had to give up his plan for an American Empire.

Napoleon feared that England might take Louisiana from France. He would rather get rid of it than have this happen. Napoleon was greatly in need of money to carry on his wars. The French people would not give this money to him. They wanted no more war.

United States buys Louisiana. President Jefferson advised Livingston, who was Ambassador to France, to buy Florida and New Orleans from Napoleon. The President sent Monroe to help Livingston make this purchase. Before Monroe reached France, a French minister of Napoleon asked Livingston how much money the United States would give for all of the Louisiana Territory. Livingston waited until Monroe arrived before making a decision. After careful discussion they decided to buy the territory for the United States. The whole Louisiana Territory was bought for $15,000,000. In 1803, the United States took possession of it.

Louisiana helps the growth of the United States. The purchase of Louisiana was very important. It more than doubled the area of the United States. The United States now had full control of the Mississippi and the port of New Orleans. It also gave us rich and productive farm lands. European nations were kept from building colonies in this territory. Vast forests and mines of value added to the wealth of the country. People from the Southwest began moving into this new land. Later, thirteen new states were formed from this territory.

Exploring the Louisiana Territory. Long before Thomas Jefferson became President, he desired to send explorers into this land. He wanted to find out about the trees, plants, animals, minerals, and any other re-

Upper Louisiana Territory is transferred to the Americans at St. Louis in 1804
Culver

sources that were there. Now that the Louisiana Territory belonged to the United States, he was more anxious than ever to have this land explored.

In 1804, President Jefferson appointed Meriwether Lewis of Virginia and William Clark, brother of George Rogers Clark of Kentucky, to lead the exploration party. With about forty men, they started from St. Louis in 1804. They traveled up the Missouri River and by winter were in what is now the state of North Dakota. Although they had come to the end of the land in the Louisiana claim, they did not remain there.

Early in the spring of 1805, the exploring party started out again with a French trapper and his Indian wife Sacajawea (sa-ka-ja-way'-a) as guides. They journeyed through the Rocky Mountains, along the Columbia River to the Pacific Coast. It was partly due to the work of Lewis and Clark that the United States later claimed the Oregon country.

In 1806, these hardy explorers returned. Captain Lewis went immediately to Washington and reported his findings to President Jefferson. This gave Jefferson valuable information about the new territory and the Far West. Afterwards, maps were made which were valuable to the people who later went across the continent to the Pacific Ocean.

War with the African Pirates. From the deep inlets along the coasts of Morocco, Algiers, Tunis, and Tripoli, pirates set out to attack trading vessels on the Mediterranean Sea. They demanded tributes or bribes from all the nations of the West. If bribes were not paid, they attacked the shipping vessels and made slaves of the sailors.

These Barbary Pirates grew bolder and increased their demands. The older and larger nations hesitated about attempting to stop these pirates. President Jefferson decided that the United States must do something. Instead of sending money for bribes he sent a fleet of warships. The pirates were attacked and defeated. In 1805, the ruler of Tripoli asked for peace. The pirates gave no more trouble until 1815.

Americans can be justly proud of our Marines and of our Navy in conquering these pirates. For daring to fight for what was just and right, Americans won respect for

Algiers today. It was from this city that Barbary Pirates sailed to prey on American shipping

their country. They were trustworthy, loyal, and brave.

Jefferson is reelected in 1804. During his first term, President Jefferson gained the confidence of most of the people. Even New England, which strongly opposed him and his party, gave him great support in the second election. He won by a large majority.

Taxes were lower because the expenses of running the government were cut down. Through the skill of the Secretary of the Treasury, Albert Gallatin, the national debt had been reduced. Most of the people were pleased with the purchase of Louisiana. Trade had been protected because the pirates in the African states were forced to stop attacking our commerce. The national government had become more democratic. Jefferson had tried to be fair to all the people in every section of the country. His great desire was to unite the nation.

During his second term, difficult problems arose because of the wars in Europe. President Jefferson was most anxious to keep peace and remain friendly with all nations. How could this best be done since England and France were interfering with America's neutral rights?

3. Neutrality, the Right of a Free Nation

Blockade of European ports. In 1805, war again broke out between England and France. Most Americans wished to remain neutral. England and France depended upon neutral countries to bring them supplies. American commerce profited greatly by trade with both of these countries.

Napoleon knew that England had to get most of the necessities of life from other countries. In order to stop British trade he decided to blockade all the ports on the continent of Europe. Soon he became bold enough to stop even neutral ships from entering British ports. He hoped by this plan, known as the "Continental System," to destroy England.

England tried to stop French trade. The British issued "Orders in Council," which forbade all neutral trade with France. English captains were ordered to seize any ship, French or neutral, which entered or left a French port. All neutral ships going to Europe had first to enter an English harbor for inspection. If these ships carried goods for France, the goods were taken from the ship.

The "Chesapeake" Affair. In 1807, the American warship *Chesapeake* left Norfolk, Virginia. Not far from the coast the *Leopard,* a British man-of-war, ordered it to stop. The brave American captain refused to stop. Immediately the *Leopard* fired upon the *Chesapeake* and three Americans were killed and eighteen wounded. The *Chesapeake* was forced to surrender. The English commander took four sailors whom he claimed were deserters. Our nation demanded an apology. Our government insisted that the English respect our neutral rights and stop seizing and searching American ships. England paid no attention to our demands.

The Embargo Act. President Jefferson did not want to go to war if it could be avoided. He hoped to settle the trouble peacefully. He persuaded Congress to pass an act which would forbid any American ship to go to a foreign port for trade. Congress passed this Embargo Act in December, 1807. It was thought that the British would need American goods so badly that they would stop seizing ships and sailors.

America was mistaken, for this act hurt the United States more than it did either England or France. Warehouses were closed, ships were idle, goods rotted on the docks and in the ships. Sailors could find no work. Many ship captains disobeyed the law. Others who were honest turned to different ways of earning a living. Some shipowners and merchants began to build factories to make articles which could not be obtained from Europe.

The farmers of the West and South were very much opposed to the Embargo Act. The merchants and shippers of New England strongly resented their loss of trade. The Americans had lost millions of dollars in trade and goods. Jefferson's plan was a failure. Finally, Congress was forced to repeal the Embargo Act.

The Non-Intercourse Act. Jefferson still hoped to prevent war. He realized that it was dangerous to have vessels on the open seas. After the Embargo Act had been repealed, another law, called the Non-Intercourse Act, was passed on March 1, 1809. By this act, trade with France and all parts of the British Empire was forbidden. However, trade was allowed with all other countries. Our ships again sailed the seas, but the profits were not so high, and merchants were not satisfied. Finally, this act, too, was repealed.

Do you remember these words and phrases?

blockade	swivel chair	ambassador
capital	secret agreement	embargo
ballots	neutral rights	inlets
campaign	French minister	pirates
duel	exploration party	capitol

Things to talk about

1. Thomas Jefferson spent much time working so that his fellow-Americans would be allowed to use their God-given rights. Can you name some of the things he obtained for the people?

2. If you had been in Washington for President Jefferson's inaugural address, what would have interested you most in his speech?

3. Why was President Jefferson so anxious for the United

States to remain neutral and to keep out of European wars? How did he keep America out of war?

Matching Test

Can you match the names in Column A with the correct items in Column B?

Column A	Column B
1. Albert Gallatin	a. French Emperor
2. Francis Scott Key	b. famous Chief Justice of the Supreme Court
3. Meriwether Lewis	
4. Citizen Genêt	d. Secretary of the Treasury
5. Napoleon	e. engineer who planned the city of Washington
6. John Adams	
7. Major L'Enfant	f. ambassador to France
8. George Washington	g. explored the Louisiana Territory
9. Thomas Jefferson	
10. John Marshall	h. Secretary of State
11. James Madison	i. challenged Hamilton to a duel
12. Aaron Burr	j. defeated for President in 1800
13. John Jay	
14. Robert Livingston	

Selection Test

Can you pick out the incorrect reason in each of the following?

1. The Louisiana Purchase was one of the most successful land deals ever made because
   a. it gave the United States control of the Mississippi River.
   b. it cost only $10,000,000.
   c. it doubled the size of the United States.
   d. it made the national government stronger.

2. Thomas Jefferson was a great statesman because
   a. he wrote the Declaration of Independence.
   b. he kept the United States out of war.
   c. he had great faith in the ability of the common people to govern themselves.
   d. he liked Hamilton's plans for raising money.

3. The United States won the respect of European nations because
   a. she borrowed warships from England to stop the pirates from robbing merchant vessels.
   b. she would not pay bribes to the Barbary Pirates.
   c. she sent a fleet to the African coast to punish the pirates.
   d. she defeated the Barbary Pirates and stopped their raids.

148

CHAPTER II

A SECOND WAR FOR INDEPENDENCE

Year after year Americans found it increasingly difficult to keep out of war. No one tried harder than Thomas Jefferson to remain neutral. However, his efforts to prevent war were not acceptable to the people of the United States.

In 1810, many of the older Congressmen were not reelected. The younger group that replaced them was highly in favor of attacking Great Britian. Led by Henry Clay and John C. Calhoun, these "War Hawks" represented the spirit of the West.

In this chapter we shall study the War of 1812. We shall notice the growing independence of the western frontiersmen and the anger of the people against the British. We shall see how this finally led Congress to declare war after James Madison was elected President.

1. Causes of the War of 1812

Impressment of seamen. The quarrel over the right to trade with any nation was not the only reason for our unfriendly feeling towards England. Impressment of seamen caused many bitter and lasting arguments. Because England was at war with France, she needed many warships and many sailors to man them. Most Englishmen did not want to join the Navy because the wages were low, the working conditions were bad, and the officers were often brutal.

Many Englishmen left the service of England, became American citizens, and worked as sailors on American ships. England did not recognize their right to do this. She insisted that a man who was "once an Englishman" was "always an Englishman." She carried her idea so far as to search American vessels for any of these men. If she found any, she took them and put them back into the English Navy. This practice is called impressment of seamen.

Very often, the men taken were native-born Americans. Although the United States government protested strongly against such actions, England continued taking Americans and making them serve on English ships. In 1812, when the war began, the State Department had the names of over six thousand American citizens who had been forced to serve in the English Navy.

Indian attacks on our western frontier. Deeper ill-feeling against England was aroused by the stories that the English had been encouraging the Indians to attack our western frontier. The English were accused of supplying guns and powder used by the attacking Indians. The Americans could never prove this charge, however. The Indians resented being pushed farther and farther west by the white men. Tecumseh (te-cum'-seh), an intelli-

General Harrison attacks the Indians at Tippecanoe

Culver

gent Indian chief, realized that these Americans were slowly but surely taking lands from his people. He formed a league to keep the white people out of his territory.

In 1811, Tecumseh went South to get more Indian tribes to join his league against the white men. While he was absent, William Henry Harrison, the governor of the territory, attacked the Indian village at Tippecanoe (tip-pe-ca'-noo). It was a hard battle in which the Indians were defeated and forced to abandon their lands. Harrison's forces entered the Indian village and burned it. Tecumseh and his people moved farther west.

War is declared. Jefferson had tried to follow Washington's plan of neutrality. He used every possible means to force foreign nations to respect America's rights and its desire for peace. You remember the Embargo and Non-Intercourse Acts by which he tried to prevent war. These acts harmed the United States more than they harmed European countries.

When James Madison became President in 1809, he, too, was most anxious to keep America out of war. Nevertheless, both

James Madison   *Culver*

England and France continued to interfere with America's rights on the sea. Although America had reasons to declare war on France, many people believed we had greater reasons to attack England.

A group of young men, interested in the development of the West, had become members of Congress. Among these were Henry Clay of Kentucky and John C. Calhoun (cal-hoon') of South Carolina. They were so anxious for the United States to declare war against England that they became known as the "War-Hawks."

These Westerners believed that the English had done more damage to us on the seas than the French had done. They also claimed that English fur traders were giving guns and ammunition to the Indians so that they could attack our frontier. They hoped to conquer the neighboring lands.

These young Congressmen kept demanding war. They finally convinced President Madison that they were right. War was declared against England on June 18, 1812.

This war might have been avoided if means of communication at that time were as good as they are today. When Congress declared war, England was planning to stop the search of American vessels. Because neither knew of the plans of the other, England and the United States were at war for the second time.

2. The War on Land

America unprepared for war. The United States declared war even though the New England states, the richest and the most densely populated part of the country, opposed it. President Jefferson's plan to save money had weakened our Army and Navy. The militia supplied by the states was poorly trained. Most American officers were old men. A Navy of twelve swift sailing vessels faced the British fleet of more than a thousand. There was little money in the Treasury to pay for another war.

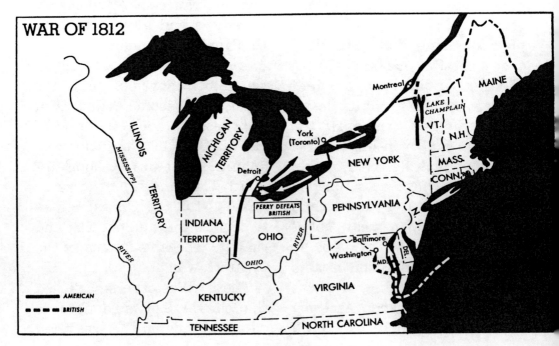

WAR OF 1812

The invasion of Canada. The "War-Hawks" and other members of Congress who voted for a declaration of war thought it would be easy to invade Canada. They were very much mistaken.

Plans were made to enter Canada from three different points. One army was to start from Detroit, another to cross the Niagara River, the third was to go up the valley of Lake Champlain. All were to meet at the Canadian border and proceed to capture Montreal and Quebec. The whole plan was a failure.

General Hull, commander of the fort at Detroit, was supposed to start for Canada. When he heard that the British were approaching, he made no effort to protect the fort; he merely surrendered. General Van Rensselaer (van ren'-saler) conquered the English at Queenstown but was unable to proceed to the Canadian border. The New York militia refused to cross their state line so the English captured this army.

The third army, under General Dearborn, reached the Canadian border but had to turn back because the other two forces were not there to help. The conquest of Canada, which the "War-Hawks" believed could be completed in a month, failed.

Burning of Washington. In April, 1814, the British sailed up Chesapeake Bay and landed their forces on the shores of the Patuxent River in Maryland. From there they marched into the undefended city of Washington and set fire to the White House, to the Capitol, and to several other public buildings. President Madison saved as many valuables as he could before he fled to Virginia. However, about a million and a half dollars worth of damage was done.

The British fleet then tried to take Baltimore, but failed. After an all-night bombing of Fort McHenry, it had to retreat because the cannon from this small fort damaged many of the British warships.

Our national anthem. Francis Scott Key was an American who had gone aboard one of the British ships to arrange for an exchange of prisoners. Forced to stay over night, he watched the bombardment of Fort McHenry.

In the morning, as the sun rose over the fort, he could see the American flag flying in the breeze. It inspired him to write

Francis Scott Key writes the "Star-Spangled Banner" during the bombardment of Fort McHenry

the immortal words of "The Star-Spangled Banner." This patriotic song was made the national anthem by an act of Congress on March 3, 1931.

Whenever you sing "The Star-Spangled Banner," think of the ideals for which America stands. Thank Almighty God that this Land of Our Lady has become "the land of the free and the home of the brave." Pray that our flag will ever continue to be a symbol of freedom, justice, peace, and prosperity.

3. The Naval War

War on the seas. The War of 1812 was not successful on land. Since the main reason for the war was to gain freedom of the seas for American trade, sea battles were most important.

After seven months of fighting, our small Navy was able to boast that it had captured five hundred merchantmen and three British frigates. Not one American frigate had surrendered to a British vessel.

Great Britain resented such success and sent vessels to patrol the Atlantic seacoast. In spite of a complete British blockade of our coast, the

American merchant marine seriously threatened English vessels. Our fast ships almost stopped all trade in the English Channel. By the end of the war, the Americans had captured more than thirteen hundred vessels and more than forty million dollars worth of goods.

The *Constitution,* commanded by Captain Issac Hull, was a famous American vessel. In August, 1812, she attacked the British ship *Guerriere* (ger-i-air′) in the Gulf of St. Lawrence. In thirty minutes, most of the crew were killed and the ship was completely destroyed. In December, 1812 the *Constitution* captured another British vessel, the *Java.*

After two battles, the *Constitution* was so little damaged that she was nicknamed *Old Ironsides.* In 1830, she was to be destroyed, but Oliver Wendell Holmes saved this famous frigate from destruction. He wrote a poem entitled "Old Ironsides." As a result of this poem, people became so interested in preserving the ship that it was decided not to scrap it. "Old Ironsides" was com-

The *Constitution* has defeated the *Guerriére*

pletely overhauled and restored to its original form in 1928. Since then it has been kept as a national memorial at the Charlestown Navy Yard, Charlestown, Massachusetts.

War on the Great Lakes. The Americans determined to win back Detroit and the Northwest Territory. To do this, they planned to gain control of Lake Erie. The Navy Department assigned Commodore Oliver Hazard Perry to the task. Perry had to build his own boats. He obtained the timber from the woodlands along the shore of the Lake. Finally, he had nine ships built and went into action against the British.

In a furious battle, Perry lost his ship, the *Lawrence*. Rowing through fierce bullet fire, he directed the battle from another ship and won. The British were obliged to surrender.

Perry announced his victory by saying: "We met the enemy and they our ours: two ships, two brigs, one schooner, and one sloop." Perry's courage and determination to fight amidst such difficulties should be a great example for us.

Perry at the Battle of Lake Erie

Culver

The victory made it possible for General Harrison to recapture the fort at Detroit which General Hull had surrendered. The great lands of the Northwest again belonged to the United States.

The Battle of Lake Champlain. In order to end the war, the British planned to gain control of New York by invading the state from Canada. In this way, they hoped to separate New England from the rest of the nation. Before they could do this, they would have to capture an American fleet of sixteen vessels stationed on Lake Champlain. The commander of this fleet was Thomas Macdonough, a hero of the war with the Barbary Pirates.

Macdonough met the British and defeated them in a brilliant victory. The British forces marching southward began to retreat as soon as they heard of the defeat. This great American victory stopped the British invasion from Canada.

4. The War Comes to an End

The Battle of New Orleans. The British commanders still had hope. They thought that the American forces at New Orleans could be captured easily. This would give the British control of the Mississippi and crip-ple American trade. They expected very little resistance from the American forces.

Much to their surprise, General Jackson had fortified the city with huge bales of cotton. When the British attacked, the American riflemen stationed themselves behind these bales of cotton. From their excellent positions, they shot down nearly two thousand British regulars, including their commander. The American losses were very small.

During this battle, the Ursuline Sisters cared for the wounded. When victory was announced, a Mass of thanksgiving was celebrated at the Cathedral of New Orleans. Jackson, with many of his soldiers, attended and offered thanks to God for their victory.

Although this was a great victory for America, it was a battle that should never have been fought. It is often referred to as the "Battle of Slow News." Two weeks before it was fought, the peace treaty between England and the United States had been signed and the war was over. Word of the treaty did not reach the soldiers, for there was no cables or radios to tell them that peace had been declared.

Statue of General Jackson, hero of the Battle of New Orleans. In the background
is the Cathedral of Saint Louis

The Hartford Convention. The Federalists of New England were very much opposed to the War of 1812. They had voted against it in Congress. The blockade of the Atlantic coast by the British caused business to come practically to a standstill. New Englanders were even considering breaking away from the Union.

It was suggested that a convention be held in Hartford, Connecticut. Representatives from all the New England States attended the convention. The sessions were held in secret. Three delegates were chosen to go to Washington. They were instructed to demand Constitutional Amendments which would give more rights to the states.

When these delegates arrived at Washington, they were surprised to find great rejoicing. The war was ended and the news of Jackson's victory had just been received. No one paid any attention to these delegates from New England or to their complaints. The only effect was a greater dislike for the Federalist Party.

The Treaty of Ghent. On December 24, 1814, the treaty of peace between England and the United States was signed at Ghent (gant), Belgium. The treaty provided that all territory gained during the war should be returned to the nation from which it had been taken. It also said that the dispute over the Canadian boundaries should be settled at a later date by representatives of both countries.

Words you should know

impressment	national anthem	brig
conquest	national memorial	sloop
league	densely populated	frigate
bombardment	spirit of the West	symbol

Some things to talk about

1. Were the rights of Americans respected when England and France seized American ships and seamen?
2. Was England right in her claim: "Once an Englishman, always an Englishman?"
3. Imagine you were one of the Americans who wanted the United States to declare war on Great Britain. Tell why you wanted war.

Do you remember?

1. An intelligent Indian Chief who was forced to give up his lands and move farther west.
2. The hero at Lake Erie.
3. Something important agreed upon Christmas Eve, 1814.
4. The three generals who led the forces which planned to invade Canada.
5. The nickname given to the famous American vessel, the *Constitution*.

Fill in the blanks with the correct word or words

1. In 1811, William H. Harrison attacked the Indian village of _____.
2. Men from the West, anxious for war, were called_____.
3. People of New England bitterly opposed the War of _____.
4. In 1814, the British attacked the undefeated city of _____.
5. Our national anthem, the _____ was written by _____.
6. To regain Detroit from the British, Americans planned to get control of _____.
7. _____ was in command of the American fleet on Lake _____.
8. The "Battle of Slow News" was fought at _____.

CHAPTER III

EFFECTS OF THE WAR OF 1812

Looking over the chapter. The War of 1812 was so important to us that it is rightly called the "Second War of Independence." It gave the American people greater confidence in their country. America showed the nations it was capable of protecting its rights and thereby gained their respect. From now on it took its place among the family of nations.

In this chapter you will see that Americans were becoming more interested in the advancement and welfare of their country. You will also learn how President Monroe told the nations of Europe that no part of the American continents was open to European colonization.

1. The United States Becomes More United and Independent

Results of the War of 1812. Before this war, European nations acknowledged our independence, but they had little respect for us as a nation. The fact that we dared to declare war against such a strong power as England gained for us the respect of all European nations. In the future, Europe would be more likely to let us manage our own affairs.

The close of the War of 1812 marked the beginning of a new period in the history of the United States. People had a great love and loyalty for their country. The good of the nation was considered more important than the good of the individual states. Americans turned their backs upon the warring nations of Europe. They gave their time and attention to the building up of their own country. Even New Englanders put aside their bitter feelings and became loyal supporters of the government. This spirit of working together for the good of all is called national unity. National unity should be our ideal today.

Americans wished the United States to become a rich, powerful nation. They wanted the manufacturing and agriculture to become more important. The people expected the government to build roads and canals to improve transportation and to help business. Americans were willing to be taxed for these improvements, for they no longer feared a strong central government. One lesson learned from the War of 1812 was that the government must be strong to defend and protect the nation.

Growth of American industries. America had become interested in manufacturing because the Embargo Act had stopped merchant ships from trading with foreign countries. It was hard to get manufactured goods from Europe. Jefferson and Madison urged the Americans who had money to build their own factories. Factory owners and workers began to be looked upon as patriots. The textile mills of New England and the iron foundries of Pennsylvania began during this period.

The War of 1812 helped to

An early iron furnace in Pennsylvania

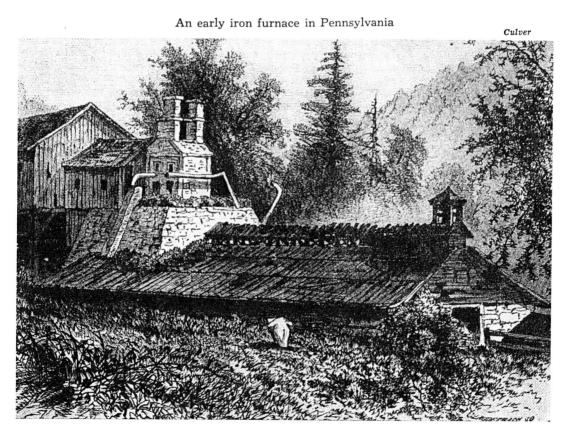

Brown Brothers

A modern steel mill. Compare this picture with that of the early iron furnace

build up the manufacturing industry. Because of the English blockade people were not able to get manufactured goods from Europe; so they built new factories in the United States. Today, the United States is one of the leading manufacturing countries in the world.

A tariff for protection. After the War of 1812, American factory owners complained that European goods were coming into the country again. They were being sold at a lower price than American-made goods. English factories had been in business

longer and had stored up large quantities of goods. After the war English manufacturers hoped to sell their goods at cheap prices in America.

This meant that orders for American-made goods were smaller. Americans were forced to close their factories, and unemployment caused great hardships. The people became alarmed.

To help factory owners and workers, Congress passed the first protective tariff in 1816. A protective tariff is a tax placed on goods coming into the United States from other countries. The tax is set high enough to make foreign goods cost more in this country than American-made goods. People will then buy American products.

An era of good feeling. The Federalists were strongly opposed to the War of 1812. The Hartford Convention had been called by members of the Federalist party in hope of preventing war. Rufus King, the Federalist candidate in the election of 1816, was defeated. James Monroe, a Republican of Virginia, was elected.

With this election an era of good feeling began. The country was more united than ever before. After the Federalist Party disappeared, there was only one party, the Democratic-Republican, started by Thomas Jefferson. Good will was so general that President Monroe ran for reelction in 1820 without an opponent. Only one electoral vote was cast against Monroe. The elector who cast it wanted George Washington to have the honor of being the only President elected with the consent of all.

Shortly after President Monroe was inaugurated he made a tour of the New England

Culver
James Monroe

States. He was so well received that the newspapers began to speak of him as the herald of "an era of good feeling." Since then Monroe's administration has been called the "Era of Good Feeling."

From 1816 to 1825 the national government tried to please every group. It gave help to the farmer. It gave the manufacturer a protective tariff. A second United States Bank was established. Americans were united in their efforts to develop their nation.

Westward expansion. Until 1803, the western boundary of the United States was the Mississippi River. After the purchase

Settlers on their way into the new Western territories

of Louisiana it extended to the Rocky Mountains. By treaties made with the Indians and with the English after the War of 1812, other large areas were opened for settlement.

People were not slow to take advantage of the opportunities offered them. More and more settlers pushed westward to the newer territories. The West was rapidly growing. From 1812 to 1820, five new states joined the Union. These were Louisiana, Indiana, Mississippi, Illinois, and Alabama.

This meant the West had more representatives in Congress. These men asked Congress for cheaper land and better transportation. In 1820, a land law was passed by Congress which satisfied the Westerners. The West also received aid from the federal government to help build roads and canals.

2. Disagreement over Important Questions

Sectional rivalry. Congressmen from the North and South began to resent demands of the Westerners for government aid to help the growth of the West.

A spirit of rivalry was growing among the different parts of the country. As a result, they did not agree on important questions. The North, interested in manufacturing and shipping, was favoring high tariff. The South, engaged in the growing of cotton, tobacco, rice, and sugar was against high tariff. Southerners claimed the tariff was increasing their expenses, for they had to pay higher prices for manufactured articles. The West joined the South in its opposition to the tariff because it, too, was producing many agricultural products.

There was quarrelling among the different parts of the country about federal aid for the building of roads and canals. Some argued that the individual states should be responsible for the expenses of internal improvements. Slavery was another question which caused great trouble. As each section of the country grew larger and stronger, it developed its own particular interests. These were the reasons for the rivalry and clash of opinions among the different sections.

The slavery question. The slavery problem grew out of a difference of opinion between the North and the South. Slave labor was not profitable in the North because machines did most of the work in the factories. The Northern manufacturers found it cheaper to hire workers at low wages to tend the machines, rather than to buy slaves.

Slavery was forbidden by the Northwest Ordinance of 1787. Therefore, the states formed from the Northwest Territory were free states. In 1808, during President Jefferson's second term, Congress passed a law forbidding any more slaves to be brought into the United States. By 1800, slavery had disappeared in seven of the thirteen original states north of Maryland.

In the South, men like George Washington, Thomas Jefferson, Patrick Henry, and James Madison were against slavery. But other Southerners wanted slaves to work on their plantations. The invention of the cotton gin increased the demand for slave workers. Southern planters knew that slaves could work well in the cotton fields; so they bought more slaves.

The cotton industry helped to spread slavery. Even many of those people who did not own slaves believed that prosperity would end in the South if the slaves were freed.

The Missouri Compromise. In 1819, trouble began when Missouri asked to be admitted as a free state. At that time there was an equal number of free states and slave states. For two years, there were lengthy discussions and bitter disputes in Congress over the slavery question. Then Maine asked to be admitted as a free state.

Henry Clay, the peacemaker, finally succeeded in getting the Congressmen to come to an agreement. Each side gave in on some points. This agreement was called the Missouri Compromise. Maine came in as a free state, and Missouri as a slave state. No more slave states would be admitted to the Union north of the Missouri boundary in all of the Louisiana Territory.

3. The Monroe Doctrine — A New Policy

Dangers from Europe. After the American and French Revolutions, many of the Spanish Colonies in America fought for and gained their independence from Spain. The United States feared more trouble from Europe, because some countries joined together and promised to help Spain regain her colonies.

Another event which disturbed Americans was an attempt by Russia to control the Bering Sea and the Pacific coast of North America. This territory north of the fifty-first parallel was already claimed by England and the United States. Russia finally accepted the parallel 54° 40′ as the southern boundary of her territory.

American foreign policy established by the Monroe Doctrine. George Washington had set forth our foreign policy in his farewell address. He realized the need to keep out of European wars. President James Monroe tried to heed this advice. In December, 1823, he sent to Congress his annual message in which he made three important points of our foreign policy very clear: (1) The American continents were no longer open to European colonization; (2) The European countries must not interfere with the new republics of South America; (3) The United States would keep out of European politics.

This policy was called the "Monroe Doctrine." For almost one hundred years, the "Monroe Doctrine" was the guiding plan which helped American diplomats settle many international problems.

Bishop John England. While American leaders were building up a spirit of unity and good will among the people, Bishop John England was working hard to help the Catholics in the South. He was as much interested in the souls of the Negroes as in those of other Catholics. He even started a school for colored children and got Sisters to teach them.

In 1820, Bishop England had come from Ireland to do missionary work in the United States. He was made the first Bishop of Charleston. His diocese included not only South Carolina, but also North Carolina and Georgia.

Although the South was strongly Protestant, Bishop England, in a very short time, became as popular with the Protestants as he was with the Catholics. Protestants asked him to speak at public affairs, and in 1826 he was invited to make a speech before Congress. Bishop England had won the respect of the Southern people.

The first Catholic newspaper, *The United States Catholic Miscellany* was started by Bishop England in 1822. He wanted people to know the truths of religion; so he wrote many interesting articles for the paper.

Culver

John Quincy Adams

To him is given much credit for the meeting of the First Provincial Council of Baltimore in 1829. Bishop England did great work for the Church in America.

3. John Quincy Adams Becomes President

The Election of 1824. In 1824, there was only one political party, the Democratic-Republican, but it had four candidates for President. These candidates were Andrew Jackson, Henry Clay, John Quincy Adams, and William Crawford.

When the votes were counted Andrew Jackson had received the highest number, but not the majority. The majority means more than half of all the votes. To determine who should be President, the names of the three candiates who received the highest number of votes were sent to the House of Representatives. The House declared John Adams elected. Andrew Jackson knew that Henry Clay had arranged for his friends to vote for Adams. When Clay was appointed Secretary of State, Jackson's followers claimed that he had been cheated out of the Presidency.

New Parties Formed. With Jackson as leader, these men formed a new political party. Those who favored Andrew Jackson were called Democratic-Republicans. Those who favored John Quincy Adams were called National Republicans.

During the next four years, the followers of Andrew Jackson did everything in their power to defeat the aims of President Adams. They wished to build up a party which would make certain the election of Andrew Jackson in 1828.

President Adams. John Quincy Adams, the son of the second President of the United States, believed that the welfare of his country should be given first consideration. He was capable, honest, sincere, and hard-working but he was not popular with the people. All his life President Adams had held positions of trust in the government. Men respected him for his ability.

After four difficult years, President Adams was defeated by Andrew Jackson, the founder of the new Democratic Party. The Federalists had brought about form and authority in government. The Jeffersonian Democrats had given it freedom of action. Now it was ready to be placed in the hands of the common people for whom it had been established.

Words and phrases you should know

prosperity	protective tariff	peacemaker
electoral	internal improvements	canals
herald	loyal supporters	handicapped

Selection Test

Select the word or group of words which will make each of the following statements true.

1. The War of 1812 is known as the "Second War of Independence" because the United States

a. gained more territory

b. became more united and independent

c. promised to help Spain

d. bought the Louisiana Territory from France

2. American manufacturing was built up by

a. the War of 1812

b. the election of Jefferson

c. the Monroe Doctrine

d. slavery

3. A protective tariff causes

a. higher prices on imported goods

b. unemployment

c. lower prices on goods manufactured in the country

d. great hardship

4. The Monroe Doctrine was announced

a. in 1812

b. in 1808

c. in 1820

d. in 1823

5. John Quincy Adams was elected President of the United States by

a. the people

b. electors

c. the House of Representatives

d. the Senate

6. The War of 1812 was an important event in the administration of

a. James Monroe

b. James Madison

c. John Quincy Adams

d. Thomas Jefferson

7. The most important result of the War of 1812 was

a. the preventing of impressment of seamen

b. the gaining of new territory

c. the strengthening of national unity

d. the settling of the slavery question

8. High tariff was favored by the

a. South

b. West

c. farmers

d. North

9. Bishop England came from Ireland to help build up the Catholic Church in

a. the South

b. the North

c. the Southwest

d. the Northwest

Checking your knowledge of Unit Four

I. Choose words or phrases in Column B which are closely related to word or phrases in Column A.

Column A

1. National Capitol
2. America for Americans
3. Election of 1824
4. Battle of New Orleans
5. Era of Good Feeling

Column B

a. John Quincy Adams

b. explorers of the Louisiana Territory

c. Albert Gallatin

d. decided to buy Louisiana

6. Livingston and Monroe
7. Barbary Pirates
8. Lewis and Clark
9. Chesapeake Affair
10. John Calhoun

e. burned by the British
f. 1807
g. Andrew Jackson
h. Stephen Decatur
i. War Hawk
j. James Monroe
k. 1800
l. Tripoli
m. Monroe Doctrine

II. Have you studied enough? From the list of words below choose the one which correctly answers each question.

Henry Clay
Commodore Perry
Bishop England
Captain Hull
Thomas Jefferson

House of Representatives
Washington, D. C.
James Monroe
Constitution at sea
cotton gin

1816
Leopard
1804

1. How was the election of 1800 decided?
2. What ship is known as "Old Ironsides?"
3. Where did President Jefferson take the oath of office?
4. Whom did President Jefferson send to France to help Livingston purchase the Louisiana Territory?
5. What statesman was responsible for the Missouri Compromise?
6. Who was the hero of the battle of Lake Erie?
7. What bishop was invited to make a speech before Congress in 1826?
8. What English warship fired upon the *Chesapeake* and killed three Americans?
9. What American general recaptured Detroit from the English?
10. Who was the captain of the warship *Constitution* when she captured the *Guerriere*?
11. When was the first protective tariff law passed?
12. Who wanted the Embargo Act passed?
13. Where were most of the important battles of the War of 1812 fought?
14. What invention increased the demand for slave trade?
15. When was the Twelfth Amendment added to the Constitution?

III. Below is a list of important people you have met in this Unit. How many facts can you tell about them?

Albert Gallatin

John Marshall

John Quincy Adams
James Madison
Meriwether Lewis
Tecumseh

Thomas Jefferson
Andrew Jackson
James Monroe
Oliver Perry

IV. Tell an important event which happened at each of the following places.

Washington, D. C.
Lake Erie
Louisiana
Ghent
Detroit

Tippecanoe Creek
Lake Champlain
New Orleans
Hartford
Baltimore

V. Find examples in this Unit which show:

1. Honesty, justice, and exactness in political leaders.
2. Thanksgiving to God for success.
3. Interest in the common good of the people.
4. Refusal of Americans to pay unjust demands.

VI. Give dates of the following:

1. First protective tariff
2. Lewis and Clark start expedition
3. Monroe Doctrine
4. Embargo Act
5. Lousiana Purchase
6. Thomas Jefferson becomes President
7. War with England

VII. Some activities to aid in mastering information in this Unit.

1. Continue your work on the Classroom Scrapbook. Collect all the pictures you can of persons, places, or things related to this Unit.
2. Read the poem "Old Ironsides" to the class.
3. Make a map of the city of Washington, D. C., showing how Major L'Enfant planned the city, locating important buildings and monuments.
4. Write a letter to President Jefferson urging him to buy the Louisiana Territory. State advantages of possessing this land. Show the importance of the control of the Mississippi River by the United States for farmers in the Northwest Territory.
5. Draw a cartoon about one of the following: Monroe Doctrine, War Hawks and the War of 1812, Hartford Convention.
6. Show the films: Thomas Jefferson and Monticello; Romance of Louisiana; Song of a Nation.

Mary and Religion

MEANING. Jesus is eternal Wisdom, who made Mary His Mother. As His Mother, she is the Seat of Wisdom. The Church applies to her the words of the Bible: "It is she that teacheth the knowledge of God" (Wisdom: 8:4). She does this by giving us an example of following Jesus through our religion.

APPLICATION. In a true democracy, religion is practiced freely. Religion is a duty owed to God. The practice of it is an obligation, and the way of life it demands is shown by Mary's devotion to her Son Jesus. Mary, as Seat of Wisdom, guides all in the practice and teachings of her Son's religion—the Catholic Church.

Prayer

Seat of wisdom, *pray for us.*

Litany of the Blessed Virgin

LORD, have mercy on us.
Christ, have mercy on us.
Lord, have mercy on us.
God the Son, Redeemer of the world, have mercy on us.
God, the Holy Ghost, have mercy on us.
Holy Trinity, one God, have mercy on us.
Christ, hear us.
Christ, graciously hear us.
God the Father of heaven, have mercy on us.
Holy Mary,[1]
Holy Mother of God,
Holy Virgin of virgins,
Mother of Christ,
Mother of divine grace,
Mother most pure,
Mother most chaste,
Mother inviolate,
Mother undefiled,
Mother most amiable,
Mother most admirable,
Mother of good counsel,
Mother of our Creator,
Mother of our Saviour,
Virgin most prudent,
Virgin most venerable,
Virgin most renowned,
    [1] Pray for us.

Virgin most powerful,
Virgin most merciful,
Virgin most faithful,
Mirror of justice,
Seat of Wisdom,
Cause of our joy,
Spiritual vessel,
Vessel of honor,
Singular vessel of devotion,
Mystical Rose,
Tower of David,
Tower of ivory,
House of gold,
Ark of the covenant,
Gate of heaven,
Morning star,
Health of the sick,
Refuge of sinners,
Comforter of the afflicted,
Help of Christians,
Queen of angels,
Queen of patriarchs,
Queen of prophets,
Queen of apostles,
Queen of martyrs,
Queen of confessors,
Queen of virgins,
Queen of all saints,
Queen conceived without original sin,

Queen assumed into heaven,
Queen of the most holy Rosary,
Queen of peace.
Lamb of God, who takest away the sins of the world, spare us, O Lord.
Lamb of God, who takest away the sins of the world, graciously hear us, O Lord.
Lamb of God, who takest away the sins of the world, have mercy on us.
Christ, hear us. Christ, graciously hear us.
℣. Pray for us, O holy Mother of God. ℟. That we may be made worthy of the promises of Christ.

Let us pray

Grant, we beseech Thee, O Lord God, unto us Thy servants, that we may rejoice in continual health of mind and body; and, by the glorious intercession of blessed Mary ever Virgin, may be delivered from present sadness, and enter into the joy of Thine eternal gladness. Through Christ our Lord. Amen.

An indulgence of 7 years. A plenary indulgence once a month on the usual conditions for the daily devout recitation of this Litany with its versicle and prayer (See "The Raccolta," the official work of indulgenced prayers, page 216).

MARY AS A GUIDE THROUGH LIFE. The free will of man accepts the guidance of Mary in the way of life. This guidance of Mary is part of our religion. It affects our home life, our association with our fellow man, our civic obligations, our career in life, and our acceptance of life's problems.

Courtesy of Rev. J. B. Carol, O. F. M.

UNIT FIVE

WESTWARD TO THE MISSISSIPPI

CHAPTER 1—SETTLEMENTS IN THE SOUTHWEST

Western Land Attracts Settlers
    Southwest Open for Settlement
    Routes to the West
Pioneers Move into the Southwest
    Reasons for Going West
    Settlements in Kentucky and Tennessee
Missionaries Work among Pioneers
    Bishop Flaget—First Bishop of Bardstown Diocese
    Work of Father Gallitzin

CHAPTER II—SETTLEMENTS IN THE NORTHWEST

Pioneers Settle North of the Ohio River
    Plans for settling and governing Northwest Territory
    Early settlements in Ohio and at Chicago
    New means of travel
    Missionaries—Father Gibault; Father Richard
Comparison of Settlements in Northwest and Southwest
Indian Troubles on the Frontier
    General Wayne conquers Indians in Northwest
    General Jackson conquers Indians in Southwest
    Purchase of Florida

CHAPTER III—LIFE OF THE PIONEER

Living Conditions on the Frontier
    Homes—recreation—religion
    Rapid growth of the West
    Trade and business increase
    People become more democratic

UNIT FIVE

WESTWARD TO THE MISSISSIPPI

BY THE YEAR 1800, America was already becoming a great nation. The people were enjoying the rights and privileges stated in the Declaration of Independence.

The War of 1812 helped to develop a spirit of nationalism among Americans. They were proud to be citizens of this great nation which had such high ideals. The people recognized their duty to protect American ideals. They had confidence in their nation.

The United States lost no territory by the War of 1812. By the purchase of the Louisiana Territory from France, a vast stretch of land was added to the country. Moreover, the land west of the Appalachian Mountains to the Mississippi River was not yet settled. Americans

hoped that with the help of Divine Providence their nation would grow and expand until it reached from sea to sea.

We shall now study the Western movement, the settlement of the land east of the Mississippi. We shall learn how the beautiful peninsula of Florida became part of the United States. We shall follow the pioneers on their difficult travels through mountain gaps, along Indian trails and into the wilderness, and up and down the rivers in their sturdy flatboats.

New names will be added to our list of American heroes. There will be names of valiant men who blazed the trial for the frontiersmen. There will be those of heroic priests and bishops who planted the seed of faith on the Western frontier.

CHAPTER I

SETTLEMENTS IN THE SOUTHWEST

Over the mountains. The territory extending from the Appalachian Mountains to the Mississippi River was known as "the West." Trappers and hunters, who returned to settlements after weeks of adventure in the Indian territory of the West, told glowing stories of the beauty and wealth of those rich lands. The constant repetition of these stories filled the people of the East with a desire to better their condition. The spirit of adventure moved them to make plans for crossing the Appalachians into the new territory.

In studying this chapter we shall see some of the hardships which were endured by the early settlers of the West. We should be grateful to the brave pioneers who gained for us many of the rights of freedom and justice that we enjoy. What virtues do you think these early pioneers must have possessed?

1. Western Lands Attract Adventurers

The West of the early days. To the dwellers along the eastern seacoast, "the West" meant a vast land beyond the Appalachian Mountains. France, in 1763, had lost her claim to this territory, and it was given over to England by the Treaty of Paris. Even before American independence was gained, groups of colonists had moved to "the West." These groups were called pioneers. They cleared the land and built log-cabin homes. The Indians feared the loss of their hunting grounds, which were being destroyed, and resented the settlers. Under the Indian leadership of Chief Pontiac (pon'-ti-ak), pioneers were murdered, their homes and crops burned, and English forts captured. The English sent an army against the Indians and defeated them. Finally, treaties were made with the Indians. **Colonists forbidden to settle be-**

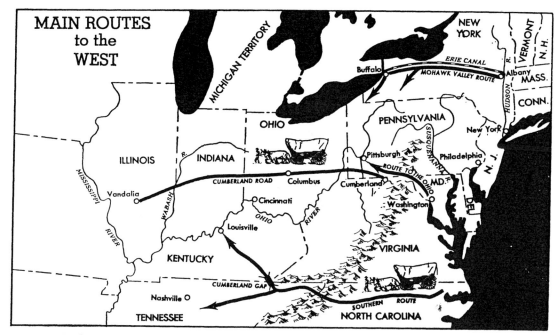

MAIN ROUTES to the WEST

yond the Appalachians. In 1763 and 1774 Great Britain had passed laws forbidding American colonists to settle beyond the Appalachians. There were several reasons why England objected to such settlements. In this territory fur-bearing animals were found and England had profited by her fur trading. If the forests were cleared for settlements a valuable business would be lost.

England also claimed that if her colonies extended to the Mississippi it would be difficult to govern and to protect them. She wanted both peace among the Indians and contentment among the fur trappers. However, in spite of England's orders, American pioneers braved many dangers to settle beyond the Appalachians.

Travel was not easy in those days. There were no roads, only Indian trails or natural passes between the mountains, or paths along the waterways. The people suffered miseries and hardships on their journeys westward.

Routes to the West. The great Appalachian Mountains were a barrier to travel. Let us look at some of the routes used to reach the lands of the West.

One path across New York State followed the valleys of the Hudson and Mohawk Rivers. This passage could be followed until the Allegheny River or some branch of the Ohio or Mississippi was reached. Some

Rafts like these were used by many settlers on their way to new homes in the West

travelers decided to settle along the shores of the Great Lakes. Others ventured into the interior of the country in flatboats.

Another route westward was entirely by water. On rafts, packed with their household goods firmly tied together, whole families drifted down the Susquehanna, (sus-kwee-han'-na), Ohio, Monongahela (moe-non-ga-he'-la) or other smaller rivers. The pioneers guided these clumsy crafts with long, stout poles. Flatboats could carry more people and a larger cargo than the rafts.

Still another route passed the Cumberland Gap, in the mountain ridges between Kentucky and Tennessee. This route later became known as the famous Wilderness Road. It was the route used by Daniel Boone in blazing the trail to the West. This was the most traveled route in the early pioneer days.

2. Pioneers Move Into the Southwest

Reasons for settling the Southwest. Many frontiersmen were anxious to move into the Southwest. This territory included Western Pennsylvania,

Western Virginia, Kentucky and Tennessee. It was located beyond the Allegheny Mountains and south of the Ohio River. Even though the pioneers met with danger and hardships, their spirit of adventure urged many of them onward. These people longed for a place in which they might live with greater freedom than in the East. Some of the Eastern states would not permit people to vote unless they owned property or belonged to a particular church. These settlers were determined to be free from such regulations in the West.

The rich, fertile lands of Kentucky and Tennessee attracted settlers to the Southwest. The land of rich plantation owners in the South was wearing out from too much planting. The farmers needed new land and found it in the West. In newspapers and booklets the West was described as a place of boundless opportunity. The land of this region was being sold at a very low price so that even poor people could buy a place for a home and a farm.

Some people from European countries, instead of settling in the colonies, joined these hardy, fearless pioneers in their journey to the new settlements.

These immigrants could not afford to purchase land elsewhere. Here they could claim free land.

Settlement of Kentucky. Among the most daring of the frontiersmen was Daniel Boone who led settlers into Kentucky. He had been born in Pennsylvania, but his father moved the family to North Carolina while Daniel was still a small boy. Daniel loved to hunt. He became an excellent scout, able to walk through the woods as silently as an Indian. At sixteen he was known as the best hunter in North Carolina.

Although Daniel had no opportunity to go to school, he learned to read, to write, to do arithmetic, and to use the instruments of a surveyor. All this knowledge helped him as leader of his people in their new land beyond the mountains.

When the boy became a young man, he married Rebecca Bryan. For a while Boone settled down as a farmer with his wife, but the spirit of adventure was so strong in him that farming proved to be too quiet a life. He spent months away from home exploring the wilderness.

In 1769, Daniel Boone and a few of his companions ventured

Daniel Boone leads a group of settlers into Kentucky

through Cumberland Gap into Kentucky. Upon discovering a hunter's paradise there the pioneers' hearts were filled with joy. It was two years before Boone returned to North Carolina.

Boonesborough. In 1773, Boone decided to move to Kentucky. He persuaded a few families to go with him to the blue grass country, as it is called. These people endured many hardships on their travels and it was not until 1775 that they finally made a settlement. They called this settlement Boonesborough after the famous trail blazer.

Many, many times these first pioneers of Kentucky were attacked by the Indians. Boone's oldest boy was killed by them. The pioneer leader himself and several of his companions were captured by the Shawnee Indians in 1778 while they were searching for salt. Boone was adopted by the Indian chief, Blackfish, who admired his courage. Boone lived with these Indians for some time before he was able to return to his own people.

Once Boone overheard the Indians planning for an attack upon Boonesborough. He dared not stay any longer but cautiously escaped through the woods. He arrived at Boonesborough in time to warn the pioneers. They fortified their settlement so well that the Indian attack failed.

Many other settlers followed these pioneers into the blue grass country. In 1792, when Kentucky was admitted to the Union as a state, there were nearly a hundred thousand people living there. It was the first new state to be formed west of the Appalachians.

The settlement of Tennessee. At the time of the settlement of Kentucky, James Robertson blazed a trail into Tennessee. The settlers formed a little colony and organized a democratic government for themselves at Wataugo (wa-taw′-go). The colony adopted a constitution which granted its citizens freedom to worship as they pleased and the right to vote in all elections.

When Robertson left Wataugo to open a new settlement at Nashville, John Sevier (se-veer′), replaced him. Sevier was another sturdy pioneer interested in the western movement and he became the leader of the people. He fortified the settlement against the British and defended the people against the Indians. With Robertson and Sevier as leaders, many settlers came to the Tennessee Valley and opened settlements there. In 1796, Tennessee was admitted to the Union as another state.

3. Missionaries Work Among the Pioneers

Catholic Pioneers. The first Catholics known to have settled in Kentucky were William Coomes and his family. Other Catholic settlers came to Kentucky from Maryland. Many immigrants from Ireland also settled there.

After these Catholic pioneers settled in the new lands, many of them were in danger of losing their faith because there were so few priests to minister to them. Bishop Carroll of Baltimore had sent some priests to Kentucky. However, the distance between the settlements was so great, and travel was so slow and dangerous that many of these people seldom saw a priest. Consequently these pioneers could not go to Mass, receive the sacraments, nor be instructed in their religion. Added to this, many of them married non-Catholics, for there

Early Settlers dwelt far from churches and schools.
Missionaries had to penetrate far into the wilderness

were only a few Catholics in these settlements. It is surprising that so many kept their faith without the ordinary means of getting God's graces and helps.

It was due chiefly to the hard work of Father Stephen Badin (bah'-din) that the Church was established in Kentucky. Dominican Fathers from England also worked as missionaries among the pioneers. These priests built the first Dominican church at St. Rose, near Bardstown, Kentucky.

Diocese of Bardstown. The mis-sionaries met with much success in preserving and spreading the faith among the pioneers. Reverend Benedict Joseph Flaget (flay-zhay'), a Sulpician (sul-pish'-an), was appointed the first bishop of the diocese of Bardstown, which Pope Pius VII established in 1808.

A pioneer village at Loretto. Among the other early pioneers who dared to cross the great Appalachian barrier were the settlers of the little town of Loretto in Western Pennsylvania. In 1788, Captain Michael

McGuire, a former officer in the Revolutionary Army, purchased this tract of land near the top of the Allegheny Mountains in Pennsylvania. His family braved the hardships of pioneer travel to come with him from Maryland to Western Pennsylvania.

There, in the midst of a dense forest, McGuire built a log cabin and cleared some land. His nearest neighbor was more than twenty miles away. The Captain was soon joined by relatives and friends, who founded what was called McGuire's Settlement. Later, it was called Clearfield, and finally Loretto. When Captain McGuire died in 1793, he left Bishop Carroll four hundred acres of land.

Father Gallitzin. Father Demetrius Gallitzin (gal-litz'-in), one of the most noted early missionaries, ministered to the people in the Southwest. This priest's father was a Russian prince and his mother was a baptized Catholic. Demetrius was born at the Hague in Holland in 1770. When Prince Demetrius was seventeen years of age he became a Catholic. He came to America in 1792 using the name Augustin Smith. After a short time in America, he asked Bishop Carroll to permit him to study for the priesthood at St. Mary's Seminary in Baltimore. He was ordained on March 18, 1795, the first one to receive all the priestly orders within the limits of the original thirteen colonies.

Out of his own fortune he bought land next to the four hundred acres that Captain McGuire gave to the Church. He asked Bishop Carroll's permission to work as a pioneer priest among the settlers in the Alleghenies.

Father Gallitzin helped his people a great deal. He cared not only for their souls but also for their bodies. He also taught them the best European methods of road building. He set up a saw mill, a tannery, and a flour mill for the use of the settlers. This great prince, priest, and missionary showed a courage and a devotion which ranks him high as a heroic leader of the people. On many occasions he risked his life to carry on his work. Father Gallitzin was one of the most famous missionaries of the West. Father Gallitzin also wrote books about the Catholic religion. These were among the earliest books of this kind printed in America. This priest was not only a missionary, but a Catholic author.

Using the new words

trappers	barrier	tannery
boundless	immigrants	surveyors
pioneers	blazing	frontiersman

Copy the following definitions. From the list above find word that matches each definition.

1. People who are among the first to move into a new part of a country and settle there.
2. Persons who come into a country or region to live.
3. Persons who measure the land to establish boundaries and positions.
4. One who lives on the outer edge of a settled section of a country.
5. People who trap wild animals for their furs.
6. Place where hides are tanned and made into leather.
7. Something stopping progress or preventing approach.
8. Not limited.
9. Making known a path or marking out.

Interesting things to talk about

1. If you had lived in Maryland and had wished to join the pioneers journeying to Kentucky, how would you have traveled? By which route?
2. Missionaries went with the pioneers to the new West. In what ways did they help the people to become better Catholics? better citizens?

Match these "firsts"

Column A	Column B
1. First settlement in Western Pennsylvania	Daniel Boone and companions
2. First Catholic family to settle in Kentucky	Benedict Joseph Flaget
3. First Bishop of Bardstown	William Coomes
4. First pioneers of Kentucky	Demetrius Gallitzin
5. First to receive all priestly orders within limits of the 13 original colonies.	John Sevier and his followers
	Stephen Badin

Map study

Draw a map like the one on page 177. Locate and print these places on it.

Appalachian Mountains	Cumberland Gap	Ohio River
Mississippi River	Boonesborough	Bardstown

184

Completion Test

On a sheet of paper complete the following statements by writing the correct word or words.

1. The territory extending from the Appalachians to the Mississippi was called _____

2. Pioneers were killed and English forts destroyed by _____, an Indian chief.

3. A passage through the mountains between Kentucky and Tennessee was called _____.

4. The first town settled in Kentucky was _____

5. Kentucky was admitted to the Union in _____

6. A prince, priest and missionary, who helped the settlers of Western Pennsylvania, was _____

7. The State of Tennessee was admitted to the Union in _____

8. The diocese of Bardstown was established in _____

9. The government set up at Wataugo, Tennessee gave the settlers two important rights: _____ and _____

Selection Test

Find the incorrect statement.

1. Pioneers moved into the Southwest because they longed for a place in which they might live with greater freedom.
   Pioneers moved into the Southwest because the West was described as a place of boundless opportunity.
   Pioneers moved into the Southwest because the land of this region was being sold at a very low price.
   Pioneers moved into the Southwest because they were always friendly with the Indians there.

2. Daniel Boone was a daring frontiersman.
   Daniel Boone was a good student in school.
   Daniel Boone was married to Rebecca Bryan.
   Daniel Boone was adopted by an Indian Chief.

3. Many Catholic pioneers were in danger of losing their faith.
   Many Catholic pioneers married non-Catholics.
   Many Catholic pioneers settled in Loretto.
   Many Catholic pioneers came to Kentucky from Spain.

4. The Treaty of Paris was signed in 1763.
   The Treaty of Paris gave the land beyond the Applachians to England.
   The Treaty of Paris gave over the Cumberland Gap to France.
   The Treaty of Paris took from France her claim to "the West."

SETTLEMENTS IN THE NORTHWEST

Getting Ready to Go On. You have been following these early pioneers on their difficult journeys through mountain passes and along Indian trails to the new settlements, Kentucky and Tennessee. You were very much interested in the efforts of the missionaries to keep alive the faith among the people.

You will now study how the Northwest was settled, and find out how the government helped the people who settled there. You will also learn about the troubles these people had with the Indians. You will see how the Church sent missionaries to take care of the spiritual needs of her children.

As you study this chapter, comparisons will be made. You will notice differences between these pioneers and those of the Southwest region. Their form of government and their methods of dealing with the Indians will attract your attention.

1. Pioneers Settle North of the Ohio River

Northwest Territory. As early as 1778 the territory around the Great Lakes and north of the Ohio River had been taken from the English by George Rogers Clark. Later, the states whose charters had granted them land in this district gave up their land to the government.

Land Act of 1785. In 1785, Congress passed laws for the surveying of this Northwest Territory. This Land Act also provided that tracts should be sold at auction to the highest bidder. Sometimes this land was sold for as little as two dollars an acre. The money received from these sales was used to pay the war debt and the expenses of the government.

Land companies bought large tracts and advertised the new country most favorably. So many settlers left the East that the older states became alarmed and discouraged emigration.

After many years, the government decided to give away land to anyone who promised to live on it and cultivate it. These pioneer settlers were called "squatters."

The Northwest Ordinance. You remember the famous Northwest Ordinance passed by Congress in 1787. It provided for the government of the Northwest Territory. The states formed under this government were to have the same rights as the thirteen original states. Slavery was forbidden. Provisions were made for education, and religious freedom was granted. The Ordinance of 1787 was the most important work of the government under the Articles of Confederation.

Here is a sentence taken from the Ordinance of 1787. You should be very interested in what it says. "Knowledge, religion, and morality being necessary to good government and the happiness of mankind, schools and the means of education shall forever be encouraged." This should help you to appreciate more the freedom to practice your religion and the

The great city of Cleveland has grown from a small settlement

Brown Brothers

privilege of receiving a Catholic education. Too often, one takes these things for granted.

Early Beginnings in Ohio. In the spring of 1788, General Rufus Putnam of Massachusetts led a group of settlers from the New England states to the Northwest Territory. They traveled on horseback and in slow wagon trains. Some of them built flatboats and continued their journey by water. They floated down the Ohio River to the place where it joined the Muskingum River. They landed and built a settlement which they called Marietta. This was the first town in the Northwest.

Under the leadership of Judges Symmes (sims) a group from New Jersey founded Cincinnati further down the river. This town soon became one of the most important in the Northwest Territory.

In 1796, Moses Cleveland, with a group of pioneers from Connecticut, settled on the shores of Lake Erie. From this settlement grew the city of Cleveland.

In 1803, the territory which included these and other com-

An air view of modern Chicago

munities was admitted to the Union as the state of Ohio.

Chicago. During the War of 1812, Fort Dearborn, on the shores of Lake Michigan, was lost to the English. In 1816, this fort was rebuilt. In time a settlement grew up around it which was called Chicago. Because of its splendid location on Lake Michigan and its rich farming regions, Chicago became the second largest city in the United States.

New means of travel. The people who settled in the Northwest followed the routes that the earlier frontiersmen used, besides the new ones which they themselves discovered. These people traveled either on foot, on horseback, by wagon or stage coach. They carried with them as much of their household goods as possible.

Many of the pioneers traveled in the Conestoga (con-a-stoe'-ga) or covered wagon. This type of wagon was named after Conestoga Creek in Pennsylvania. It was near this creek that the first covered wagon of this type was made. In these wagons, the pioneer families carried food, furniture, and cattle. They even slept in them at night. The Conestoga wagon looked like a boat on wheels,

with a large rounded canvas spread over it. Painted in bright colors and drawn by many horses, these vehicles made quite a sight. West of the Mississippi River covered wagons were called prairie schooners. Why do you think they were given this name?

Rapid growth of the Northwest. Shortly after Congress passed the Northwest Ordinance in 1787, a rush to the new territory began. For several years settlers came to the Northwest region in large numbers. By 1820, three states, Ohio, Indiana, and Illinois, had been formed from this territory. All sorts of people moved in—rich and poor, young and old. They were anxious to make use of the opportunities and freedoms offered them.

Catholics in the Northwest. A small number of the pioneers in the Ohio Valley were Catholics. Priests, ready for any hardships, followed these pioneers. At each settlement that he visited the priest would go to one of the homes. Here the people would gather to hear Mass and to receive the sacraments. There were no churches. At times, the priests' labors and sacrifices were truly heroic. Very often they had to travel

A Conestoga wagon in front of a country inn

hundreds of miles from one settlement to another.

Bishop Flaget, who had charge of both the Northwest and the states of Kentucky and Tennessee, sent missionaries from Kentucky to work among the Catholics in the Ohio Valley. As early as 1811, an attempt was made to organize the Catholics of this district.

Diocese of Cincinnati. In 1814, Bishop Flaget visited the settlement at Cincinnati. He found practically a wilderness with only a few scattered log cabins. The bishop said Mass at one of these cabins. He asked the people to build a church. They were willing and anxious to do so, but had to build it outside of the settlement. There was a law which would not permit them to build one within the settlement.

In 1821, Ohio was made a diocese. Father Edward Fenwick, a Dominican, was appointed bishop. Before he was made bishop, the law forbidding the building of chuches in the Cincinnati settlement was repealed. Immediately, Bishop Fenwick had the new church brought into this settlement.

This church became Bishop Fenwick's cathedral. The diocese had about fifty Catholic families. Ten years later, at the death of its bishop, the Catholic population had increased to seven thousand.

Father Pierre Gibault, a patriot priest. You already know about Father Gibault who helped George Rogers Clark in the Revolution. Father Gibault was a great patriot and a powerful missionary. Born in Montreal, Canada, in 1737, he was educated and ordained priest at the Quebec Seminary. In spite of many difficulties, and in the face of grave danger, Father Gibault worked very hard for the good of the pioneer Catholics. Many Catholics who had become careless began to practice their religion once more.

Father Gabriel Richard, a heroic leader. Father Gabriel Richard, a French refugee, came to Baltimore in 1792. This priest was sent to do missionary work in the Illinois territory. He was loved among his parishoners and accomplished a tremendous amount of good for the pioneer Catholics there.

Father Richard then went to Detroit, which was a military post. Besides attending to his duties at the post, he became interested in the Indian missions. He did splendid work among the Indians.

In 1808, this zealous priest visited Baltimore and brought back a printing press. He was now able to print a newspaper. This was the first newspaper printed in Michigan. It contained much news of interest to Catholics. Next, pamphlets and books were printed to tell the people about the social, political, and religious happenings of the community.

During the War of 1812, Father Richard was arrested by the British and sent to Canada. He was held captive until the war ended. This was done because of his great influence with the people. As soon as Father Richard was released, he returned to his parish in Detroit. The people liked him so well that they elected him to be their representative in Congress in 1823. He is the only Catholic priest who ever served as a representative in Congress.

Comparison of Northwest and Southwest settlements. The pioneers of the Northwest were more fortunate than those of the Southwest. In the Northwest, they were governed by federal laws. The national government surveyed the land and laid out the tracts. The government sent soldiers to protect the settlers. These soldiers built roads and forts. They protected the people from Indian attacks.

The settlers of the Southwest had to mark out their own trails and face the dangers of Indian attacks. They had to adopt a form of government for themselves. Because the tracts were not laid out for the people in the Southwest, there were constant disputes about land boundaries.

The settlers differed, too, in their way of life. Some in the Southwest were plantation owners who brought their slaves with them. Others were backwoodsmen. In the North-

"Mad" Anthony Wayne

west there were many farmers, carpenters, and skilled workers who were used to doing their own work.

2. Indian Troubles on the Frontier

"Mad Anthony" Wayne conquers Indians in Ohio. All the settlers had great difficulties with the Indians. The different tribes resented the white men taking over their hunting grounds. Often the Indians treated them cruelly. The Indians were not entirely to blame. The white man had not always been fair to them. Many treaties were made and broken. Most of these treaties had favored the white man in regard to the territory north of the Ohio River.

There was so much trouble with the Indians in Ohio that President Washington sent soldiers to stop the uprisings. The soldiers were not successful. Later, Washington asked Anthony Wayne, nicknamed "Mad Anthony" because of his daring and courageous acts during the Revolutionary War, to take command.

For more than a year, Wayne trained his men to fight Indian fashion. In 1794, he attacked and defeated the Indians at Fallen Timbers near Toledo, Ohio. Two years later Wayne and the Indians signed a treaty at Fort Greenville. In this treaty the Indians agreed to give the land north of the Ohio to the Americans. This brought many years of peace to the settlers of the Northwest.

The Indians did not attack white settlers in the Northwest again until 1811. Then Tecumseh urged the tribes to unite and drive the white man from the West. Again they were defeated by the Americans.

Indian troubles in the Southwest. The most troublesome Indians in the Southwest were the Creeks and the Seminoles. In 1813, the Creeks attacked and killed many of the settlers in Alabama. The United States Government was aroused and sent soldiers under the leadership of Andrew Jackson to conquer the Creeks. In 1814, at the Battle of Horseshoe Bend, Jackson completely defeated these Indians. A treaty was made and the Indians gave up much of their land.

After the Indians were defeated, thousands of people moved into this territory. They cleared the forest and built farms. The states of Louisiana, Mississippi, and Alabama were made from this territory.

The Seminoles, who were kinsmen of the Creeks, lived in the Florida peninsula, where they frequently raided American villages. In 1817, General Jackson was sent there to settle the Indian uprisings. He not only defeated the Indians, but also seized Spanish settlements. During one of these raids, General Jackson captured and put to death two Englishmen. Jackson claimed that these men encouraged the attacking Indians and gave military supplies to them.

Great Britain was angry. Spain was also stirred up because her territory had been invaded by American troops. There was cause for war between America and European nations. President Monroe declared that Jackson had acted without the authority of the government. Spain was given back her ports and American troops were withdrawn from Florida.

Purchase of Florida. For a long time, it was thought that Western Florida, which included the territory along the Gulf of Mexico, was part of the Louisiana Territory. Spain claimed both the peninsula south of Georgia and western Florida. However, she did very little to settle this land. Indians, runaway slaves, and criminals found the territory along the Gulf of Mexico a convenient place in which to hide. These outlaws banded together and made raids on the neighboring states. Many lives were lost and much property was destroyed during these raids.

John Quincy Adams warned Spain that she must keep order in the territory or sell it to the United States. Spanish governors found it impossible to keep order. In 1819, a treaty was arranged, and Spain agreed to sell Florida to the United States for five million dollars. This agreement was not carried out until 1821. Then the territory of the United States extended to the Gulf of Mexico.

Words you should know

tracts

squatter

backwoodsmen

auction

kinsmen

outlaws

Things to talk about

1. Some of the Eastern states owned land in the Northwest Territory. They gave this land to the government. What use did the government make of this land?

2. Congress organized the government of the Northwest by the Ordinance of 1787. What rights were assured the people by this law?

3. Self-sacrificing missionaries suffered great hardships to keep the faith alive and to bring it to all sections of the Northwest. Who were those missionaries and what did they do?

4. Show how the Catholic pioneers needed courage, determination, and great will power to keep their faith.

Reasons Test

Can you find one reason in each group which is incorrect?

1. The pioneers of the Northwest were more fortunate than those of the Southwest because
   a. the United States government sent soldiers to protect them.
   b. the national government surveyed the land and laid out the claims.
   c. they had no quarrels at all with the Indians.
   d. the men were tradesmen, farmers, or skilled workers.

2. General Jackson, while settling the Indian uprisings in Florida, captured and put to death two Englishmen because he claimed

a. that these men gave military supplies to Indians.
b. that they deserved such a fate.
c. that President Monroe said it was all right to do so.
d. that they encouraged attacking Indians.

3. Catholic priests followed the pioneers into the Northwest because

a. they wanted to minister to the Catholics.
b. they wished to spread the Catholic faith.
c. they did not like the places they left.
d. they knew the Catholic settlers needed them.

4. The Northwest Ordinance was an important law because

a. it provided for the government of the Northwest Territory.
b. the states formed under this government were denied the same rights as the thirteen original states.
c. provisions were made for education and religious freedom.
d. slavery was to be forbidden.

Matching Test

Match Column A with Column B.

Column A	*Column B*
1. Land Act	a. Indians of Northwest
2. Father Gibault	b. Cincinnati
3. Judge Symmes	c. 1787
4. Fort Dearborn	d. Bill of Rights
5. Battle of Horseshoe Bend	e. Chicago
6. Purchase of Florida	f. 1785
7. "Mad Anthony" Wayne	g. General Jackson
8. Northwest Ordinance	h. Spain
	i. Famous missionary
	j. England
	k. Catholic priest representative in Congress

195

CHAPTER III

LIFE OF THE PIONEERS

On the frontier. You have already studied about the dangers which the brave pioneers had to face. Neither the hardships of the journey nor the attacks of the Indians discouraged them.

Now you will learn how the settlers built their homes, obtained food and clothing, and provided for the education of their children. You will see how people of different religions were friendly with each other. You will find out how the East was helped by the growth of the West.

1. Living Conditions on the Frontier

Frontier homes. The pioneer family built its one-room cabin from heavy logs cut down and dragged from the forest. The cracks between the logs were filled with clay and moss to keep out the rain and the snow. Against one end of the log cabin was built a large outside chimney made of rough stones or logs. The chimney allowed the smoke from the open fireplace to escape. The rooms were lighted by the fire in the fireplace or by homemade candles.

Benches, chairs, tables, and beds also were made from lumber from the forests. Some of the beds were fastened to the wall, and the bedding was usually made from the skins of animals.

Deer horns or antlers were nailed over the door in each house. These made a convenient rack for the guns, which were necessary for frontier life. Gunpowder was kept nearby.

Food. At first, food was scarce. After the crops were harvested, there was a good supply of corn, hominy, and wheat. Bread and pies could be made. Deer, bear, pheasants, and wild turkey provided the meat. The food was wholesome, though plain.

Clothing. These early pioneers

196

did not have to worry about the style of their clothing. Animal skin was the usual source of clothing material. Caps were made from raccoon skins. Skirts and trousers were cut of buckskins. Jackets, shoes, and moccasins were made from deerskin.

It was not until later that the women and girls put their knowledge of weaving to practical use. They wove cloth from flax grown in the fields. In this way, they could have homespun as well as knitted clothing.

Work. Hard work faced the frontiersmen at every step. They needed great strength to clear the lands and to prepare them for homes and farming. Corn, cotton, and tobacco crops needed constant care. The problem of getting crops to market was a difficult one. Wagons were few, roads were bad, and distances were great. Boys and girls had to do their share of the hard work.

Education. There was little opportunity for education because schools were few and poor. Trained teachers were not available and books were hard

An old-time school room

Culver

197

to get. Children went to school only during the winter months because they were needed to help with the work on the farm at other times of the year. Reading, writing, and arithmetic were the principal subjects taught.

Social life and recreation. Family life was vigorous and pleasant. There was very little time for social life and recreation. The pioneer combined work with play whenever possible. When a new settler was ready to build his log cabin, he sent word to his neighbors. A "log-rolling party" then took place. People gathered from far and near. They all worked together, and in a few hours the cabin was finished. Afterwards, a big dinner was served. Dancing and singing ended the day.

At harvest time the neighbors from miles around gathered for a "husking bee." At the bee they removed the dry outside covering of each ear of corn.

When it was time to make apple butter the neighbors gathered to pare the apples.

Such gatherings were planned to make work easier and more pleasant. News of the territory was exchanged at these events. This spirit of working together helped the pioneers to develop community life.

Their neighborly charity kept them closer to God through service to one another. Whole families worked, played, and prayed together. This was the source of their success and happiness.

Religion. Most of these early pioneers were God-fearing people who were faithful to their religious duties. Although not all of one faith, they respected each other's beliefs. Each group wanted its own church. In some towns there were as many as five or six churches. The continuous labors of missionaries made the frontiersmen better Christians and, therefore, better Americans.

2. Rapid Growth of the Frontier

Settlers pour into the West. Each year greater numbers journeyed to the West to enjoy greater freedom of life. Good farming land was cheap, and forests furnished valuable lumber products. Fur-bearing animals were plentiful. Large quantities of salt, iron, coal, and lead were found.

Trade and business increased. There were so many products in the West that a very profitable trade with the Eastern states began. To improve this

A scene on the Erie Canal

trade the government built roads, canals, and railroads. The Cumberland Road helped business with Philadelphia and Baltimore. The Erie Canal furnished a direct route from New York to the West. In general, conditions improved throughout the country.

Spirit of democracy grows. The early pioneers came from all walks of life. Among them were doctors, lawyers, skilled workmen, woodsmen, plantation owners, and laborers. No matter from where these people came, what was their position in life, their greatest pride was that they were Americans.

There was a generous spirit among these people. Though busily engaged in building and farming, each settler was willing to give his neighbor a helping hand. These early pioneers left a mark upon American life and set an example for all other Americans.

Each one considered himself the equal of his neighbor. Every man in the West had the right to vote. Everywhere men began to show a greater interest in the government. The new democratic form of government had the interests of all at heart.

The pioneers have left us a heritage of which we should be proud. Their lives and works should help us to love and appreciate America. We should be willing at all times to sacrifice ourselves in order that our country may remain "the land of the free and the home of the brave."

Words you should know

a husking bee	hominy	buckskin
log-rolling	homespun	moccasins
heritage	antlers	pheasants
perseverence	vigorous	raccoon

Things to talk about

1. Show how the love of freedom and the spirit of equality caused American families to go West.

2. The pioneers' homes and their ways of living were different from yours. Name some of the differences.

3. The West developed a new type of American. How did the American pioneers differ from the people of the original colonies.

4. Tell why the early Amercan pioneers worked so hard, made such great sacrifices, and depended so much upon God to take care of them.

True or false

Some of these statements are *false*. Make these statements *true* by writing them correctly.

1. Most of the homes of the early frontiersmen had but one room.

2. The furniture of the pioneer home was rough and crude.

3. Their houses were lighted by gas.

4. Wild deer, bears, pheasants, and turkeys provided meat for the early settlers.

5. Most of the clothing of the pioneers was made from the skins of animals.

6. Flax was planted so as to provide thread for weaving.

7. Life on the frontier was hard, but the people were happy.

8. Boys and girls on the frontier did not have much chance to go to school.

9. The pioneers helped one another, and often shared their goods with their neighbors.

10. Corn husking on the frontier was an excuse for a party.

11. Many of the early pioneers were God-fearing people.

12. The greater number of Catholics who settled the West came from New England.

13. A good pioneer should have courage, determination, and a willingness to suffer hardships.

14. Early western pioneers contributed very little to the growth of the United States.

15. The frontiersmen loved freedom and believed in the spirit of equality.

16. Cheap and fertile farm land attracted people from the East to the West.

17. The pioneers, for the most part, came from educated and the wealthy classes of people.

18. In the West only property owners could vote.

19. There was a lack of religious intolerance among the early western people.

20. The early West played a large part in making the West more democratic.

Checking your knowledge of Unit Five

I. Can you name the people who did the things listed below?

1. the explorer who captured the Northwest Territory from the English

2. the Indian chief who resented Western pioneers

3. the patriot priest who helped Clark in the Revolution

4. the bishop who sent missionaries from Kentucky to Ohio

5. the general who conquered the Indians in Ohio

6. the man who led a group of people from New Jersey to settle Cincinnati

7. the best hunter in North Carolina

8. the Massachusetts general who made a settlement at Marietta

9. the first bishop of Ohio

10. the man who blazed a trial into Tennessee

11. the priest who built the first Catholic Church at Loretto, Pennsylvana

12. the leader who defeated the Creek Indians in Alabama in 1814

II. Time marches on—Match these events with the dates.

Column A	Column B
1. Spain agreed to sell Florida	a. 1783
2. Settlement at Boonesborough, Kentucky	b. 1785
3. Founding of diocese of Bardstown, Kentucky	c. 1787
4. The Land Act	d. 1808
5. Founding of diocese of Cincinnati, Ohio	e. 1812
6. Northwest Ordinance	f. 1819
	h. 1824
	g. 1821

III. Can you tell an important fact connected with each place?

1. Cleveland
2. Tennessee
3. Chicago
4. Cumberland Gap
5. Loretto
6. Detroit
7. Kentucky
8. Florida
9. Ohio

IV. Write a short composition of one of the following topics.

1. Flatboats
2. The Toll Roads
3. Pioneer Children
4. Conestoga Wagons

V. In this Unit find examples which show:

1. charity being practiced by the people
2. the need of working together to succeed
3. courage and perserverance
4. people sharing God's gifts
5. that the pioneers were free to practice their religion

VI. Choose the words or expressions which best complete the statement.

1. A famous frontiersman who opened a trail to Kentucky
   a. Captain McGuire
   b. Daniel Boone
   c. Rufus Putnam
   d. Andrew Jackson
2. A turnpike is a
   a. canal
   b. river
   c. wagon
   d. road
3. The United States purchased Florida from
   a. Spain
   b. England
   c. France
   d. Canada
4. The route through Cumberland Gap was known as the
   a. Genesee Road
   b. Erie Road
   c. Wlderness Road
   d. Indian Road
5. Father Richard was elected as a representative to Congress in
   a. 1823
   b. 1810
   c. 1800
   d. 1812

VII. Some activities to aid in mastering information in this Unit.

1. Continue your work on the Classroom Scrapbook. Collect and label pictures of pioneers and their work.

2. Hold a quiz show. Have each pupil write five questions on this Unit. The Quiz Master will collect questions, and choose the best ones. Then he will select five or six pupils to answer the questions.

3. Dramatize scenes from this Unit.

4. Write a radio play about people settling in the Northwest or Southwest.

5. Imagine you had gone West before 1800. Write a letter to your grandmother telling about the trip or describing your new home.

6. Look up outside information and report to the class on an Indian uprising in the old West.

7. Draw a picture of a log cabin or a log school house.

8. Give an illustrated talk on a family moving from the East or South to Chicago in 1800. Compare the trip taken then with a similar one taken today. The class will help collect or make material to make your speech interesting.

9. Plan a debate; Resolved: That the life of the pioneer was better than modern life.

10. Construct a pioneer settlement on a sand table.

Class Quiz

1. Give three reasons why the people in the East were willing to leave their homes and go to the western wilderness.

2. Name some of the difficulties and dangers the people met with in moving westward.

3. When was Kentucky admitted to the Union? Tennessee?

4. Why is Father Gallitzin considered a great missionary?

5. What plans did the government make for the settling of the Northwest Territory?

6. In what way did life on the frontier help people to become more democratic?

7. Was it wrong for the pioneers to drive the Indians from their hunting grounds and take their lands from them? Why?

8. Give two reasons why the government sent General Jackson to Florida.

9. Name three qualities necessary for a good frontiersman.

10. Compare a pioneer home with your modern home.

Mary and Fortitude

MEANING. The Church reminds us that because of her purity of soul, Mary is more beautiful than the sun, and like the morning star, she is more beautiful than all the stars: "For she is more beautiful than the sun, and above all the order of the stars" (Wisdom: 7:29). The Church tells us that we should prefer to have a soul that is beautiful with grace. Thus, we should not be unhappy if we are born poor, or sick, or homely. We shall be happy if we imitate Mary's life of purity.

APPLICATION. Sickness, disease, limited abilities and misfortune are handicaps of life. To be reconciled to such handicaps is the reward of trust in God. Religion offers true happiness. Mary and her Son accepted a life of hard work and suffering. Let Mary be a guide as the Morning Star.

Prayer

Morning Star, *pray for us.*

Litany of the Blessed Virgin

LORD, have mercy on us.
Christ, have mercy on us.
Lord, have mercy on us.
God the Son, Redeemer of the world, have mercy on us.
God, the Holy Ghost, have mercy on us.
Holy Trinity, one God, have mercy on us.
Christ, hear us.
Christ, graciously hear us.
God the Father of heaven, have mercy on us.
Holy Mary,[1]
Holy Mother of God,
Holy Virgin of virgins,
Mother of Christ,
Mother of divine grace,
Mother most pure,
Mother most chaste,
Mother inviolate,
Mother undefiled,
Mother most amiable,
Mother most admirable,
Mother of good counsel,
Mother of our Creator,
Mother of our Saviour,
Virgin most prudent,
Virgin most venerable,
Virgin most renowned,

[1] Pray for us.

Virgin most powerful,
Virgin most merciful,
Virgin most faithful,
Mirror of justice,
Seat of wisdom,
Cause of our joy,
Spiritual vessel,
Vessel of honor,
Singular vessel of devotion,
Mystical Rose,
Tower of David,
Tower of ivory,
House of gold,
Ark of the covenant,
Gate of heaven,
Morning star,
Health of the sick,
Refuge of sinners,
Comforter of the afflicted,
Help of Christians,
Queen of angels,
Queen of patriarchs,
Queen of prophets,
Queen of apostles,
Queen of martyrs,
Queen of confessors,
Queen of virgins,
Queen of all saints,
Queen conceived without original sin,

Queen assumed into heaven,
Queen of the most holy Rosary,
Queen of peace.
Lamb of God, who takest away the sins of the world, spare us, O Lord.
Lamb of God, who takest away the sins of the world, graciously hear us, O Lord.
Lamb of God, who takest away the sins of the world, have mercy on us.
Christ, hear us. Christ, graciously hear us.
℣. Pray for us, O holy Mother of God. ℟. That we may be made worthy of the promises of Christ.

Let us pray
Grant, we beseech Thee, O Lord God, unto us Thy servants, that we may rejoice in continual health of mind and body; and, by the glorious intercession of blessed Mary ever Virgin, may be delivered from present sadness, and enter into the joy of Thine eternal gladness. Through Christ our Lord. Amen.

An indulgence of 7 years. A plenary indulgence once a month on the usual conditions for the daily devout recitation of this Litany with its versicle and prayer (See "The Raccolta," the official work of indulgenced prayers, page 216).

MARY AS A GUIDE THROUGH LIFE. The free will of man accepts the guidance of Mary in the way of life. This guidance of Mary is part of our religion. It affects our home life, our association with our fellow man, our civic obligations, our career in life, and our acceptance of life's problems.

Courtesy of Rev. J. B. Carol, O. F. M.

UNIT SIX

CHANGES IN AMERICAN WAY OF LIFE

CHAPTER I—EARLY EDUCATION IN AMERICA

Education in Colonial Times
Education after the Revolution
Archbishop Carroll—His Interest in Catholic Education
First Catholic Schools in the United States
Education in the Old West
Beginning of Public Education in the Northwest
Difficulties in Establishing Public School System
Catholic Schools in the Old West
The Work of Father Gabriel Richard
Missionaries Start Schools in Kentucky
First Provincial Council

CHAPTER II—EARLY LITERATURE AND ART IN AMERICA

Writers—Irving, Cooper, and Bryant
Artists—Stuart, Copley, West, and Trumbull
Architects—Latrobe and Bulfinch

CHAPTER III—INVENTIONS IMPROVE AMERICAN WAY OF LIFE

Inventions Help Industries, Trade and Travel
Factories and Mills Begin in New England
Cotton Industry Grows—Invention of Cotton Gin
Growth of Iron Industries
Improvements in Transportation
    Roads Built by Private Companies and National
      Government
    Canals—Steamboats—Railroads

UNIT SIX

CHANGES IN AMERICAN WAY OF LIFE

BY 1820, THE WEST had changed from a wilderness to a settled region. North and south of the Ohio River, villages, towns, and cities had grown up. Population increased. Several states were formed from this Western land and were admitted to the Union. The people in these states were given the same rights and privileges as those living in the thirteen original states.

Life in the West was more simple than in the East. Most men in the West owned their own homes, worked on their own farms, or were in business for themselves. These people were really their own masters. They discussed public affairs freely and elected their own governmental representatives.

All this helped to create a spirit of independence and equality. In time, their example helped the people of the older states to have a broader view of their freedoms. As a result, the East and the West became more strongly united.

In this Unit, you will study about the schools in early America. You will see how many American leaders and many people helped to provide free schools for all children. You will become acquainted with early American writers, artists, and architects. You will learn why early inventors played so important a part in industry and transportation.

CHAPTER I

EARLY EDUCATION IN AMERICA

Education aids freedom and happiness. The pioneers had little opportunity to attend to the education of their children. They did the best they could under the circumstances. As soon as they were settled, they made every effort to provide better schools. Education was very important, as these children were to be the future guardians of the precious freedoms that had cost their parents so much.

1. Education in Colonial Times

The first schools in America were church schools. In 1629, the Franciscans established free schools for the Indians. Franciscan priests and brothers traveled through the countries of Spanish America and into New Mexico and Florida. Here they built mission schools. They taught religion, art, manual training, and agriculture.

Augustinians, Dominicans, Jesuits, and other missionary priests were also interested in the Indians. These priests opened primary schools in which they themselves taught. They made every effort to educate the Indians and to make them Christians.

Some of these priests wrote books in the Indian languages so that Indians could learn more easily. They taught Latin and Spanish to the brighter ones. While all this was being done for the Indians, the Spanish settlers did not neglect their own children. Schools were also opened for them.

French missionary priests who came to America with the explorers also taught the Indians. French settlements had their own parish schools and the priest was usually the teacher. Religion, reading, writing and arithmetic were the main subjects taught.

In the English colonies, too, the first schools were church

schools. Reading was considered the most important subject, because everyone was expected to be able to read the Bible. Boys who wanted to become ministers attended higher grade schools called grammar schools. In 1633, the Dutch Reformed Church opened a school in New York.

Schools in New England. The people in New England did more for the education of their children than the people of the other colonies. They sent their children to a "Dame School," a private school kept by a village woman in her home. Here the children learned the alphabet and were taught to read simple words. They studied a little arithmetic and sometimes the Protestant catechism.

After attending the Dame School, some of the boys continued their studies in a school taught by a minister or a hired school master. Parents wanted their boys to be very well educated.

Girls seldom went beyond the Dame School. Members of the family taught them how to keep house, how to can foods, to cook, and to sew. It was expected that the girls would be housewives.

As early as 1642, Massachu-

Brown Brothers
Phillips Exeter Academy today

setts passed a law requiring all children to be taught to read. In 1647, another law was passed. This compelled every town of fifty families to have a grammar school. For many years these laws were not enforced. In time, however, town after town started schools. By 1700, there were small schools throughout Massachusetts and some other New England colonies.

By 1790, there were many private academies under church control in New England. The wealthy boys from all the colonies went to these academies. The well-known Phillips Exeter Academy and Phillips Andover

Academy date back to these early days.

Boston Latin School was opened in 1635. It prepared boys for Harvard College, where they could study to be clergymen or lawyers. The following year Harvard College was opened at Cambridge, Massachusetts. This is the oldest college in the United States. By 1769, three other colleges were established in New England. There was Yale in Connecticut; Brown in Rhode Island; and Dartmouth in New Hampshire. **Schools in the Middle Colonies.**

The legislatures of New York, New Jersey, Pennsylvania, and Delaware paid little attention to education. Maryland, however, made attempts to open public schools, but was not successful. In Pennsylvania, Benjamin Franklin opened a school for older boys to help them study surveying and navigation. Later this school became the University of Pennsylvania.

The churches provided some schools. These were paid for by the members of a particular church. These schools gave more time to the teaching of re-

William and Mary College, Williamsburg

Culver

ligion than to reading, writing, and arithmetic. The Quaker schools in Pennsylvania were the exceptions. Here the children were taught to read and write and to master some useful trade.

Where there were no church schools, the children were taught sometimes by a minister or by a school master. Those who could afford it were sent to one of the colleges in the United States or to Europe for higher education.

Schools in the South. In the Southern colonies there were no public schools and very few church schools or private academies. The plantation owners hired private tutors to live on the plantation and to teach their children. The very rich planters, like the people in the middle colonies, sent their boys abroad to be educated. In 1622, William and Mary College at Williamsburg, Virginia, was opened.

The poorer children in the South had to learn what they could from the older members of their families. This was unfortunate, because usually parents and older members of the family were not educated. Sometimes a missionary would set up a school in an open field.

Such schools were called "Field Schools." The missionaries taught the children a great deal.

In colonial times the school day was long, the teachers were severe, but the results were good. Not all children were able to attend school. Many boys went to live in the home of a master tradesman. Little by little they learned his trade, until they themselves became masters. Then they could open their own shops.

Books were scarce. Children in early America learned to read and spell from the catechism and the New England Primer. This primer was a small book

A hornbook

which contained the alphabet, rhymes, prayers, and lessons from the Bible. Because of the scarcity of books, the teacher sometimes had to take a book apart and give a page to each child. To preserve these loose pages, each one was placed between two transparent sheets of cowhorn. Such pages were called Hornbooks.

How different are the school books of today! They contain interesting stories and beautiful pictures. Everything has been done to make schools more interesting and pleasant.

2. Education after the Revolutionary War

Beginning of free schools. As soon as the United States gained its independence, many people began to see the great need of education. Knowing that Massachusetts and other New England states were supporting their schools by taxation, other states decided to use the same plan.

District schools were opened in Pennsylvania, New York, and New Jersey. Each district had to be rather small, for most children had to walk to school. The tax money allotted to each school was not always enough for the expenses, so the parents were obliged to pay a small tuition fee. Each school had only one teacher who taught all the classes. The pupils were ungraded and the school term lasted only a few months.

After the War of 1812, a movement began to provide free education through the eight grades for all children. Normal schools had to be established to train teachers to work in the schools. Little thought was given to free high schools until after the Civil War. However, there was a high school opened in Boston, Massachusetts, in 1821, and another in Philadelphia in 1839.

Today, all states have laws requiring children to attend school. Young people with very little money have opportunities to get even a college education if they are good workers. Many grown-ups attend free evening schools to improve their education and to get better jobs.

Other means of education. While the school is necessary for education, it is not as important as the home and the church. Good home training forms worthwhile habits that help one all through life. The Church works with the home in training children to know and to do what is right. The Catholic Church insists that parents see to it that their children's spiritual wel-

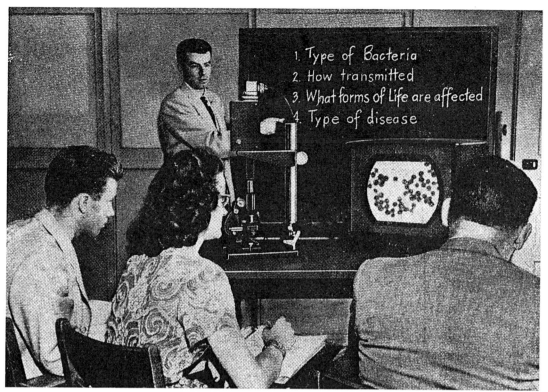

1. Type of Bacteria
2. How transmitted
3. What forms of Life are affected
4. Type of disease

Brown Brothers

Television can be a help in learning

fare is taken care of. That is why parishes build parochial schools.

Another means of education is books. Benjamin Franklin started a lending library in Philadelphia in 1731. Nearly all cities and towns now have public libraries. Other valuable means of education are newspapers, magazines, moving pictures, radio, and television. These, however, need careful supervision.

3. Bishop Carroll's Interest in Catholic Education

Religious freedom. Many colonists came to America for religious freedom. Great was their disappointment when they found that here, too, people were denied this freedom. Catholics, especially, were ill-treated because of their religious belief. Everything possible was done to make it difficult for them to practice their religion.

These Catholic colonists, when needed to defend their country against England, forgot the injustice shown them and fought side by side with the other colonists. They numbered about thirty-eight per cent of the Continental Army. The part they played in the war proved them to be true patriots.

When the leaders of America met at Philadelphia to plan the Constitution, Father John Carroll wrote a letter asking them for freedom of religion for Catholics. They granted his request indirectly when they put into the Constitution, "No religious test shall ever be required as a qualification to any office of public trust under the United States." The Bill of Rights, too, guaranteed religious freedom to all.

The first Bishop of the United

Archbishop Carroll
Brown Brothers

States. Bishop Carroll was born in Maryland in 1735. His saintly and intelligent mother taught him until he was ready to attend a Jesuit school in Maryland. After completing his studies there, the boy was sent to a Catholic college in France. While there he decided to become a Jesuit priest. Father Carroll taught in a Jesuit College until the Jesuits were driven from France in 1773.

Father Carroll returned home to Maryland in 1774. There he learned that the Catholics had been deprived of their churches and schools. Father Carroll used to say Mass in his own home. Fearing that the people might grow weak in their faith, he became a missionary and devoted his time entirely to their spiritual welfare.

In 1784, Father Carroll was put in charge of all missions and missionaries in the United States. Pope Pius VI appointed him Bishop of Baltimore in 1789. His diocese included the whole United States. The Catholic Church was now really established in America. Bishop Carroll's appointment took place in the same year that George Washington became the first President of the United States.

Through the influence and hard work of Bishop Carroll and his priests the Church grew rapidly. By 1808, four dioceses were set up: Bardstown, Boston, New York, and Philadelphia. Baltimore became an Archdiocese and Bishop Carroll became an Archbishop.

Catholic colleges and seminaries. As early as 1640, the Jesuits planned to open a Catholic college in Maryland, but were not permitted to do so. In 1789, at the request of Bishop Carroll, the Jesuits opened Georgetown College. The bishop needed a school to train young men to the priesthood. For years, Georgetown University in Washington, D. C., has educated men who have become leaders in both Church and state. In 1818, the University of St. Louis was established. It, too, has done great work.

When Father Carroll was made bishop there were about thirty thousand Catholics under his charge. Forty priests scattered all over the United States could not take care of

Georgetown University's first building

this large number. A seminary and experienced priests were needed to train boys studying for the priesthood.

About this time, priests were being driven from France because of the French Revolution. This was Bishop Carroll's opportunity to invite the French Sulpicians (sul-pish'-ans) to come to the United States to teach. Bishop Carroll founded St. Mary's Seminary at Baltimore in 1791 for these Suplicians. This is one of the leading seminaries in the United States today. Students from all parts of the country are trained there for the priesthood. In 1806, the Sulpicians opened another seminary in Maryland at Emmitsburg.

Archbishop Carroll worked hard to provide every means possible to help Catholics practice their religion and to spread the Catholic faith. When he died in 1815, the Catholic Church was better known, more people were practicing their faith, and the Church had a strong foothold in the United States.

Bishop Fenwick opened a seminary at Cincinnati, Ohio, in 1829. Here young men from the Northwest territory were trained to be priests.

The Ursuline Sisters. As early as 1727, the Ursuline Sisters came from France to New Orleans, Louisiana. There they opened a school for girls. All classes of people could attend—the rich, the poor, the Negro and the Indian.

After the Louisiana Purchase, the Sisters feared that the government would close their schools. In reply to a letter they wrote to President Jefferson, he told the Sisters that the Constitution guaranteed their rights. Today, the Ursuline Sisters have schools in New Orleans and throughout the United States.

The first Catholic school in Massachusetts was opened by the Ursuline Sisters in the part of Charlestown now known as Somerville. This was a school for girls. Protestants as well as Catholics attended. It was considered one of the best schools in Boston.

The growth of Catholic schools and churches did not please the enemies of the Church. Their feeling against the Catholics grew stronger and stronger. In 1834, someone set fire to the Sisters' Convent at Charlestown, and it burned to the ground.

The first nun fom New England.

Before convent schools opened in New England, many Protestants sent their daughters to Catholic schools in Canada. Ethan Allen, the hero of Ticonderoga, sent his daughter, Fanny, to one of these schools. She not only received a good Catholic education, but God gave her the gift of faith and a religious vocation. In 1810, she returned to her home in Vermont, before entering the convent in Canada. She was the first nun from New England.

The Visitation Sisters. Miss Alice Lalor, a young lady from Ireland, came to Philadelphia with her parents in 1797. Two years later, she and two other young ladies became teachers in the Academy of the Poor Clares at Georgetown, Maryland. Teaching was not the usual work of these Sisters, but they were doing it to help Bishop Carroll in his plan to educate children. In 1804, the Poor Clares returned to France and Alice Lalor and the other two young ladies continued their work. Other girls joined them, and in 1816 the group became known as the Visitation Sisters. These Sisters opened the first free school in the District of Columbia.

Mother Seton — An American Foundress. Elizabeth Ann Bay-

Mother Seton

ley was born in New York City just one year before the American Revolution began. She grew up with the country, and dearly loved this Land of Our Lady. Her father, a famous doctor, taught her well and developed in her a great love for reading. She especially liked reading about the lives of God's heroes and heroines.

When Elizabeth grew up, she married William Seton, the son of one of the wealthiest New York families. Sometime afterwards, William became ill. So that he might regain his health, he and his family took a trip to Italy. There William became constantly weaker and died at

217

Leghorn. Elizabeth and her children were cared for by a prominent Catholic family in Leghorn. From them she learned about the Catholic faith and became interested in the Church.

When she returned to America in 1805, Elizabeth Ann Seton was baptized a Catholic at Saint Peter's Church, New York. Her family was very angry with her and refused to help her support herself and her family. She opened a small school in New York. Then, in 1806, Bishop Carroll gave her permission to begin a school in Baltimore. She was very successful there. Right from the beginning God blessed her work.

Shortly after this, in 1809, Mrs. Seton started a religious community. Several women joined her at Emmitsburg, Maryland. These were the first Sisters of Charity in the United States. The Community grew rapidly. Today their schools, hospitals, and orphanages are found in every part of the country. Mother Seton began the parochial school system in America. Today, the parochial schools are sending well-trained students into all walks of life.

4. Education in the Old West

Beginnings of public education in the Northwest. Before the Constitution was adopted many of our great leaders had seen the need of education. If the people were to govern themselves, they must be educated. Otherwise, they could not make wise decisions or vote intelligently.

The settlers of the Northwest were assured of free education by the Ordinance of 1787. The government provided log cabins or one-room buildings for schoolhouses. Very few children could receive an education because it was so difficult to reach the few schools that were built. Many others could not attend because they were needed to work on the farm or to help at home. School was in session only during the winter months.

Effort to establish public schools. Leaders in education had to fight a hard battle to establish free education and to get trained teachers. Many public-spirited men and women devoted much time and energy to this task. Because the people were asked to contribute to the support of the schools, trouble arose. Those who had no children asked, "Why should I spend money to educate other people's children?" Others said that free education was not a charity, but a right. It was not until schools were supported by taxes that the public school system was established.

Perhaps the one who did the most to arouse the public to the need of educating all classes of people was Thomas Jefferson. He firmly believed in the education of the common people.

Although many educational leaders were working to establish free schools, Horace Mann became the best known educator in the country. He was a Massachusetts lawyer who gave up his law practice to interest people in public education. He pleaded with the legislature of Massachusetts to do something about free public schools. Mann was appointed Secretary of the Massachusetts State Board of Education in 1837.

In 1839, he persuaded the state authorities to found a public school system in Massachusetts. During this time he greatly improved conditions in the schools. His work in education aided not only Massachusetts, but the whole United States. Leaders in education, influenced by Horace Mann, began working for the establishment of free schools in their respective states.

Catholic schools in the West. The public schools did not teach religion. Because Catholic parents wanted their children properly instructed in the Faith, they had to build parochial schools. The missionary became the teacher as well as the father of souls. He was often aided by groups of young ladies who offered their services.

Father Gabriel Richard. You have studied about some of the work done by Father Richard. He also did a great deal for Catholic education. To him belongs the credit of opening the first teacher training-school in the United States.

Catholic schools begin in Kentucky. After 1785, so many Catholic people had settled in the West that the priests could not do all the work of instruction without help. Therefore, religious Communities of women were founded in Kentucky. These Communities were: The Sisters of Loretto, the Sisters of Charity of Nazareth, and the Dominican Sisters of Saint Catharine. Bishop Flaget, called "The Saint of Kentucky," gave his blessing to these Sisters and to their work in his territory.

Sisters of Loretto. Father Nerinckx (ner'-inks), the Apostle of Kentucky, realized the need of training children to know, love, and serve God. He was not able to do this himself on account of his many duties. His problem was solved by Mary Rhodes, a young lady who had moved from Baltimore. Having been trained at the Visitation Academy at Georgetown, Mary was prepared to take over the noble work of teaching.

Soon other girls joined her. They decided to make teaching their life work. Father Nerinckx trained them to become Sisters. Bishop Flaget gave his approval. This religious Community, known as the Sisters of Loretto, was established in 1812. These Sisters now have many schools in the United States and missions in China.

Sisters of Charity of Nazareth. In 1812, Father John David, seeing the need of Catholic teachers, formed a Community of girls from pioneer families in Kentucky. These young ladies were willing to give their lives to God's service. Bishop Flaget appealed to Mother Seton for

The Visitation Academy at Georgetown

Brown Brothers

Sisters to train these girls. She had so few that she could not send him any Sisters.

Father David trained the girls to be as much as possible like Mother Seton's Sisters of Charity. They are known as the Sisters of Charity of Nazareth. Their work is in hospitals, schools, orphanages, and in foreign missions.

Dominican Sisters of Saint Catharine of Siena. Father Samuel T. Wilson, a Dominican, saw the great need of Catholic education for the children of his district. He decided to establish a Community of Dominican Sisters. Although there were already two groups of teaching Sisters in Kentucky, they were unable to care for the needs of the increasing population. In order to get girls to join this Community, Father Wilson preached about the great need of Sisters to help teach the word of God amongst His little

ones. Several brave and generous young women volunteered for this great work. He began at once to train them.

Filled with the courage and zeal of Saint Dominic, these Sisters started teaching God's truth to the children in a small log cabin near Springfield. Today, Sisters of this same Community are working in schools and hospitals in many states and in Puerto Rico.

The First Provincial Council. Catholic parochial schools were gradually growing in numbers, but more were needed. In 1829, a meeting called a Provincial Council was held at Baltimore. Bishops, priests, and seminarians attended the meeting. One of the chief topics discussed was the absolute need for more parochial schools in which the young could be "taught the principles of faith and morality, while being instructed in letters."

New words to use

founders	district schools	supervision
tutor	New England Primer	university
hornbook	religious Community	tuition
archdiocese	Dame School	archbishop

How well can you talk about these topics?

1. After the War of 1812, some American leaders started a crusade for free public schools. Why did they do this? Why did so many people oppose free tax-supported schools?

2. The Catholic Church has always been interested in education. Can you tell some of the things Archbishop Carroll did for Catholic education? Can you name other bishops and priests who established schools and spent much time teaching and training people? Can you discuss their work?

3. Happy people spend some time helping and doing kind deeds for others. Those who devote their lives entirely to God's service are most happy. How many different kinds of priests, Brothers, and Sisters have you met? What kind of work do they do?

Do you remember

1. The oldest college founded in the United States was _____.

2. The Catholic Church was established in the United States in _____.

3. Children in _____ attended Dame Schools.

4. The first free school in the District of Columbia was opened by _____.

5. The first seminary in the United States was opened in the year _____ at _____.

6. _____ was the first bishop in the United States.

7. In 1727, the Ursuline Sisters opened a school for girls in _____.

8. The parochial school system in the United States was begun by _____.

9. _____ believed in the education of the ordinary citizen.

10. _____ asked the people of New York to build schools and hire teachers.

11. The free school system spread more quickly in the states of the _____ than in the states of the _____.

12. The first teacher-training school in the United States was opened by _____.

13. The Sisters of _____ were founded in _____ by Father Nerinckx.

14. The Sisters of Charity of Nazareth were established at Kentucky in _____.

15. The first American Dominican Sisters were founded in 1822 at _____.

16. In _____ Massachusetts passed a law requiring every town of fifty families to have a primary school.

17. At the First Provincial Council held in _____ the bishops discussed the need of Catholic schools.

18. Parochial schools teach the same subjects as the public schools and also _____.

EARLY LITERATURE AND ART IN AMERICA

Clinching old ideas. American leaders made great efforts to establish a school system in the United States. They did not give up until all the states provided free public schools for all classes of children. While these men were fighting for public schools, bishops and priests were struggling to found parish schools so that children could receive spiritual as well as intellectual training. Catholics had to build and support the parish schools as well as to pay taxes for the support of the public schools. Parents were willing to do this in order to fulfill their duty and use the right given them by God to educate their children.

Progress in education created an interest in literature and art. Writers and artists wrote stories and painted pictures about their country and its heroes. The works of these men made America better known and loved.

In this chapter we shall study about the early writers, artists, and architects and see what they did for America.

1. Authors and Poets Write About American Life

Washington Irving. Washington Irving, the "Father of American Literature," was born in New York City in 1783. He had tried law and business for some time, but later turned to writing as a means of earning a living.

As a boy, he liked to listen to the tales about the old Dutch customs of the people who lived in the Hudson River Valley. In 1809, he wrote the *Knickerbocker History of New York.* This book tells in a delightful way the tales of Dutch times when New York was New Amsterdam. It contains many stories Irving had listened to so

Washington Irving

Washington Irving was the first American writer to be acknowledged by European nations. Because he wrote the lives of Columbus and Washington, he is considered a historian.

James Fenimore Cooper. James Fenimore Cooper was born in New Jersey in 1789. He spent his youth roaming through the forest. There he learned to love the wild animals and to know about the Indians and the pioneers. As a young man, Cooper went to Yale College. Later, he became an officer in the Navy, but resigned. In 1821, he wrote the first real American novel, *The Spy*. It is the story of a spy in the service of George Washington during the Revolutionary War.

Cooper's *Leatherstocking Tales* are adventure stories about thrilling experiences of Indians, frontiersmen, and seafaring people. The best of these stories are "The Last of the Mohicans," "The Pathfinder," and "The Pilot." In his stories, Cooper has described early American life as no one else has done. His early childhood memories of the frontier are brought into many of his books. The works of James F. Cooper caused others to take a

eagerly as a boy. This book was the first of its kind to be published in America.

Washington Irving liked to travel. While in England, he wrote sketches of things he heard and saw there. His *Sketch Book,* published in 1819, contains many stories of England and New York. The best liked of these stories are "The Legend of Sleepy Hollow" and "Rip Van Winkle." His writings caused the English people to think more kindly of Americans. Because Irving's stories described the beauties of America so well, many who read them admired the new nation.

greater pride in their country. **William Cullen Bryant.** Our first great American poet was born in 1794 in Massachusetts. As a young boy, he loved to walk in the woods and watch the birds and animals. There he learned to think more deeply about life, death, and God Who governs both.

In the poems, "Robert of Lincoln," "The Fountain," "The White-Footed Deer," and "To a Waterfowl," Bryant gave beautiful descriptions of what he saw and heard in the woods. "Thanatopsis" (than-a-top′ sis), thoughts on death, is considered his best poem. It was written when he was only seventeen years of age. His poems show his love of nature. Bryant could see, beyond the lonely waterfowl, God guiding His creatures.

Newspapers and Magazines. In 1704, the *Boston News Letter,* the first American newspaper, was printed in Massachusetts. Such care had to be taken to avoid displeasing the readers of a newspaper, that few people were interested in publishing one. Peter Zenger was the editor of the *Weekly Journal* which was published in Mount Vernon, New York. In 1735, he was arrested because he allow-

Culver
William Cullen Bryant

ed his paper to criticize some action of the governor of New York. The case was decided in his favor. This established once and for all the freedom of the press, and as a result, newspapers in the colonies became more numerous. By 1810, there were about three hundred-fifty newspapers in the United States.

Magazines soon followed the newspapers. The number of newspapers and magazines have increased so rapidly that they are now large business industries. Newspapers and magazines can do an enormous amount of good or evil. Be sure that what you read is good.

The trial of Peter Zenger

The First Catholic Newspaper.
The United States Catholic Miscellany was the first real Catholic newspaper. It was published in 1822 by Bishop England in Charleston, South Carolina. Soon, two other Catholic papers appeared; *The Truth Teller* in New York in 1825, and *The Pilot* in Boston in 1829. Now many dioceses have weekly newspapers.

2. American Artists Begin Their Work

Early American painters. Most of the first American artists painted portraits. Photography had not been developed and cameras were unknown at this time. People of wealth who wanted a picture of themselves or of their families had an artist paint it. Other pictures showing happenings connected with the history of the times were also painted. A few artists painted outdoor scenes.

Benjamin West. Benjamin West, a gifted young artist from Philadelphia, started painting in Italy and England where he spent most of his life. He became a favorite of the English

King and painted portraits of the royal family. Desiring to pass his talents on to others, he became a great teacher of artists.

Two of his noted pictures, which are of interest to Americans, are "The Death of General Wolfe" and "Penn's Treaty with the Indians."

Although West was a Quaker, he painted a picture of the Holy Family for Father Farmer, S.J. He did this to show his appreciation to Father Farmer for introducing him to prominent Italian people. This picture is still at St. Joseph's Church in Philadelphia.

Gilbert Stuart. No doubt the best known American portrait painter is Gilbert Stuart, who was born in Rhode Island in 1755. As a youth, he became the pupil of Benjamin West.

Stuart lived for a while in Europe, and after the Revolutionary War he came back to the United States. He painted pictures of the early Presidents and other well-known Americans. The one with which we are most familiar is that of George Washington.

John Singleton Copley. John Singleton Copley, another of West's pupils and a distinguished portrait painter, was born in

Gilbert Stuart

Culver

Boston, Massachusetts, in 1738. Copies of his portraits of John Adams and John Hancock adorn many public buildings.

Charles W. Peale. Charles W. Peale, another artist, painted pictures of American heroes. His style of painting was much like that of members of the Royal Academy in England. Peale's painting of George Washington is his best known picture.

The Pennsylvania Academy of Fine Arts, opened in 1805, and the National Academy of Fine Arts, opened in New York in 1826, were established through the efforts of Peale and others. Although this man

Trumbull's picture. "The Surrender of Cornwallis."

was not a great artist himself, he started a lively interest in art in America.

John Trumbull. John Trumbull painted both portraits and colorful scenes from the American Revolution. In 1830, after the National Capitol in Washington was completed, he was asked to paint four historical pictures to adorn its walls. Everyone is acquainted with one of these, "The Signing of the Declaration of Independence." Another popular scene is "Cornwallis Surrendering at Yorktown." Copies of these paintings are to be found in many public buildings.

These early artists, through their paintings, have done much to help Americans love their country and its heroes. Through these pictures people of each generation have learned to recognize early American leaders and the founders of this great nation.

Cartoons. Cartoon drawing has long been popular. Candidates for public office and those holding positions in the government are often made sport of by cartoonists. Some of the drawings give an exact picture of a person or happening. Others ridicule people or events. The majority of people who would never read or listen to a discussion about public affairs, will look at a cartoon. This type of drawing not only acquaints people with the happenings in public life, but sometimes changes popular opinion on questions of the times.

Colonial architecture. The wealthy colonists usually modeled their homes on the style of architecture that was popular in Europe. People who came from England built homes in in the Georgian style of architecture. Those from Holland fashioned their homes in the Dutch style.

Houses modeled after colonial homes can be seen in all parts of the United States. The houses are large and two or three stories high. These houses have many windows, very big rooms, and high ceilings. In many of them, there are fireplaces. Some of the old colonial homes have become American shrines which tourists visit each year.

In parts of New England there is another type of colonial architecture. Around the village green a group of small dwellings and a meeting-house can be seen. These buildings, although small and simple, are beautiful.

Classical architecture. After the Revolutionary War, some of the homes and public buildings were designed according to the style of buildings of ancient Greece and Rome. Such buildings had many columns and porticos. This style of architecture is called classical.

Thomas Jefferson, an architect as well as a statesman, followed this style in the buildings he planned. His home at Monticello, the University of Virginia, and the State House at Richmond, were all modeled after this classical architecture.

Benjamin Latrobe, an English architect and engineer, came to America in 1796. Shortly after his arrival, he drew up plans for the Bank of the United States, the Bank at Philadelphia, and the Art Academy. He was one of the architects who drew plans for the National Capitol at Washington.

Although Latrobe was not a Catholic he designed the Cathedral of the Assumption in Baltimore. He was a friend of

The State Capitol at Richmond, designed by Thomas Jefferson

Archbishop Carroll. Latrobe devoted much time to the building of the Baltimore Cathedral, and would not accept any salary for his services.

Charles Bulfinch designed many public buildings and churches in New England. He was the architect who drew plans for the Massachusetts and Connecticut State Capitols. After the National Capitol at Washington was burned by the British in 1814, he was one of the architects who planned its rebuilding.

American buildings were for a long time copies of European architecture. However, as time went on, the nation made great progress in architecture. In recent times, America has contributed much to this field, particularly in the building of skyscrapers. She has not only developed new styles of architecture, but also new methods in building.

Mastering new words

literature	artist	architecture
adorn	tales	cartoonist
novel	architect	photography
portrait	editor	talents

Selection Test

Choose the word or group of words which will complete the sentences below correctly.

1. "The Death of General Wolfe" was painted by
   a. Gilbert Stuart
   b. Benjamin West
   c. Charles Peale
   d. John Trumbull
2. Washington Irving wrote
   a. "Rip Van Winkle"
   b. "The Last of the Mohicans"
   c. "The Pioneers
   d. "To a Water Fowl"
3. A noted architect was
   a. James F. Cooper
   b. John S. Copley
   c. William C. Bryant

d. Charles Bulfinch
4. The American writer who wrote books about Indians, frontiersmen, and the Revolutionary War was
   a. Bryant
   b. Cooper
   c. Franklin
   d. Irving
5. William C. Bryant was born in
   a. New York
   b. Virginia
   c. Massachusetts
   d. New Jersey

Matching Test

Column A
1. Gilbert Stuart
2. James F. Cooper
3. Washington Irving
4. Catholic newspaper
5. Benjamin West
6. Cartoons
7. Type of Architecture
8. William C. Bryant

Column B
a. Bishop England
b. John S. Copley
c. Painting of the Holy Family
c. Famous picture of George Washington
d. Painting of the Holy Family
e. Classical
f. Archbishop Carroll
g. "Last of the Mohicans"
h. Father of American Literature
i. Pen Drawings
j. Architect who planned National Capitol
k. The first American poet

CHAPTER III

INVENTIONS IMPROVE AMERICAN WAY OF LIFE

A glance backward. We have been watching the early settlers of our country overcome many and great difficulties in building up a vast new nation. We have seen how these people found ways to safeguard their human rights by a system of democratic government and a system of free education for all.

We have studied American authors who wrote about the history and beauties of their country. We recall how they told about the thrilling events in the American Revolution, the trouble with the Indians, and early frontier life. These writers and artists hoped by their works to inspire Americans with a greater love and appreciation of their country. They wanted to make the United States better known and respected in Europe.

Meanwhile, the early settlers had many unsolved problems, especially in the fields of industry and transportation. In this chapter, we shall learn the important part inventors played in America's progress in these fields.

1. Inventions Help Industry to Grow

Samuel Slater — the father of American manufacturing. Since 1769, England had invented new machines for the spinning of thread and the weaving of cloth. As a result, her factories were making large quantities of cloth and selling them to other countries. To keep this trade for herself she forbade the selling of these machines or models of them to any other country. Moreover, she would not permit anyone who knew anything about the machines to leave England.

In spite of all this, in 1789, Samuel Slater, who had worked for seven years in English factories, managed to travel to New York. He had always looked upon America as a land of opportunity. Slater wrote to Moses Brown, a wealthy factory owner in Rhode Island, who wanted the United States to become a great manufacturing country. Brown was so interested that he hired Slater to build spinning machines like those used in the English mills. After months of hard work, Slater successfully drew from memory plans for the machines.

In 1793, the first cotton mill in the United States was opened in Pawtucket, Rhode Island. Factory after factory was built. The invention of these machines brought the spinning of yarn out of the home into the factory. Samuel Slater is called the "Father of American Manufacturing."

Francis Lowell. Spinning thread by machine was a big success. Francis C. Lowell, a Boston merchant, believed that weaving could also be done by machine. Lowell went to England in 1810 and tried to get models or drawings of weaving machines, but he failed. However, he visited several English mills and noted carefully the construction of the machines and studied their parts.

When Lowell returned to the United States he built a mill at Waltham, Massachusetts. The machinery to be used in this mill had to be modeled from memory. Lowell interested other men, and with their help a new set of spinning machines and power looms were built. These machines worked so well that by 1814 the new mill at Waltham was making cotton cloth. This was the first mill in the world in which all of the work needed to change raw material into cloth was done in one building.

Later, Lowell and his companions built on the Merrimac River a cotton mill and a factory for making the machines. The town of Lowell, Massachusetts, grew up around this mill. Lowell was the first real mill town in America.

Cotton growing in the South. While the Eastern states were building up manufacturing, the people in the South were continuing to grow tobacco and cotton. Cotton was the most important crop of the South. The biggest difficulty was that its fibers had to be separated from its seeds by hand.

Cotton Gin. Eli Whitney, a young teacher from Massachusetts, visited a plantation in Georgia and saw this difficulty. Having an inventive mind, he became interested. In 1793,

Eli Whitney at work

Whitney invented a machine which could separate the cotton from the seeds. He called this new machine a "gin," which is a short word for engine.

The cotton gin, when run by hand, could do the work of ten men. Later, water or steam power was used. The importance of cotton-growing in the South increased after the invention of the cotton gin. Bales of cotton were shipped to textile mills in New England, and others were sent to factories in England and France. The cotton gin was one of the most important early inventions in the United States.

Growth of iron and coal indus- tries. Much more iron and coal were needed to build and operate the machines, tools, and furnaces for the new manufacturing industry. Large quantities of coal, iron ore, and limestone were found in Pennsylvania, Kentucky, and Ohio. Limestone was necessary to separate the iron from the ore.

At first, charcoal was used to heat the large furnaces in which the iron was smelted. Later on, soft coal replaced charcoal. This was the beginning of the iron industry. Men were beginning more and more to make use of Mother Nature's treasures. Americans were discovering the wonderful gifts that God had planted in the earth for the use of man.

As far back as colonial times, Pennsylvania had a large iron industry. So many iron works or forges had been built in and around Philadelphia that this section was called Valley Forge. **Iron stoves.** Inventions enabled the iron industry to grow. Benjamin Franklin, in 1774, invented a stove which was slowly replacing the old fireplaces in many homes.

Iron plows. In 1797, Charles Newbold of New Jersey invented an iron plow. Many of the farmers would not use it because they thought iron would poison the soil. Later, Thomas Jefferson improved this plow. In 1819, Jethro Wood of New Jersey improved this plow so that a broken part could be replaced easily. Then the thrifty farmers recognized its value and began to use it.

Guns. Guns were also made of iron. At first, they were fashioned entirely by hand. This was very slow. In 1798, Eli Whitney had discovered a quicker and cheaper way to make guns. He wrote to the government for a contract to manufacture them and he obtained it.

Whitney had to build a factory before he could make the machine which in turn could produce all the different parts for the complete guns. Building this factory took a long time, and the officials in Washington sent for Whitney to explain his delay. As Whitney was explaining he gave each one several parts of a gun. He then selected the proper parts, fitted them together, and made a perfect rifle before their eyes. He continued doing this until ten guns were put together and fired. Whitney was questioned no longer regarding his contract. Officials at Washington were willing to wait. When guns were needed for the War of 1812, Whitney supplied them.

Inventions benefit Americans. Everyone was trying to do work in the shortest time and the easiest way. Men with inventive minds were attempting to devise machines to take the place of hand labor. Before long, reapers, sewing machines, and other time saving machines were invented. These saved not only time, but manual labor, and unnecessary expense as well. Everyone began to recognize that work done by hand could no longer compete with machine work.

Next year, you will study about many inventors and the great things they accomplished. Some of their inventions helped in making use of natural resources, especially oil, rubber and iron. Others increased business, because means of communication and travel were improved. The discovery of all the wonderful gifts of God and the ways in which they can be used should lead us to thank God daily and to use His gifts only for the good of our neighbor and for our own welfare.

2. Improvements in Transportation Help Trade and Travel

The Lancaster Turnpike. The

growth in industry required an improvement in the means of transportation. The first paved road in the United States, the Lancaster Turnpike, was completed in 1794. It connected Philadelphia with Lancaster in Pennsylvania.

The Lancaster Turnpike was a macadam road, which means it was surfaced with crushed stone. This name was given because John L. Macadam, a Scotsman living in England, was the first road builder to use crushed stone for paving roads. Anyone wanting to use the turnpike had to pay a toll, or tax. Roads having toll gates were called turnpikes. The money collected helped to pay for the building of the road and to keep it in repair.

The success of the Lancaster Road caused a great increase in the road-building business. Roads were being built by private companies to connect all the important cities in the East, especially New York, Boston, and Baltimore.

The Cumberland Road. There were some parts of the United States that could not pay for roads; yet, roads were needed badly. In 1806, Congress set aside $30,000 for the building of a road from Cumberland, Maryland, to Wheeling, West Virginia.

This was a big undertaking. Work began in 1811 and was not completed until 1820. The government spent seven million dollars on the Cumberland Road.

This highway was the route most commonly used in traveling from East to West. Thousands of settlers traveled it in their journeys to their new homes in the West. The road proved so valuable that later it was extended to the Mississippi. Then it became known as the National Road. Since then, road building has advanced rapidly. State highways now connect all important parts of the United States.

The Erie Canal. The newly-built roads were a great improvement over the old ways of travel. The cost of transporting goods by land was much more expensive than by water. Where there were no bodies of water to connect cities, canals were built. These early canals had to be dug by hand, and the earth carried away in wheelbarrows. Steam shovels had not yet been invented.

In 1813, to encourage trade between New York and the West, De Witt Clinton, Gover-

236

nor of New York, started work on the Erie Canal. This canal was to connect Albany on the Hudson River with Buffalo on Lake Erie. It was completed in 1825.

There was a great celebration for the official opening of the Erie Canal. A procession of boats, decorated with flags, went through the canal from Buffalo to Albany. These boats then sailed down the Hudson River to New York Harbor. Governor Clinton poured into the Atlantic a barrel of water which had been carried from Lake Erie. This act was to signify that the Great Lakes were being joined to the Atlantic Ocean.

The Erie Canal became the most important canal in the United States. It lessened the cost of transportation, and it helped to make New York City the leading commercial center.

Other canals. The Erie Canal was not the only one which was successfully built and used. Among others, there were the Ohio Canal and the Illinois and Michigan Canal. The Ohio Canal joined the Ohio River

Governor Clinton pours Lake Erie water into the Atlantic

Culver

with Lake Erie. The Illinois and Michigan Canal connected the Illinois River with Lake Michigan. This canal helped Chicago to become the great city that it is today.

Passengers and freight boats were used on the canals. Many pioneers made use of passenger boats to journey to the West.

Steamboats. In 1769, James Watt, a native of Scotland, invented a steam engine for pumping water. Soon, others tried using a steam engine to run boats. In 1774, James Rum-sey made a steamboat which was used for a short time on the Potomac River.

Between 1786 and 1791, John Fitch, a silversmith and gunmaker of Trenton, New Jersey, built three large passenger steamboats. These made trips between Philadelphia and Trenton, New Jersey. Because of a lack of money, Fitch had to stop running the boats. At this time, very few people traveled on steamboats.

Robert Fulton and his steamboat. Robert Fulton, a young American, went to Europe to study

Robert Fulton's *Clermont* sails proudly up the Hudson

art, but became more interested in building steamboats. He drew up plans for a steamboat, which was soon built and given a trial on the Seine River. However, France was not interested in Fulton's project, and Napoleon was too busy with wars.

After returning to New York, Fulton built a steamboat which he named the *Clermont*. Robert Livingston, then American ambassador to France, gave Fulton the necessary money. He also obtained for the inventor the exclusive right to run steamboats on the Hudson River.

In August, 1807, at four miles an hour, the *Clermont* started from New York and proudly sailed up the Hudson River to Albany. It made the trip in thirty-two hours. The return trip to New York took only thirty hours. Crowds of people stood along the banks of the Hudson River watching the strange-looking boat move steadily up stream. Fulton was the only one who believed the steamboat would actually make the trip to Albany and back to New York. When the *Clermont* was being built, many had called it "Fulton's Folly." Now they were convinced that the steamboat would be a success.

Fulton kept improving the steamboat. Before long, there were several steamboats carrying passengers and freight up and down the Hudson. In a few years, steamboats were used on all the large rivers and on the Great Lakes. The invention of the steamboat was one of the greatest improvements in transportation.

Early railroads. While Americans were busy building steamboats, the English were engaged in another important project. In 1814, George Stephenson, an English miner, built a small steam engine which hauled carloads of coal from the mines. By 1825, he had improved his steam engine so much that the railroads used the new model to haul their passenger coaches and freight cars.

Men in America became much interested in the English railroads. They decided to build railroads in this country. However, Americans used horsepower instead of steam. In 1827, the first railroad was begun. It was called the Baltimore and Ohio. On July 4, 1828, Charles Carroll of Carrollton drove the first spike for the rails. As he did so, he said, "I consider this among the most important acts of my life, second only to my signing of the Declaration of Independence, if indeed it is second to that."

Before many years, steam engines imported from England took the place of horses, which the railroads had been using. In England, these engines ran without difficulty because the railroads there were built on level land. However, they could not make the curves or the hills over which the Baltimore and Ohio railroad traveled. For this reason, it was feared that pulling cars with steam power would be a failure.

In 1830, Peter Cooper solved this problem by inventing a small locomotive which he called the "Tom Thumb." This engine pulled two cars at the speed of thirteen miles an hour.

From this small beginning, railroads increased in number. Today, many of the leading cities in the United States have become great railroad centers.

America marches onward. The United States was on its way to a successful future. It had grown from a few small colonies to a young, rugged nation

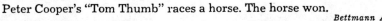
Peter Cooper's "Tom Thumb" races a horse. The horse won.

Bettmann Archive

which had much to be proud of. Its people had conquered the wilderness, and had successfully overcome the many obstacles they had met.

Most of all it could glory in the democratic form of government "of the people, for the people, by the people."

Churches were established throughout the country. Schools were preparing the younger generation to be worthy citizens of this great land. American art and literature were becoming known at home and abroad. Many improvements had been made in transportation, manufacturing, and all industries. The United States was ready to take its place among other nations of the world.

Things to talk over with the class

1. Inventors have to have great patience, to work hard, and to make great sacrifices. Name three inventors and mention something invented by each which helped the American way of life.
2. According to God's plan, man is obliged to share what he has and what he knows with other people for their good. What do you think of the laws passed by England in the 1800's regarding textile machines and textile workers?
3. The invention of the steamboat, the building of canals and better roads brought about many changes in the way of living in America. Can you tell some of the benefits obtained from these things?

Test yourself on these words

inventor
locomotive
devise
smelt

inventive mind
power looms
passenger coaches
macadam road

textile
forges
charcoal
canal

Can you tell why

1. Samuel Slater is called the Father of Manufacturing in America?
2. cotton growing became the leading industry in the South?
3. most of the early factories in America started in New England?
4. better transportation was needed in America?
5. the inventions caused the iron industry to grow?

Do you remember

1. what inventions led to better transportation?
2. by whom the first steam engine was invented?
3. who hired Samuel Slater to put up a spinning mill in Pawtucket?
4. how Valley Forge got its name?
5. how the Erie Canal helped New York to become a leading city?

Making connections

1. National Road
   a. Pittsburgh to Cincinnati
   b. New York to Philadelphia
   c. Maryland to Illinois
2. Erie Canal
   a. DeWitt Clinton
   b. James Monroe
   c. Andrew Jackson
3. Toll
   a. policeman
   b. tax
   c. prize
4. Tom Thumb
   a. game
   b. politician
   c. steam locomotive
5. A Gin
   a. ocean liner
   b. tailor shop
   c. engine
6. The Lancaster Turnpike
   a. Baltimore and Ohio
   b. macadam road
   c. The Turner House

Checking your knowledge of Unit Six

1. I wrote "The Spy."
2. My steamboat, the *Clermont,* steamed down the Hudson River to New York in 1825.
3. I published the first successful Catholic newspaper.
4. I invented a steam engine to pump water.
5. I drove the first spike for the Baltimore and Ohio Railroad.
6. I influenced the people of New York State to build a canal.
7. I built the first spinning machine in the United States.
8. I built a small locomotive called "Tom Thumb."
9. My diocese included the whole of the United States.
10. I painted four historical pictures for the new National Capitol Building.

Below are listed some important events. Arrange them in the order in which they happened and give date of each.

1. Erie Canal completed.
2. First American newspaper.
3. The *Clermont* steamed down the Hudson River.
4. Cotton mill opened at Lowell, Massachusetts.
5. Whitney invented cotton gin.

6. Mother Seton founded Sisters of Charity in the United States.
7. Baltimore and Ohio Railroad begun.
8. Oldest college in the United States.
9. Bishop Carroll, first bishop in the United States.
10. Cumberland Road completed.

The class officers will copy the names listed below on separate slips of paper. Each pupil will draw one or two names. Write or prepare a "thumb-nail sketch" of the person whose name you drew. A thumb-nail sketch is a biography told in six or seven sentences. Use books or encyclopedias from the library for additional information.

1. Archbishop John Carroll
2. Eli Whitney
3. Peter Cooper
4. Horace Mann
5. Mother Seton
6. Washington Irving
7. Father Gabriel Richard
8. Benjamin West
9. Samuel Slater
10. Robert Fulton
11. William Cullen Bryant
12. Benjamin Franklin
13. Bishop Flaget
14. Charles Bulfinch
15. James Fenimore Cooper
16. Francis Lowell
17. John Fitch
18. Gilbert Stuart
19. Governor DeWitt Clinton
20. Bishop England

Connect some person, event, or date with each of the following.

1. Pawtucket, R. I.
2. Emmitsburg, Maryland
3. Lancaster, Pennsylvania
4. Mount Vernon, New York
5. Washington, D. C.
6. New Orleans, Louisiana
7. Baltimore, Maryland
8. Albany, New York
9. Cambridge, Massachusetts
10. Lowell, Massachusetts

Match Column B with Column A.

Column A	Column B
1. Jethro Wood	a. governor, built Erie Canal
2. Horace Mann	b. nature poet
3. Benjamin Latrobe	c. free education for every child
4. Charles Carroll	d. toll roads
5. DeWitt Clinton	e. skyscraper
6. Bishop Carroll	f. inventor of the "Tom Thumb"
7. by 1769	g. trial helped to establish freedom of the press
8. turnpikes	h. four colleges in New England
9. 1829	i. lending library in Philadelphia
10. John Fitch	

11. colonial architecture
12. Peter Zenger
13. Bishop Fenwick
14. William C. Bryant
15. recent architecture
16. Eli Whitney
17. Peter Cooper
18. Charles Bulfinch
19. 1731
20. Samuel Slater

j. first Provincial Council
k. New England architect
l. improved the iron plow
m. opened a seminary in Cincin-cinnati
n. built steamboats
o. architect of the Cathedral in Baltimore

Find in this Unit an example which shows:

1. Devotion to a noble cause.
2. Sacrifices made in the cause of education.
3. Making use of God-given talents.
4. Spirit of friendliness.
5. Sharing material and non-material good.

Some activities to help master the information in this Unit.

1. Continue work on the Class-room Scrapbook by collecting pictures of buildings which show the different types of architecture. See if you can find pictures of the early artists.
2. Make a chart showing the important inventions, names of inventors, and dates.
3. Make an illustrated map of the United States showing the location of the first railroad, of the first cotton mill, the first spinnng mill. Mark the places where the iron and coal industries are located; the Cumberland Road and the Lancaster Turnpike.
4. Make a frieze showing the different ways of travel in the United States up to 1830. Dis-

cuss in class one of these subjects.

5. Choose one of these topics. Look up some interesting information and report to the class.

Early Railroads
Washington Irving
Father Gabriel Richard
stage coaches
The Erie Canal
Conestoga Wagon

6. Plan to visit a mill or factory in your city or town. Make a list of questions that you would like answered.
7. Prepare a radio news broadcast. Imagine the cotton gin or some other machine has just been invented. Tell the people about it.

THE DECLARATION OF INDEPENDENCE

Reasons for Declaration.

When, in the course of human events, it becomes necessary for one people to dissolve the political bonds which have connected them with another, and to assume among the powers of the earth the separate and equal station to which the laws of nature and of nature's God entitle them, a decent respect to the opinions of mankind requires that they should declare the causes which impell them to the separation.

Rights given by the Creator.

We hold these truths to be self-evident: That all men are created equal; that they are endowed by their creator with certain inalienable rights; that among these are life, liberty, and the pursuit of happiness. That to secure these rights, governments are instituted among men, deriving their just powers from the consent of the governed; that, whenever any form of government becomes destructive of these ends, it is the right of the people to alter or to abolish it, and to institute its powers in such form, as to them shall seem most likely to effect their safety and happiness. Prudence, indeed, will dictate that governments long established should not be changed for light and transient causes; and accordingly all experience hath shown that mankind are more disposed to suffer, while evils are sufferable, than to right themselves by abolishing the forms to which they are accustomed. But when a long train of abuses and usurpations, pursuing invariably the same object, evinces a design to reduce them under absolute despotism, it is their right, it is their duty, to throw off such government and to provide new guards for their future security. Such has been the patient suffering of these colonies, and such is now the necessity which constrains them to alter their former systems of government.

The tyranny of the British King.

The history of the present king of Great Britain is a history of repeated injuries, and usurpations, all having in direct object the establishment of an absolute tyranny over these states. To prove this, let facts be submitted to a candid world.

1. He has refused his assent to laws the most wholesome and necessary for the public good.

2. He has forbidden his governors to pass laws of immediate and pressing importance, unless suspended in their operation till his assent should be obtained, and when so suspended he has utterly neglected to attend to them.

3. He has refused to pass other laws for the accommodation of large districts of people, unless those people would relinquish the right of representation in the legislature — a right inestimable to them and formidable to tyrants only.

4. He has called together legislative bodies, at places unusual, uncomfortable, and distant from the repository of their public records, for the sole purpose of fatiguing them into compliance with his measures.

5. He has dissolved representative houses repeatedly for opposing with manly firmness his invasions on the rights of the people.

6. He has refused for a long time after such dissolutions to cause others to be elected; whereby the legislative powers incapable of annihilation, have returned to the people at large for their exercise: the state remaining, in the meantime, exposed to all the dangers of invasion from without and convulsions within.

7. He has endeavored to prevent the population of these states; for that purpose obstructing the laws for naturalization of foreigners; refusing to pass others to encourage their migration hither, and raising the conditions of new appropriations of lands.

8. He has obstructed the administration of justice by refusing his assent to laws for establishing his judiciary powers.

9. He has made judges dependent on his will alone for the tenure of their offices and the amount and payment of their salaries.

10. He has erected a multitude of new offices and sent hither swarms of officers to harass our people and eat out their substance.

11. He has kept among us, in times of peace, standing armies without the consent of our legislature.

12. He has affected to render the military independent of and superior to the civil power.

13. He has combined with others to subject us to a jurisdiction foreign to our constitutions and unacknowledged by our laws, giving his assent to their acts of pretended legislation.

14. For quartering large bodies of armed troops among us;

15. For protecting them by a mock trial from punishment for any murders which they should commit on the inhabitants of these states;

16. For cutting off our trade with all parts of the world;

17. For imposing taxes on us without our consent;

18. For depriving us in many cases of the benefits of trial by jury;

19. For transporting us beyond seas to be tried for pretended offenses;

20. For abolishing the free system of English laws in a neighboring province, establishing therein an arbitary government, and enlarging its boundaries so as to render it at once an example and fit instrument for introducing the same absolute rule into these colonies;

21. For taking away our charters, abolishing our most valuable laws, and altering fundamentally the forms of our government;

22. For suspending our own legislatures and declaring themselves invested with power to legislate for us in all cases whatsoever.

23. He has abdicated government here by declaring us out of his protection and waging war against us.

24. He has plundered our seas, ravaged our coasts, burnt our towns and destroyed the lives of our people.

25. He is at this time transporting large armies of foreign mercenaries to complete the work of death, desolation, and tyranny already begun, with circumstances of cruelty and perfidy scarcely paralleled in the most barbarous ages and totally unworthy of the head of a civilized nation.

26. He has constrained our fellow citizens taken captive upon the high seas to bear arms against their country, to become the excutioners of their friends and brethren, or to fall themselves by their hands.

27. He has excited domestic insurrection amongst us, and has endeavored to bring on the

inhabitants of our frontiers the merciless Indian savages, whose known rule of warfare is an undistinguished destruction of all ages, sexes, and conditions.

In every stage of these oppressions we have petitioned for redress, in the most humble terms; our repeated petitions have been answered only by repeated injury. A prince whose character is thus marked by every act which may define a tyrant is unfit to be ruler of a free people.

Attempts to avoid separation from Britain.

Nor have we been wanting in attentions to our British brethren. We have warned them, from time to time, of attempts by their legislature to extend an unwarrantable jurisdiction over us. We have reminded them of the circumstances of our emigration and settlement here. We have appealed to their native justice and magnanimity; and we have conjured them by the ties of our common kindred to disavow these usurpations, which would inevitably interrupt our connection and correspondence. They, too, have been deaf to the voice of justice and sanguinity. We must, therefore, acquiesce in the necessity which denounces our separation, and hold them, as we hold the rest of mankind, enemies in war; in peace, friends.

Freedom declared.

We, therefore, the representatives of the United States of America, in general congress assembled, appealing to the Supreme Judge of the World for the rectitude of our intentions, do, in the name and by the authority of the good people of these colonies solemnly publish and declare that these united colonies are, and of right ought to be, free and independent states; that they are absolved from all allegiance to the British crown, and that all political connection between them and the state of Great Britain is, and ought to be, totally dissolved; and that as free and independent states they have full power to levy war, conclude peace, contract alliances, establish commerce, and to do all other acts and things which independent states may of right do. And for the support of this declaration, with firm reliance on the protection of Divine Providence, we mutually pledge to each other our lives, our fortunes, and our sacred honor.

JOHN HANCOCK

NEW HAMPSHIRE:
Josiah Bartlett, Wm. Whipple,
Matthew Thornton.

MASSACHUSETTS BAY:
Samuel Adams, John Adams,
Robert Treat,
Elbridge Gerry.

RHODE ISLAND:
Stephen Hopkins,
William Ellery.

CONNECTICUT:
Roger Sherman,
Samuel Huntington,
William Williams,
Oliver Wolcott.

NEW YORK:
Wm. Floyd,
Philip Livingston,
Francis Lewis, Lewis Morris.

NEW JERSEY:
Richard Stockton,
John Witherspoon,
Francis Hopkinson,
John Hart,
Abraham Clarke.

PENNSYLVANIA:
Robert Morris,
Benjamin Rush,
Benjamin Franklin,
John Morton,
George Clymer, James Smith,

George Taylor,
James Wilson,
George Ross.

DELAWARE:
Caesar Rodney, George Read,
Thomas M'Kean.

MARYLAND:
Samuel Chase, William Paca,
Thomas Stone,
Charles Carroll of Carrollton.

VIRGINIA:
George Wythe,
Richard Henry Lee,
Thomas Jefferson,
Benjamin Harrison,
Thomas Nelson, Jun.,
Francis Lightfoot Lee,
Carter Braxton.

NORTH CAROLINA:
William Hooper,
Joseph Hewes,
John Penn.

SOUTH CAROLINA:
Edward Rutledge,
Thomas Heyward, Jun.,
Thomas Lynch, Jun.,
Arthur Middleton.

GEORGIA:
Button Gwinnett,
Lyman Hall,
George Walton.

THE CONSTITUTION OF THE UNITED STATES

Preamble

WE THE PEOPLE of the United States, in Order to form a more perfect Union, establish Justice, insure domestic Tranquillity, provide for the common defense, promote the general Welfare, and secure the Blessings of Liberty to ourselves and our Posterity, do ordain and establish this Constitution for the United States of America.

Article I. Legislative Department

Section 1. Congress

Legislative powers.

All legislative Powers herein granted shall be vested in a Congress of the United States, which shall consist of a Senate and House of Representatives.

Section 2. House of Representatives

1. Election of members.

The House of Representatives shall be composed of Members chosen every second Year by the People of the several States, and the Electors in each State shall have the Qualifications requisite for Electors of the State Legislature.

2. Qualifications.

No Person shall be a Representative who shall not have attained to the Age of twenty-five Years, and been seven Years a Citizen of the United States, and who shall not, when elected, be an Inhabitant of that State in which he shall be chosen.

3. Apportionment.

Representatives and direct Taxes shall be apportioned among the several States which may be included within this Union, according to their respective Numbers, which shall be determined by adding to the whole Number of free Persons, including those bound to Service for a Term of Years, and excluding Indians not taxed, three fifths of all other Persons. The actual Enumeration shall be made within three Years after the first Meeting of the Congress of the United States, and within every subsequent Term of ten Years, in such Manner as they shall by Law direct. The Number of Representatives shall not exceed one for every thirty thousand, but each State shall have at least one Representative; and until such enumeration shall be made, the State of New Hampshire shall be entitled to choose three, Massachusetts eight, Rhode Island and Providence Plantations one, Connecticut five, New York six, New Jersey four, Pennsylvania eight, Delaware one, Maryland six, Virginia ten, North Carolina five, South Carolina five and Georgia three.

4. Vacancies.

When vacancies happen in the Representation from any State, the Executive Authority thereof shall issue Writs of Election to fill such Vacancies.

5. Officers; impeachment.

The House of Representatives shall choose their Speaker and other Officers; and shall have the sole Power of Impeachment.

Section 3. The Senate
1. Number and election of Senators.

The Senate of the United States shall be composed of two Senators from each State, chosen by the Legislature thereof, for six Years; and each Senator shall have one Vote.

2. Classification.

Immediately after they shall be assembled in Consequence of the first Election, they shall be divided as equally as may be into three Classes. The Seats of the Senators of the first Class shall be vacated at the Expiration of the second Year, of the second Class at the Expiration of the fourth Year, and of the third Class at the Expiration of the sixth Year, so that one third may be chosen every second Year; and if vacancies happen by Resignation, or otherwise, during the Recess of the Legislature of any State, the Executive thereof may make temporary appointments until the next meeting of the Legislature, which shall then fill such Vacancies.

3. Qualifications.

No Person shall be a Senator who shall not have attained to the Age of thirty Years, and been nine Years a Citizen of the United States, and who shall not, when elected, be an inhabitant of that State for which he shall be chosen.

4. President of the Senate.

The Vice President of the United States shall be President of the Senate, but shall have no Vote, unless they be equally divided.

5. Officers of the Senate.

The Senate shall choose their other Officers, and also a President pro tempore, in the Absence of the Vice President, or when he shall exercise the Office of President of the United States.

6. Trial of Impeachments.

The Senate shall have the sole Power to try all Impeachments. When sitting for that Purpose, they shall be on Oath or Affirmation. When the President of the United States is tried, the Chief Justice shall preside: And no Person shall be convicted without the Concurrence of two thirds of the Members present.

7. Judgment on Conviction.

Judgment in Cases of Impeachment shall not extend further than to removal from Office, and disqualification to hold and enjoy any Office of honor, Trust, or Profit under the United States: but the Party convicted shall nevertheless be liable and subject to Indictment, Trial, Judgment and Punishment, according to Law.

Section 4. Elections and Sessions
1. Elections.

The Times, Places and Manner of holding Elections for Senators and Representatives, shall be prescribed in each State by the Legislature thereof; but the Congress may at any time by Law make or alter such Regulations, except as to the Places of choosing Senators.

2. Meetings.

The Congress shall assemble at least once in every Year, and such Meeting shall be on the first Monday in December, unless they shall by Law appoint a different Day.

Section 5. Rules and Procedure
1. Conduct of business.

Each House shall be the Judge of the Elections, Returns and Qualifications of its own Members, and a Majority of each shall constitute a Quorum to do Business; but a smaller Number may adjourn from day to day and may be authorized to compel the Attendance of absent Members, in such Manner, and under such Penalties as each House may provide.

2. Proceedings.

Each House may determine the Rules of its Proceedings, punish its members for disorderly Behavior, and, with the Concurrence of two thirds, expel a Member.

3. Journal.

Each House shall keep a Journal of its Proceedings, and from time to time publish the same, excepting such Parts as may in their Judgment require

Secrecy; and the Yeas and Nays of the Members of either House on any question shall, at the Desire of one fifth of those present, be entered on the Journal.

4. Adjournment.

Neither House, during the Session of Congress, shall, without the Consent of the other, adjourn for more than three days, nor to any other Place than that in which the two Houses shall be sitting.

Section 6. Privileges and Limitations on Members

1. Compensation and privileges of members.

The Senators and Representatives shall receive a Compensation for their Services, to be ascertained by Law, and paid out of the Treasury of the United States. They shall in all Cases, except Treason, Felony and Breach of the Peace, be privileged from Arrest during their Attendance at the Session of their respective Houses, and in going to and returning from the same; and for any Speech or Debate in either House, they shall not be questioned in any other Place.

2. Limitations upon members.

No Senator or Representative shall, during the time for which he was elected, be appointed to any civil Office under the authority of the United States, which shall have been created, or the Emoluments whereof shall have been increased during such time; and no Person holding any Office under the United States, shall be a Member of either House during his Continuance in Office.

Section 7. Method of Passing Laws

1. Revenue bills.

All Bills for raising Revenue shall originate in the House of Representatives; but the Senate may propose or concur with Amendments as on other Bills.

2. Passage of bills.

Every Bill which shall have passed the House of Representatives and the Senate, shall, before it become a Law, be presented to the President of the United States; if he approve he shall sign it, but if not he shall return it, with his Objections to that House in which it shall have originated, who shall enter the objections at large on their Journal and proceed to reconsider it. If after such Reconsideration two thirds of that House shall agree to pass the Bill, it shall be sent, together with the Objections, to the other House, by which it shall likewise be reconsidered, and if approved by two thirds of that House it shall become a Law, But in all such Cases the Votes of both Houses shall be determined by Yeas and Nays, and the Names of the Persons voting for and against the Bill shall be entered on the Journal of each House respectively. If any Bill shall not be returned by the President within ten days (Sundays excepted) after it shall have been presented to him, the Same shall be a law, in like Manner as if he had signed it, unless the Congress by their Adjournment prevent its Return, in which Case it shall not be a law.

3. Veto power of President.

Every Order, Resolution, or Vote to which the Concurrence of the Senate and House of Representatives may be necessary (except on a question of Adjournment) shall be presented to the President of the United States; and before the Same shall take Effect, shall be approved by him, or being disapproved by him, shall be repassed by two thirds of the Senate and House of Representatives, according to the Rules and Limitations prescribed in the Case of a bill.

Section 8. Powers of Congress

The Congress shall have the power:

1. To lay and collect Taxes, Duties, Imports and Excises, to pay the Debts and provide for the common Defense and general Welfare of the United States; but all Duties, Imports and Excises shall be uniform throughout the United States;

2. To borrow Money on the Credit of the United States;

3. To regulate Commerce with foreign Nations, and among several States, and with the Indian Tribes;

4. To establish a uniform Rule of Naturalization, and uniform laws on the subject of Bankruptcies throughout the United States;

5. To coin Money, regulate the Value thereof, and of foreign Coin, and fix the Standard of Weights and Measures;

6. To provide for the Punishment of counterfeiting the Securities and current Coin of the United States;

7. To establish Post Offices and post roads;

8. To promote the Progress of Science and useful Arts, by securing for limited Times to Authors and Inventors the exclusive Right to their respective Writings and Discoveries;

9. To constitute Tribunals inferior to the supreme Court;

10. To define and Punish Piracies and Felonies committed on the high seas, and Offences against the Law of Nations;

11. To declare War, grant Letters of Marque and Reprisal, and make Rules concerning Captures on Land and Water;

12. To raise and support Armies, but no Appropriation of Money to that Use shall be for a longer Term than two Years;

13. To provide and maintain a Navy;

14. To make Rules for the Government and Regulation of the land and naval Forces;

15. To provide for calling forth the Militia to execute the Laws of the Union, suppress Insurrections and repel Invasions;

16. To provide for organizing, arming, and disciplining the Militia, and for governing such Part of them as may be employed in the Service of the United States, reserving to the States respectively, the Appointment of the Officers, and the Authority of training the Militia according to the discipline prescribed by Congress;

17. To exercise exclusive Legislation in all Cases whatsoever, over such District (not exceeding ten Miles square) as may, by Cession of particular States, and the Acceptance of Congress, become the Seat of the Government of the United States, and to exercise like Authority over all Places purchased by the Consent of the Legislature of the States in which the Same shall be, for the Erection of Forts, Magazines, Arsenals, dock-Yards, and other needful Buildings;—And

18. To make all Laws which shall be necessary and proper for carrying into Execution the foregoing Powers, and all other Powers vested by this Constitution in the Government of the United States, or in any Department or Officer thereof.

Section 9. Powers Denied Congress

1. The Migration or Importation of such Persons as any of the States now existing shall think proper to admit, shall not be prohibited by the Congress, prior to the Year one thousand eight hundred and eight, but a Tax or Duty may be imposed on such Importation, not exceeding ten dollars for each Person.

2. The Privilege of the Writ of Habeas Corpus shall not be suspended, unless when in

Cases of Rebellion or Invasion the public Safety may require it.

3. No Bill of Attainder or ex post facto Law shall be passed.

4. No Capitation, or other direct, Tax shall be laid, unless in Proportion to the Census or Enumeration herein before directed to be taken.

5. No tax or Duty shall be laid on Articles exported from any State.

6. No Preference shall be given by any Regulation of Commerce or Revenue to the Ports of one State over those of another: nor shall Vessels bound to, or from one State, be obliged to enter, clear, or pay Duties in another.

7. No Money shall be drawn from the Treasury, but in Consequence of Appropriations made by Law; and a regular Statement and Account of the Receipts and Expenditures of all public Money shall be published from time to time.

8. No Title of Nobility shall be granted by the United States; And no Person holding any Office of Profit or Trust under them, shall, without the Consent of the Congress, accept of any present, Emolument, Office, or Title, of any

kind whatever, from any King, Prince, or Foreign State.

Section 10. Powers Denied the States
1. General limitations.

No State shall enter into any Treaty, Alliance, or Confederation; grant Letters of Marque and Reprisal; coin Money, emit Bills of Credit; make any Thing but gold and silver Coin a Tender in Payment of Debts; pass any Bill of Attainder, ex post facto Law, or Law impairing the Obligation of Contracts, or grant any Title of Nobility.

2. Powers dependent upon Congress.

No State shall, without the Consent of the Congress, lay any Imposts or Duties on Imports or Exports, except what may be absolutely necessary for executing its inspection Laws: and the net Produce of all Duties and Imposts, laid by any State on Imports or Exports, shall be for the Use of the Treasury of the United States; and all such Laws shall be subject to the Revision and Control of the Congress.

No State shall, without the Consent of Congress, lay any Duty of Tonnage, keep Troops, or Ships of War in time of Peace, enter into any Agreement or Compact with another State, or with a foreign Power, or engage in War, unless actually invaded, or in such imminent Danger as will not admit of Delay.

Article II. Executive Department

Section 1. President and Vice-President

1. Terms of President and Vice-President.

The executive Power shall be vested in a President of the United States of America. He shall hold his Office during the Term of four Years, and, together, with the Vice President chosen for the same term, be elected as follows:

2. Electors.

Each State shall appoint, in such Manner as the Legislature thereof may direct, a Number of Electors equal to the whole Number of Senators and Representatives to which the State may be entitled in the Congress: but no Senator or Representative, or Person holding an Office of Trust or Profit under the United States, shall be appointed an Elector.

3. Electoral procedure.

The electors shall meet in their respective States, and vote by ballot for two Persons, of whom one at least shall not be an Inhabitant of the same State with themselves. And they shall make a List of the Persons voted for, and of the Number of Votes for each; which List they shall sign and certify, and transmit sealed to the Seat of the Government of the United States, directed to the President of the Senate. The President of the Senate shall, in the presence of the Senate and House of Representatives, open all Certificates, and the Votes shall then be counted. The Person having the greatest Number of Votes shall be President, if such Number be a Majority of the whole Number of Electors appointed; and if there be more than one who have such Majority and have an equal number of Votes, then the House of Representatives shall immediately choose by Ballot one of them for President; and if no person have a Majority, then from the five highest on the List the said House shall in like Manner choose the President. But in choosing the President, the Votes shall be taken by States, the Representation from each State having one Vote; a quorum for this Purpose shall consist of a Member or Members from two-thirds of the States, and a Majority of all the States shall be necessary to a Choice. In every Case, after the Choice of the President, the person having the greatest Number of Votes of the Electors shall be the Vice President. But if there should remain two or more who have equal Votes, the Senate shall choose from them by Ballot the Vice President.

4. Date of choosing electors.

The Congress may determine the Time of choosing the electors and the Day on which they shall give their Votes; which Day shall be the same throughout the United States.

5. Qualifications of the President.

No Person except a natural born Citizen or a Citizen of the United States at the time of the Adoption of this Constitution, shall be eligible to the Office of President; neither shall any person be eligible to the Office who shall not have attained to the Age of thirty five Years, and been fourteen Years a Resident within the United States.

6. Vacancy.

In Case of the Removal of the President from Office, or of his Death, Resignation, or Inability to discharge the Powers and Duties of the said Office, the same shall devolve on the Vice President, and the Congress may by Law provide for the Case of Removal, Death, Resignation, or Inability, both of the President and Vice President, declaring what Officer shall then act as President, and such Officer shall act accordingly until the Disability be removed, or a President shall be elected.

7. Compensation.

The President shall, at stated Times, receive for his Services, a Compensation, which shall neither be increased nor diminished during the Period for which he shall have been elected, and he shall not receive within that Period any other Emolument from the United States, or any of them.

8. Oath of office.

Before he enters on the execution of his Office, he shall take the following Oath or Affirmation: — "I do solemnly swear (or affirm) that I will faithfully execute the Office of President of the United States, and will to the best of my Ability, preserve, protect, and defend the Constitution of the United States."

Section 2. Powers of the President

1. Military and naval.

The President shall be Commander in Chief of the Army

and Navy of the United States, and of the Militia of the several States, when called into the actual Service of the United States; he may require the Opinion, in writing, of the principal Officer in each of the executive Departments, upon any Subject relating to the Duties of their respective Offices, and he shall have Power to grant Reprieves and Pardons for Offenses against the United States, except in Cases of Impeachment.

2. Treaties and appointments.

He shall have Power, by and with the Advice and Consent of the Senate, to make Treaties, provided two thirds of the Senators present concur; and he shall nominate, and by and with the Advice and Consent of the Senate, shall appoint Ambassadors, other public Ministers and Consuls, Judges of the Supreme Court, and all other Officers of the United States, whose Appointments are not herein otherwise provided for, and which shall be established by Law; but the Congress may by Law vest the Appointment of such inferior Officers, as they think proper, in the President alone, in the Courts of Law, or in the heads of Departments.

3. Filling of vacancies.

The President shall have Power to fill up all Vacancies that may happen during the Recess of the Senate, by granting Commissions which shall expire at the End of their next Session.

Section 3. Duties of the President

He shall from time to time give to the Congress Information of the State of the Union, and recommend to their Consideration such Measures as he shall judge necessary and expedient; he may, on extraordinary Occasions, convene both Houses, or either of them, and in Case of Disagreement between them, with respect to the Time of Adjournment, he may adjourn them to such Time as he shall think proper; he shall receive Ambassadors and other public Ministers; he shall take Care that the Laws be faithfully executed, and shall Commission all the Officers of the United States.

Section 4. Impeachment

The President, Vice President, and all civil Officers of the United States shall be removed from office on Impeachment for, and Conviction of, Treason, Bribery, and other high Crimes and Misdemeanors.

Article III. The Judicial Department

Section 1. Courts

Supreme and inferior courts.

The judicial Power of the United States shall be vested in one supreme Court, and in such inferior Courts as the Congress may from time to time ordain and establish. The Judges, both of the supreme and inferior Courts, shall hold their Offices during good Behavior, and shall, at stated Times, receive for their Services a Compensation, which shall not be diminished during their Continuance in Office.

Section 2. Jurisdiction

1. Powers.

The Judicial Power shall extend to all Cases, in Law and Equity, arising under this Constitution, the Laws of the United States, and Treaties made, or which shall be made, under their Authority;—to all Cases affecting Ambassadors, other public Ministers and Consuls; — to all Cases of admiralty and maritime Jurisdiction; —to Controversies to which the United States shall be a Party; —to Controversies between two or more States; — between a State and Citizens of different States; — between Citizens of the same State claiming Lands Under Grants of different States, and between a State, or the Citizens thereof, and foreign States, Citizens or Subjects.

2. Jurisdiction.

In all Cases affecting Ambassadors, other public Ministers and Consuls, and those in which a State shall be Party, the supreme Court shall have original Jurisdiction. In all the other Cases before mentioned, the Supreme Court shall have appellate Jurisdiction, both as to Law and Fact, with such exceptions, and under such Regulations as Congress shall make.

3. Trials.

The Trial of all Crimes, except in Cases of Impeachment, shall be by Jury; and such Trial shall be held in the State where the said Crimes shall have been committed; but when not committed within any State, the Trial shall be at such Place or Places as the Congress may by Law have directed.

Section 3. Treason

1. Definition.

Treason against the United States, shall consist only in levying War against them, or in adhering to their Enemies, giving them Aid and Comfort.

No Person shall be convicted of Treason unless on the Testimony of two Witnesses to the same overt Act, or on Confession in open Court.

2. Punishment.

The Congress shall have Power to declare the Punishment of Treason, but no Attainder of Treason shall work Corruption of Blood, or Forfeiture except during the Life of the Person Attained.

Article IV. The States

Section 1. Official Acts

Full Faith and Credit shall be given in each State to the public Acts, Records, and judicial Proceedings of every other State. And the Congress may by general Laws prescribe the Manner in which such Acts, Records and Proceedings shall be proved, and the Effect thereof.

Section 2. Privileges of Citizens

1. Privileges.

The Citizens of each State shall be entitled to all Privileges and Immunities of Citizens in the several States.

2. Fugitives.

A person charged in any State with Treason, Felony, or other Crime, who shall flee from Justice, and be found in another State, shall on Demand of the executive Authority of the State from which he fled, be delivered up to be removed to the State having jurisdiction of the Crime.

3. Fugitives from labour.

No person held to Service or Labour in one State, under the Laws thereof, escaping into another, shall, in Consequence of any Law or Regulation therein, be discharged from such Service or Labour, but shall be delivered up on Claim of the Party to whom such Service or Labour may be due. (superseded by Amendment XIII.)

Section 3. New States and Territories

1. New States.

New States may be admitted by the Congress into this Union; but no new State shall be formed or erected within the Jurisdiction of any other States; nor any State be formed by the Jurisdiction of two or more States, or Parts of States, without the Consent of the Legislatures of the States concerned as well as of the Congress.

2. U. S. territory.

The Congress shall have Power to dispose of and make all needful Rules and Regulations respecting the Territory or other Property belonging to the United States; and nothing in this Constitution shall be so construed as to Prejudice any Claims of the United States, or of any particular State.

Section 4. Protection of the States

The United States shall guarantee to every State in this Union, a Republican Form of Government, and shall protect each of them against Invasion; and on Application of the Legislature, or of the Executive (when the Legislature cannot be convened) against domestic Violence.

Article V. Amendments to the Constitution

The Congress, whenever two thirds of both Houses shall deem it necessary, shall propose Amendments to this Constitution, or, on the Application of the Legislatures of two thirds of the several States, shall call a Convention for proposing Amendments, which, in either Case, shall be valid to all Intents and Purposes, as Part of this Constitution, when ratified by the Legislatures of three fourths of the several States, or by Conventions in three fourths

thereof, as the one or the other mode of Ratification may be proposed by the Congress; Provided that no Amendment which may be made prior to the Year One thousand eight hundred and eight shall in any Manner affect the first and fourth Clauses in the Ninth Section of the first Article; and that no State, without its Consent shall be deprived of its equal Suffrage in the Senate.

Article VI. General Provisions

1. Validity of debts.

All Debts contracted and Engagements entered into, before the Adoption of this Constitution, shall be valid against the United States under this Constitution, as under the Confederation.

2. Supremacy of the Constitution.

This Constitution, and the Laws of the United States which shall be made in Pursuance thereof; and all Treaties made, or which shall be made, under the Authority of the United States, shall be the supreme Law of the Land; and the Judges in every State shall be bound thereby, any Thing in the Constitution or Laws of any State to the Contrary notwithstanding.

3. Oath.

The Senators and Representatives before mentioned, and the Members of the several State Legislatures, and all executive and judicial Officers, both of the United States and of the several States, shall be bound by Oath or Affirmation, to support this Constitution; but no religious Test shall ever be required as a Qualification to any Office or public Trust under the United States.

Article VII. Ratification of the Constitution

The Ratification of the Conventions of nine States, shall be sufficient for the Establishment of this Constitution between the States so ratifying the Same.

Done in Convention by the unanimous consent of the States present, the seventeenth day of September, in the year of our Lord one thousand seven hundred and eighty seven, and of the Independence of the United States of America the twelfth.

In witness whereof, we have hereunto subscribed our names.

GEORGE WASHINGTON

President and Deputy from Virginia.

NEW HAMPSHIRE:
John Langdon,
Nicholas Gilman.

MASSACHUSETTS:
Nathaniel Gorham,
Rufus King.

CONNECTICUT:
William Samuel Johnson,
Roger Sherman.

NEW YORK:
Alexander Hamilton.

NEW JERSEY:
William Livingston,
David Brearly,
William Patterson,
Jonathan Dayton.

PENNSYLVANIA:
Benjamin Franklin,
Thomas Mifflin,
Robert Morris,
George Clymer,
Thomas Fitzsimons,
Jared Ingersoll,
James Wilson,
Gouverneur Morris.

DELAWARE:
George Read,
Gunning Bedford, Jr.
John Dickinson,
Richard Basset,
Jacob Broom.

MARYLAND:
James McHenry,
Daniel of St. Thomas Jenifer,
Daniel Carroll.

VIRGINIA:
  John Blair,
  James Madison, Jr.

NORTH CAROLINA:
  William Blount,
  Richard Dobbs Spaight,
  Hugh Williamson.

SOUTH CAROLINA:
  John Rutledge,
  Chas. Cotesworth Pinckney,
  Charles Pinckney,
  Pierce Butler.

GEORGIA:
  Wm. Few, Abraham Baldwin.

Attest: WILLIAM JACKSON,
                    Secretary.

AMENDMENTS

I. Freedom of Religion, Speech, and the Press; Right of Assembly (1791)

Congress shall make no law respecting an establishment of religion or prohibiting the free exercise thereof; or abridging the freedom of speech or of the press, or the right of the people peaceably to assemble, and to petition the Government for a redress of grievances.

II. Right to Bear Arms (1791)

A well regulated Militia, being necessary to the security of a free State, the right of the people to keep and bear Arms, shall not be infringed.

III. Quartering of Troops (1791)

No Soldier shall, in time of peace be quartered in any house, without the consent of the owner, nor in time of war, but in a manner to be prescribed by law.

IV. Search (1791)

The right of the people to be secure in their persons, houses, papers, and effects, against unreasonable searches and seizures, shall not be violated, and no Warrants shall issue but upon probable cause, supported by Oath or affirmation, and particularly describing the place to be searched, and the persons or things to be seized.

V. Jury Trial (1791)

No person shall be held to answer for a capital, or otherwise infamous crime, unless on a presentment of indictment of a Grand Jury, except in cases arising in the land or naval forces, or in the Militia, when in actual service in time Of War or in public danger; nor shall any person be subject for the same offense to be twice put in jeopardy of life or limb; nor shall be compelled in any Criminal Case to be a witness against himself, nor be deprived of life, liberty, or property, without due process of law; nor shall private property be taken for public use, without just compensation.

VI. Rights of the Accused (1791)

In all criminal prosecutions, the accused shall enjoy the right to a speedy and public trial, by an impartial jury of the State and district wherein the crime shall have been committed, which district shall have been previously ascertained by law, and to be informed of the nature and cause of the accusation; to be confronted with the witnesses against him; to have compulsory process for obtaining Witnesses in his favor, and to have the Assistance of Counsel for his defense.

VII. Suits at Common Law (1791)

In suits at common law, where the value in controversy shall exceed twenty dollars, the right of trial by jury shall be preserved, and no fact tried by a jury shall be otherwise re-examined in any Court of the United States than according to the rules of the common law.

VIII. Excessive Bail and Punishments (1791)

Excessive bail shall not be required, nor excessive fines imposed, nor cruel and unusual punishments inflicted.

IX. Rights Reserved to the People (1791)

The enumeration in the Constitution, of certain rights, shall not be construed to deny or disparage others retained by the People.

X. Powers Reserved to States and People (1791)

The powers not delegated to the United States by the Con-
stitution, nor prohibited by it to the States, are reserved to the States respectively, or to the people.

XI. Suits Against States (1798)

The Judicial power of the United States shall not be construed to extend to any suit in law or equity, commenced or prosecuted against one of the United States by Citizens of another State, or by Citizens or Subjects of any Foreign State.

XII. Election of President and Vice-President (1804)

The Electors shall meet in their respective states, and vote by ballot for President and Vice-President, one of whom, at least, shall not be an inhabitant of the same state with themselves; they shall name in their ballots the person voted for as President, and in distinct ballots the person voted for as Vice-President, and they shall make distinct lists of all persons voted for as President, and of all persons voted for as Vice-President, and of the number of votes for each, which lists they shall sign and certify, and transmit sealed to the seat of the government of the United States, directed to the President of the Senate;—The President of the Senate shall, in the presence of the Senate and House of Representatives, open all the certificates and the votes shall then be counted;—The person having the greatest number of votes for President, shall be the President, if such a number be a majority of the whole number of Electors appointed; and if no person have such majority, then from the persons having the highest numbers not exceeding three on the list of those voted for as President, the House of Representatives shall choose immediately, by ballot, the President. But in choosing the President, the votes shall be taken by states, the representation from each state having one vote, a quorum for this purpose shall consist of a member or members from two-thirds of the states, and a majority of all the states shall be necessary to a choice. And if the House of Representatives shall not choose a President, whenever the right of choice shall devolve upon them, before the fourth day of March next following, then the Vice-President shall act as President, as in the case of the death or other constitutional disability of the President. The person having the greatest number of votes as Vice-President shall be the Vice-President, if such number be a majority of the whole number of Electors appointed, and if no person have a majority, then from the two highest numbers on the list the Senate shall choose the Vice-President; a quorum for the purpose shall consist of two-thirds of the whole number of Senators, and a majority of the whole number shall be necessary to a choice. But no person constitutionally ineligible to the office of President shall be eligible to that of Vice-President of the United States.

XIII. Abolishment of Slavery (1865)

Neither slavery nor involuntary servitude, except as punishment for crime whereof the party shall have been duly convicted, shall exist within the United States, or any place subject to their jurisdiction.

Section 2. Enforcement

Congress shall have power to enforce this article by appropriate legislation.

XIV. Citizenship (1868)

Section 1. Citizens

All persons born or naturalized in the United States, and subject to the jurisdiction thereof, are citizens of the United States and of the State wherein they reside. No State shall make or enforce any law which shall abridge the privileges or immunities of citizens of the United States; nor shall any State deprive any person of life, liberty, or property, without due process of law; nor deny to any person within its jurisdiction the equal protection of the laws.

Section 2. Representatives

Representatives shall be apportioned among the several States according to their respective numbers, counting the whole number of persons in each State, excluding Indians not taxed. But when the right to vote at any election for the choice of electors for President and Vice-President of the United States, Representatives in Congress, the Executive and Judicial officers of a State, or the members of the Legislature thereof, is denied to any of the male inhabitants of such State, being twenty-one years of age, and citizens of the United States, or in any way abridged, except for participation in rebellion, or other crime, the basis of representation therein shall be reduced in the proportion which the number of such male citizens shall bear to the whole number of male citizens twenty-one years of age in such State.

Section 3. Insurrection

No person shall be a Senator or Representative in Congress, or elector of President and Vice-President, or hold any office, civil or military, under the United States, or under any State, who, having previously taken an oath, as a member of Congress, or as an officer of the United States, or as an executive or judicial officer of any State, to support the Constitution of the United States, shall have engaged in insurrection or rebellion against the same, or given aid or comfort to the enemies thereof. But Congress may by a vote of two-thirds of each House, remove such disability.

Section 4. Public Debt

The validity of the public debt of the United States, authorized by law, including debts incurred for payment of pensions and bounties for services in suppressing insurrection or rebellion, shall not be questioned. But neither the United States nor any State shall assume or pay any debt or obligation incurred in aid of insurrection or rebellion against the United States, or any claim for the loss or emancipation of any slave; but all such debts, obligations and claims shall be held illegal and void.

Section 5. Enforcement

The Congress shall have power to enforce, by appropriate legislation, the provisions of this article.

XV. Negro Suffrage (1870)

Section 1. Negro's Right to Vote

The right of citizens of the United States to vote shall not be denied or abridged by the United States or by any State on account of race, color, or previous condition of servitude.

Section 2. Enforcement

The Congress shall have power to enforce this article by appropriate legislation.

XVI. Income Tax (1913)

The Congress shall have power to lay and collect taxes on incomes, from whatever source derived, without apportionment among the several States, and without regard to any census or enumeration.

XVII. Election of Senators (1913)

The Senate of the United States shall be composed of two Senators from each State, elected by the people thereof, for six years; and each Senator shall

have one vote. The electors in each State shall have the qualifications requisite for electors of the most numerous branch of the State Legislature.

When vacancies happen in the representation of any State in the Senate, the executive authority of such State shall issue writs of election to fill such vacancies; Provided, That the Legislature of any State may empower the executive thereof to make temporary appointment until the people fill the vacancies by election as the Legislature may direct.

This amendment shall not be so construed as to affect the election or term of any Senator chosen before it becomes valid as part of the Constitution.

XVIII. National Prohibition (1919)

After one year from the ratification of this article the manufacture, sale, or transportation of intoxicating liquors within, the Importation thereof into, or the exportation thereof from the United States and all territory subject to the jurisdiction thereof for beverage purposes is hereby prohibited.

The Congress and the several states shall have concurrent power to enforce this article by appropriate legislation.

This article shall be inoperative unless it shall have been ratified as an amendment to the Constitution by the legislatures of the several states, as provided in the Constitution, within seven years from the date of submission hereof to the states by the Congress.

XIX. Woman Suffrage (1920)
Section 1. Right of Women to Vote

The right of the citizens of the United States to vote shall not be denied or abridged by the United States or by any state on account of sex.

Section 2. Enforcement

Congress shall have power, by appropriate legislation, to enforce the provisions of this article.

XX. "Lame Duck" Amendment (1933)
Section 1. Terms of President, Vice-President, and Congressmen

The terms of the President and Vice-President shall end at noon on the 20th day of January, and the terms of Senators and Representatives at noon on the 3rd day of January, of the years in which such terms would have ended if this article had not been ratified; and the terms of their successors shall then begin.

Section 2. Sessions of Congress

The Congress shall assemble at least once in every year, and such meeting shall begin at noon on the 3rd day of January, unless they shall by law appoint a different day.

Section 3. Presidential Succession

If, at the time fixed for the beginning of the term of the President, the President elect shall have died, the Vice-President elect shall become President. If a President shall not have been chosen before the time fixed for the beginning of his term, or if the President elect shall have failed to qualify, then the Vice-President elect shall act as President until a President shall have qualified; and the Congress may by law provide for the case wherein neither a President elect nor a Vice-President elect shall have qualified, declaring who shall then act as President, or the manner in which one who is to act shall be selected, and such person shall act accordingly until a President or Vice-President shall have qualified.

Section 4. President Chosen by the House

The Congress may by law provide for the case of the death of any of the persons from whom the House of Representatives may choose a President whenever the right of choice shall have devolved upon them, and for the case of death of any of the persons from whom the Senate may choose a Vice-President whenever the right of choice shall have devolved upon them.

Section 5. Effective Date

Section 1 and 2 shall take effect on the 15th day of October following the ratification of this article.

Section 6. Ratification

This article shall be inoperative unless it shall have been ratified as an amendment to the Constitution by the legislatures of three-fourths of the several States within seven years from the date of its submission.

XXI. Repeal of Prohibition (1933)

Section 1. Repeal of Article XVIII

The eighteenth article of amendment to the Constitution of the United States is hereby repealed.

Section 2. Transportation of Liquor

The transportation or importation into any State, Territory or Possession of the United States for delivery or use thereof in of intoxicating liquors, in violation of the laws thereof, is hereby prohibited.

Section 3. Ratification

This article shall be inoperative unless it shall have been ratified as an amendment to the Constitution by conventions in the several States, as proviveed in the Constitution, within seven years from the date of the submission hereof to the States by the Congress.

XXII. Presidential Term of Office (1951)

No person shall be elected to the office of the President more than twice, and no person who has held the office of President, or acted as President for more than two years of a term to which some other person was elected President, shall be elected to the office of the President more than once. But this article shall not apply to any person holding the office of President when this article was proposed by the Congress, and shall not prevent any person who may be holding the office of President, or acting as President, during the term within which this article becomes effective, from holding the office of President or acting as President during the remainder of such term.

INDEX

member of First and Second Continental Congresses, 31, 43

one of delegates sent to seek aid of Canada, 39-40

words on driving first spike of Baltimore and Ohio railroad, 239-240

Carroll, Daniel, 85, 89

cartoons,
way of commenting on persons and happenings, 229
influence public opinion, 229

Cathedral, *See* Baltimore Cathedral

Catholic,
Americans, duties and privileges of, 79-80, 99
dioceses, four by 1808, 215
education, a privilege, 188
loyalty and numbers in Revolutionary War, 213-214
newspaper, first, 167
signer of Declaration of Independence, 43
school for Negro children, 167
schools attended by Protestants, 216-217

Catholics,
deprived of rights in Maryland, 214
pay for two school systems, 223
prominent in Revolutionary War, 39-40, 43, 54-55, 57-60

Catholic Church and rights of man, 139

census, every ten years, 96

Charleston, Mass. Navy Yard, Old Ironsides preserved at, 156

Chase, Samuel, 39

Checks and balances, system of, 97

"Chesapeake" affair, 146

Chesapeake Bay, battle of, 63

Chicago,
beginnings of, 189
helped by Illinois and Michigan Canal, 237

China missions of Loretto Sisters, 220

Cincinnati,
founded, 188
diocese founded, 190
seminary founded at, 216

Clark, Colonel George Rogers, 57, 186, 191
wins control of Ohio Valley, 57, 58
helped greatly by French priest, 57

Clark, William, 144

Clay, Henry, 149, 151, 166, 167, 168
peacemaker in Missouri compromise, 166

Clermont, makes first trip on Hudson, 238

Cleveland, Moses, 188

Cleveland, founding of, 188

Clinton, General, 55, 56

Clinton, Governor DeWitt, 109, 121
welcomes President Washington, 109
builds Erie Canal, 236-237

coal, replaces charcoal as industrial fuel, 235

College,
Brown, founded, 210
Dartmouth, founded, 210
Harvard, oldest in United States, 210
William and Mary, founded, 211
Yale, founded, 210

colonial,
architecture. *See* architecture, colonial.
homes, now tourist shrines, 229
legislatures, 17, 20

274